From Russia with Doubt

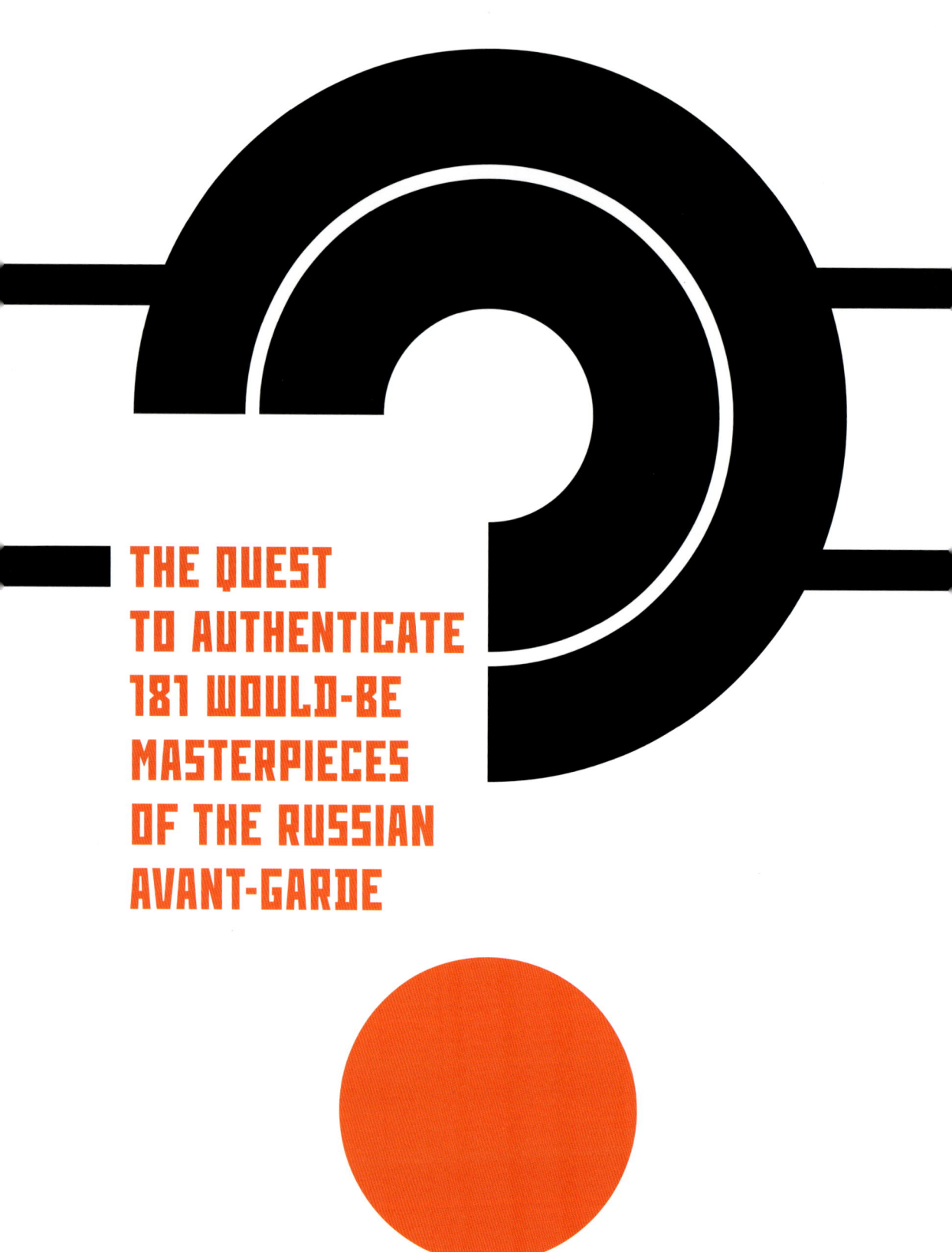

THE QUEST TO AUTHENTICATE 181 WOULD-BE MASTERPIECES OF THE RUSSIAN AVANT-GARDE

FROM RUSSIA WITH DOUBT

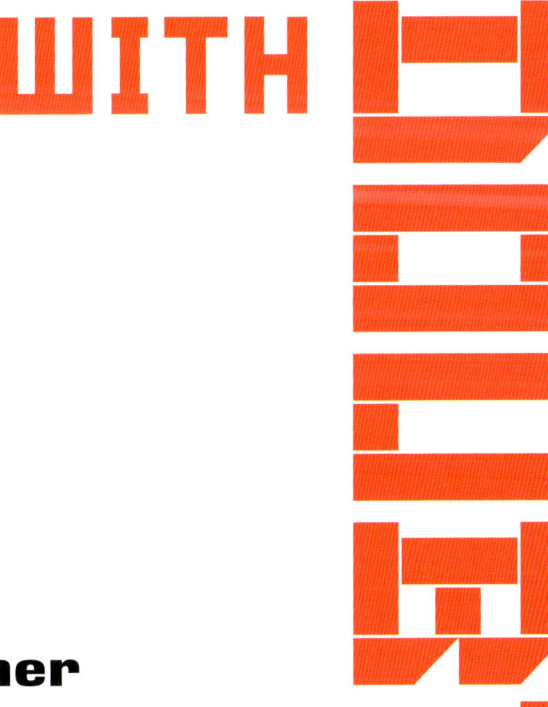

Adam Lerner

PRINCETON ARCHITECTURAL PRESS

NEW YORK

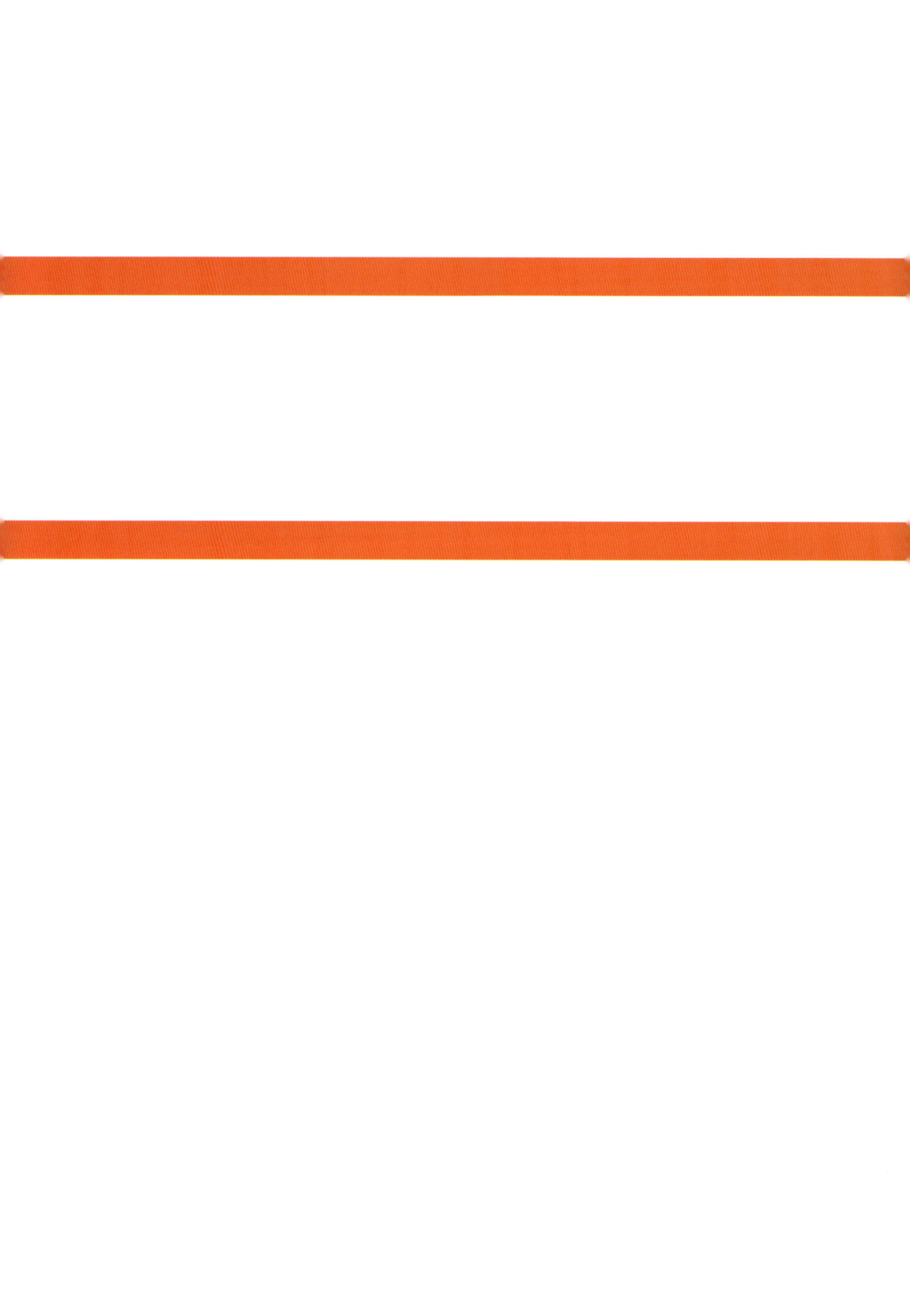

Why, sometimes I've believed as many as six impossible things before breakfast.

—Lewis Carroll, *Through the Looking Glass*

TABLE OF CONTENTS

THE STORY

PLATES

APPENDICES

INDEX OF WORKS

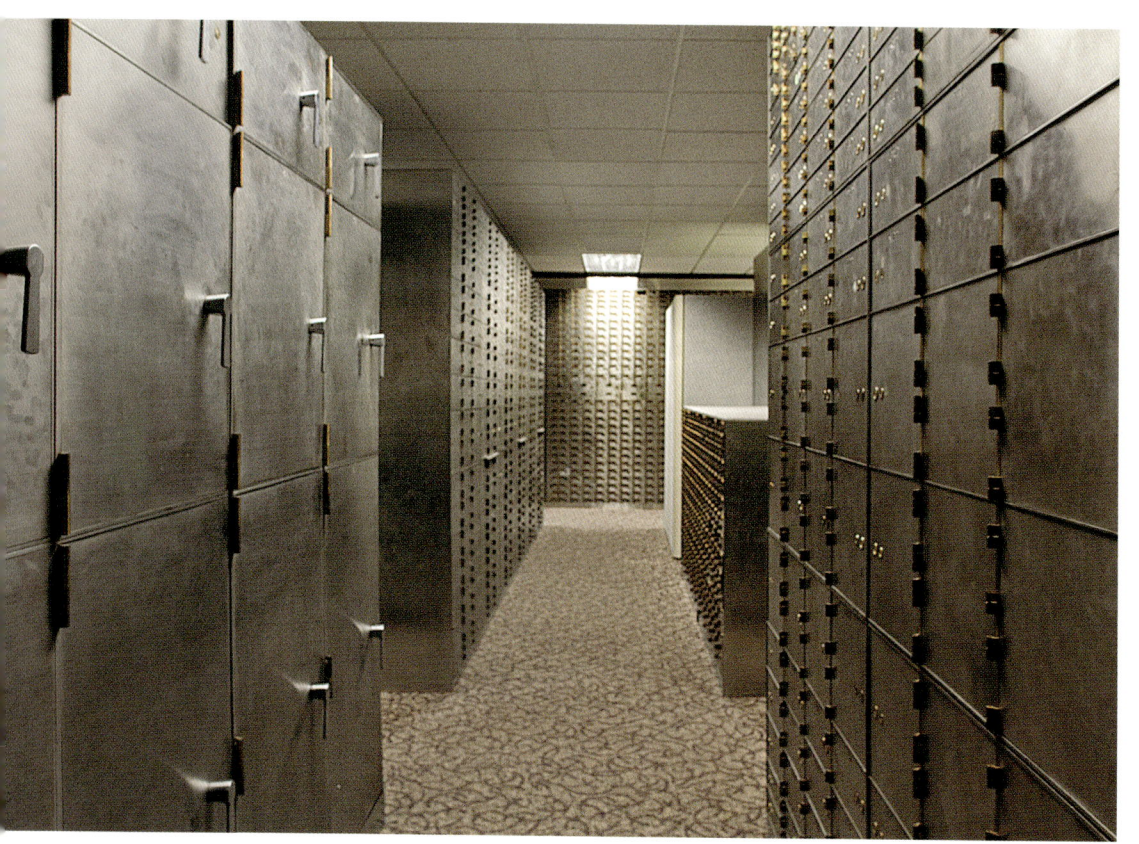

Preface

In 2007 architectural photographer Ron Pollard invited me to a bank vault in Denver's suburbs where he kept his collection of Russian avant-garde paintings, purchased from a man he met over eBay. [Fig. 1] I have to admit that at the time, I thought he was a dupe. Three years later, as director of the Museum of Contemporary Art Denver, I presented an exhibition of more than one hundred paintings from his collection. [Figs. 2–3] Now I wonder if I'm not the dupe.

Though the history of the paintings is entirely unknown, Ron is convinced that they are legitimate works from early twentieth-century Russia. His brother Roger and their friend Brad Gessner, who both amassed the collection with Ron, are also certain that the works are authentic, believing that they may have survived through neglect in some dark, forgotten storage space. Ron and his partners have a handful of fellow believers around the world. Unfortunately, none of them has much sway with experts in official art circles, and I doubt that any of my colleagues would believe that these paintings meet the minimal threshold of authenticity for an art museum.

And yet I find myself advocating for Ron.

Fig. 1 (opposite)
The bank vault in Denver where Ron stores his painting collection

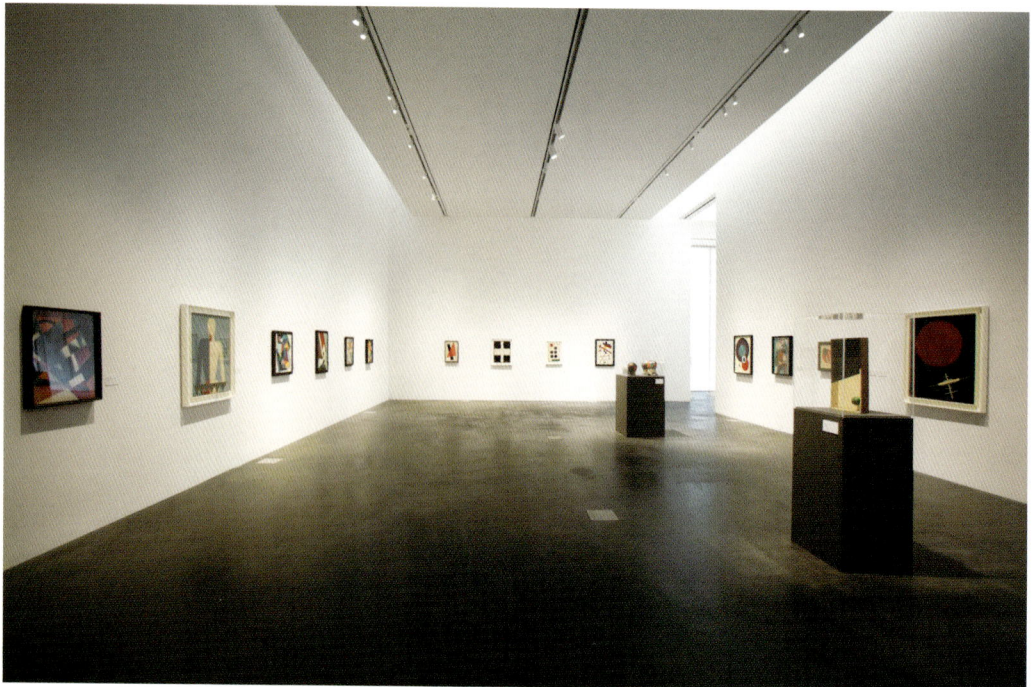

My interest in his collection of unauthenticated paintings derives in part from a personal fascination with Russian avant-garde art. I am not a scholar of this movement, but I find something magical in the circle of artists who worked in Russia around 1915, surrounding the towering figure of painter and theorist Kazimir Malevich. Their artistic inventions exploded in a burst of energy around the Russian Revolution of 1917, flourished for less than a decade, and died out under suppression by Joseph Stalin. The creations of Malevich and his circle are not only milestones in the evolution of modern art, like the works of Claude Monet, Pablo Picasso, or other giant figures, but the entire scene seems to exist in its own time and space, charged with a kind of mythic energy—perhaps because art historians are still trying to make sense of what happened in that period, whose records were buried for so long behind the iron curtain.

When I first met Ron in 2007, I was running a small art center that I had founded in Lakewood, Colorado. He walked into my office carrying two Malevich paintings. Or rather, he was carrying two works that looked exactly like Malevich paintings. He leaned the paintings

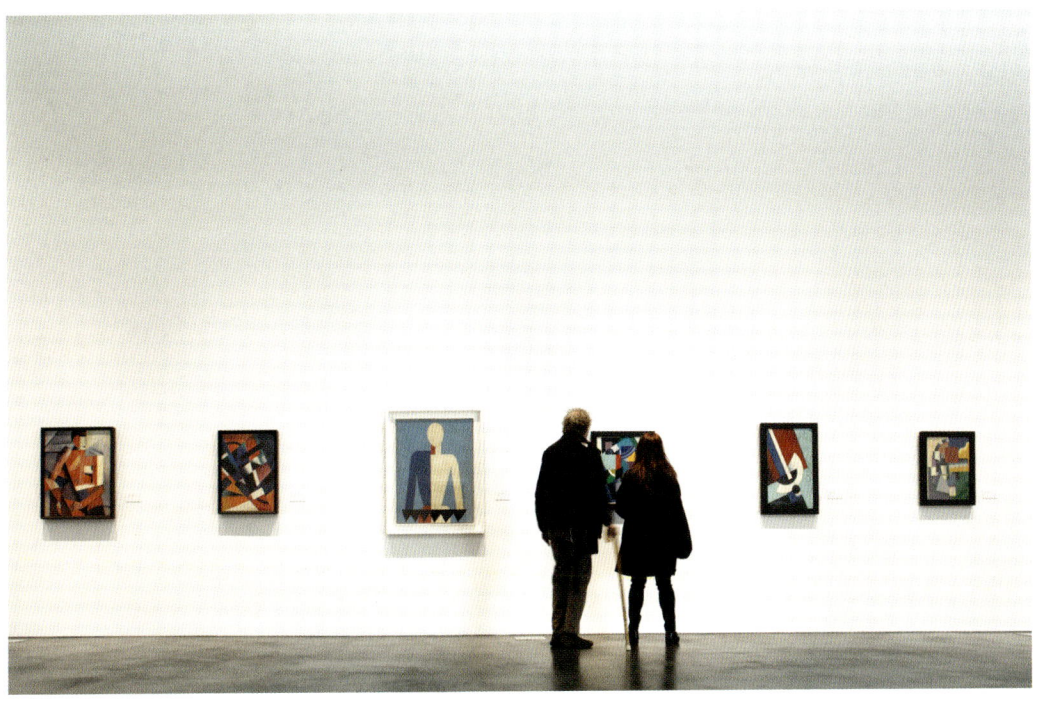

against the chair next to him while he told me the story of his collection. Talking quickly and jump-cutting from one scene to another, he told me a tale that involved conservators, lawyers, appraisers, a handwriting analyst, a science lab, an abandoned shipping container at Berlin customs, the auctioneer of a major New York auction house, refusenik Jews who smuggled paintings out of the Soviet Union in the 1970s, and an FBI agent in Salt Lake City.

I looked at the paintings. One was a simple white cross on a black background. [Fig. 37] The other was a jumble of thick, colorful lines and rectangles on a plain white background. [Fig. 54] They had the obvious signs of age: their paint was crackled and there were thin lines where the wooden stretchers supporting the canvases had creased the surface. They had the worn look of paintings that had been kept in a cellar for decades. I knew they would be worth tens of millions of dollars if they were authentic.

. Maybe it was the craziness of the story or maybe it was the quality of the paintings, but I was intrigued enough to pursue the matter further by visiting the bank vault where Ron kept a few dozen more

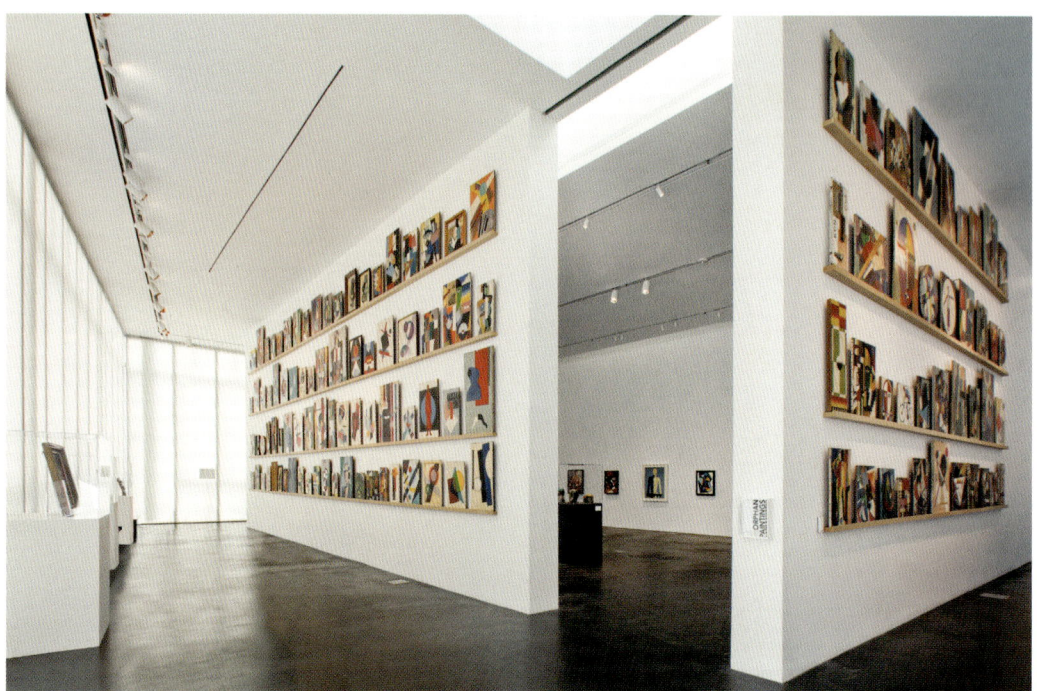

works. The vault contained not only several other unsigned paintings that closely resembled Malevich's work, but also ones that looked like they were painted by other masters of the period, such as El Lissitzky, Aleksandr Rodchenko, and Vladimir Tatlin. They were all convincingly timeworn. The wood of the stretchers was old, marked with small stamps and inscriptions that suggested that the paintings had once made the rounds through remote galleries and exhibition halls.

The paintings didn't just look authentic—they looked great. Some had the intense simplicity that Malevich gave to his works. Others had the energized complexity of artists trying to invent new forms in art or giving their own take on innovations in art that were taking place elsewhere. Some of the works looked like nothing I had seen anywhere else.

In December 2010, about a year and a half after becoming director of MCA Denver, I mounted an exhibition of Ron's collection at the museum. I felt I had the opportunity to do something different with this exhibit—not just different from typical museum practices, but different from what we experience in everyday life. Everything in our

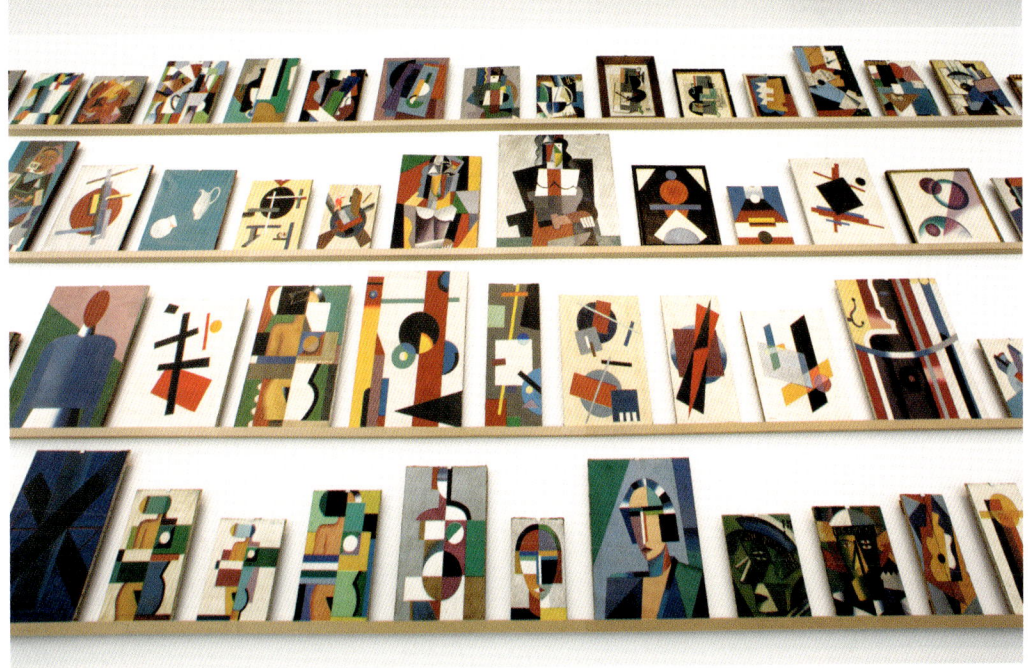

lives today is so fully known. Every object has a barcode. Everyone has a traceable genetic code. Our smartphones let us know exactly where we are. And all the analysis that objects undergo at museums—by curators, conservators, scientists, and historians—only serves to place those objects deeper and deeper into categories of knowledge and history. Everything arrives to us in the full light of day with a wealth of background information. But in Ron's collection, there is the rare opportunity to experience something different. It is more than the opportunity to look at art free from the judgments of authorities. In this collection, there is an opportunity to look at things that come from the darkness, things unknown, filled with actual mystery. I felt Ron had offered me something special.

Then again, Ron is just a guy, like a million others, who bought some stuff off of eBay. And maybe I'm just a sucker.

Acknowledgments

I am grateful to many people for helping make possible both this book and the exhibition on which it is based. Foremost, I am thankful to Ron and Roger Pollard for sharing their story with me; for trusting me enough to hand over five years of uncensored emails, invoices, reports, and other documents; and for always being available to answer my questions. I am also grateful to Ron and Roger's friends, Brad Gessner and Michel Pariseau, for their cooperation in this endeavor. I am infinitely grateful to the board of trustees of MCA Denver for encouraging me to pursue harebrained ideas like the exhibition that gave birth to this book. I want to thank my wonderful staff, especially Director of Programs and Chief of Fictions Sarah Kate Baie and Associate Curator Nora Burnett Abrams, for risking career damage by working with me on projects like this. I want to thank Mark Sofield, who first believed in Ron and helped convince me to do the same. Mark's design of the exhibition at MCA Denver was brilliant. Thanks go to Barnaby Furnas, who fueled my interest in pursuing this investigation by going with me to see Ron's bank vault filled with paintings. I am grateful to Nathan Carter and Miko McGinty, whose support I cherish. I am thrilled that they liked the exhibition at MCA Denver enough to tell their friend Paul Wagner at Princeton Architectural Press about it, and I am forever grateful to Paul for wanting to take on this book. I am thankful to Dana Schutz for her incredibly perceptive thoughts on the paintings and to Patrick Greaney for his insights on the text. Thanks to Kaitlin Maestas for her research assistance and to Rose Kalasz and Camille Paley for their help with image captions. I am deeply appreciative of Megan Carey and Nicola Brower at Princeton Architectural Press for believing in this project and for helping make it possible. I am grateful to my wife, Elissa Auther, for her endless encouragement with this project and continuous support for all of my endeavors. My ability to share ideas with her is almost a requirement for me to even have an interesting idea at all. And finally, thanks to Kristofferson for his enthusiasm.

THE STORY

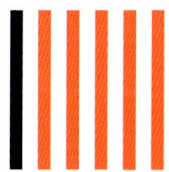

RON AND ROGER

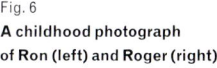

Born in 1957, Ron Pollard grew up in the suburbs of Denver alongside his close companion and younger brother by a year, Roger. As children, Ron and Roger would often ride around their neighborhood on their bicycles, looking in the dirt for objects left by previous occupants of the land. [Fig. 6] Ron had a near-legendary ability to spot arrowheads, and people said that he could locate one from fifteen feet away. He and Roger also collected insulators discarded from old telephone lines and amassed countless ornate and weathered bottles. Ron still has his collections of arrowheads, bottles, and insulators, as well as many of the other things he and Roger gathered in their childhood. Looking at these objects today, it is difficult to believe that children collected them. They are not valuable, but they have an extraordinary aesthetic quality. The insulators look

Fig. 6
A childhood photograph of Ron (left) and Roger (right)

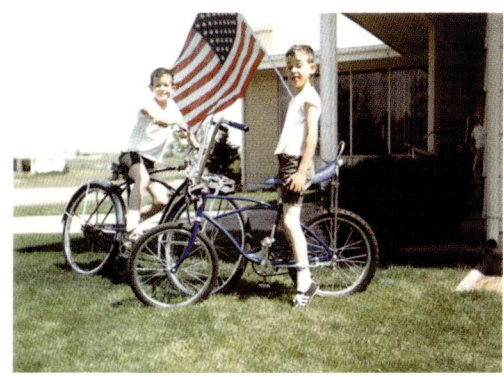

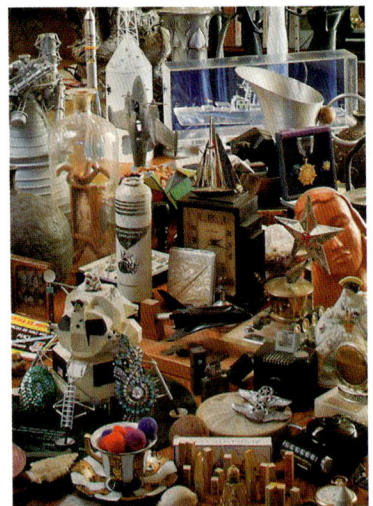

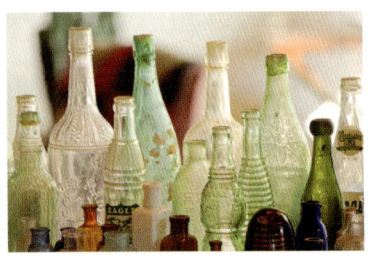

Fig. 7
Some objects from Ron's many lifelong collections

Fig. 8
Ron's bottle collection

like glass sculptures rather than functional objects, while the bottles could have been purchased in an antique shop. [Figs. 7–8]

Ron has continued his collecting hobby into adulthood. He does not hoard things, but he spends a significant amount of time on eBay, looking for modern furniture and objects whose value someone might have underestimated. He has an amateur obsession with history and a good knowledge of modern design and art. He continues to pride himself in being able to find rare objects that others overlook.

Ron may have picked up the habit of collecting from his mother, who was constantly rummaging through garage sales and thrift stores, perhaps to cope with her feelings of loss. When Roger and Ron were only six and seven years old, they lost their older brother, Richard, in a hot air balloon accident. Richard was a child prodigy who went from launching balloons in the Pollards' backyard with hot air generated from the family's barbecue grill to becoming the first U.S. National Hot Air Balloon Champion at age eighteen. Sadly, a year after winning that competition, he died in a contest in California, when a leaky valve caused his balloon to drift into high-tension wires and catch fire.

Unlike his mother, who, to fill the void, would buy rare curiosities and ordinary household objects in equal measure, Ron has always collected things for aesthetic reasons, a part of his broader artistic interests. In his youth, he pursued a career as a fine artist and attended two of the top art schools in the country. He received a Bachelor of Fine Arts from the Art Institute of Chicago and then pursued a Master of Fine Arts at the University of California, Los Angeles, where he worked with several legendary artists, including Chris Burden and Robert Heinecken, before he quit the program after his second semester. At that point it had become clear to Ron that he wanted to continue pursuing his aesthetic interests, but not as a professional artist. Instead he became an architectural photographer, shooting new buildings for a living and abandoned shopping malls as a hobby.

In contrast to Ron, whose artistic temperament leads him to rifle through dark corners and travel across the landscape, Roger possesses the family interest in flight. Like his father, a pilot who flew in the Bay of Pigs invasion, Roger joined the U.S. Air Force and had a long career as a navigator in Strategic Air Command, attaining the rank of lieutenant colonel. [Fig. 9]

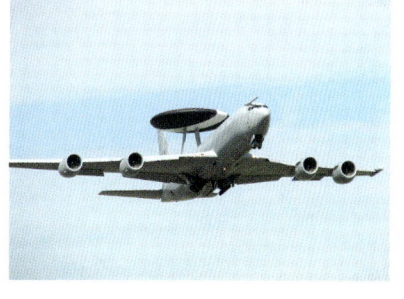

Though Ron's job keeps him focused on things on the ground and Roger's work in the Air Force gives him a perspective from the sky, their personalities take them in the opposite direction: Ron is a thinker with his head in the clouds, seeing everything in the world through philosophical eyes, while Roger is a pragmatist, approaching things from a realistic and grounded perspective.

Fig. 9
Roger was a navigator for the U.S. Air Force on this AWAC plane.

The dichotomy between realist and idealist embodied by the two brothers prefigures the central tension in this story of their collaboration on a collection of art. Earth and sky are the recurring symbols in a tale that moves back and forth between material realities and lofty ideas.

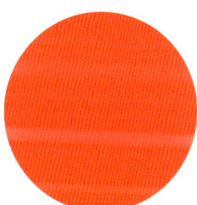

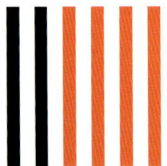

THE BEGINNING OF THE COLLECTION

The brothers started collecting the group of paintings that came to be housed in a Denver bank vault in 2004, beginning with the very practical intention of finding artwork to decorate Roger's house. At the time, Ron was interested in Russian art from the 1910s and 1920s, a period that witnessed the emergence of a unique strain of abstract art in the country. The innovative works of this era have many labels—nonobjective, constructivist, suprematist—but they are all inflected with an identifiable style that bears a family resemblance to French cubist art from around the same time. As Roger later told an FBI agent, "I was looking for some art, some paintings, and Ron said you should look for some of this constructivist stuff."[1]

While looking at paintings on eBay, Ron was struck by a few works listed by a seller in Aachen, Germany, that looked sophisticated, like the work of serious artists. Roger liked the pictures well enough, and he trusted his brother's taste, though he was nervous at first about committing to spend five hundred dollars, the amount Ron

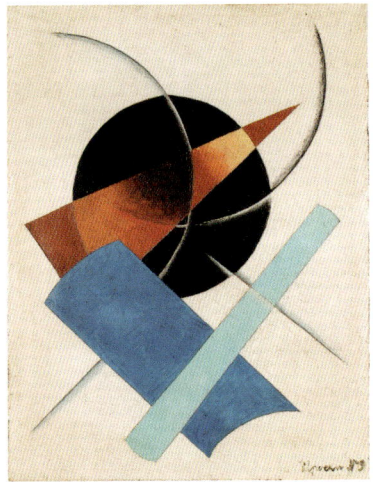 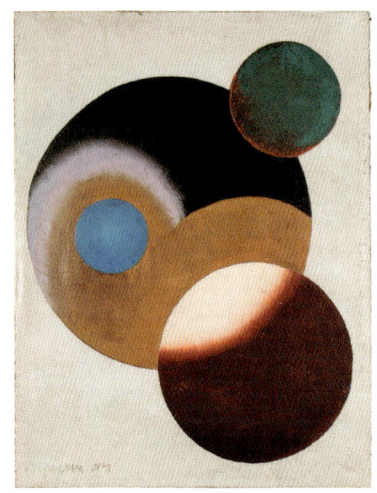

recommended they each set aside for this venture. Roger eventually succumbed, and the brothers decided they would try to acquire some of the paintings offered by the Aachen seller.

Ron began by bidding on two cubist-inspired works of human faces consisting of overlapping, hard-edged geometric forms, but he lost the auction to another buyer. A third painting from the seller was a hodgepodge of simple shapes: a circle, a triangle, and other simple forms on a plain white ground. [Fig. 10] Ron and Roger decided to pool their money this time and won the auction at 610 dollars. Ron then bid on a fourth painting, a slightly more classic cubist collage, but lost the auction to a buyer who was willing to pay 807 dollars.

After the brothers purchased their first painting from the seller, he contacted them from Germany and told them that he had a companion painting that he would sell to them directly for around the price they had paid for the first picture. [Fig. 11] Ron and Roger agreed to this so that they could each own one artwork. When the two paintings arrived in Denver about a week later, Ron felt a strong intuition that they were genuinely from the period. The colors seemed right and the brush strokes were skillful. The canvases were crackled throughout and creased along their edges from the wooden supports behind them. He saw a resemblance to the work of Russian avant-garde master Aleksandr Rodchenko, and he suspected that he might have stumbled upon a treasure trove.

Fig. 10
The first painting that Ron and Roger won together on eBay, with the inscription *Project 9*

Fig. 11
This work, with the inscription *Project 8*, **is the companion painting the brothers bought directly from the seller.**

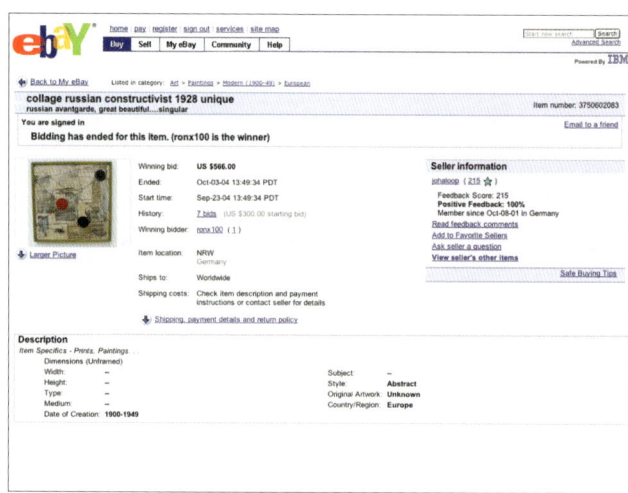

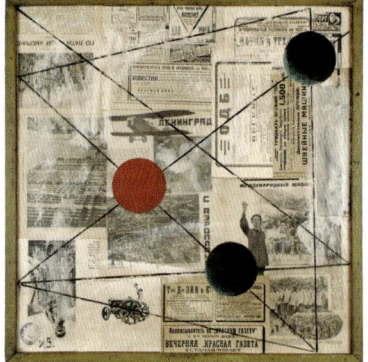

Figs. 12 + 13
Ron and Roger bought this collage for under six hundred dollars.

To confirm his suspicion Ron took the paintings to an art conservator he greatly respected and whom he had previously hired for help with another of his eBay purchases. She had worked at museums around the country and conserved works by Pablo Picasso, Georgia O'Keeffe, and many others. She even had experience with Russian icons. According to Ron, she was amazed when he brought her the two paintings. He recounted her reaction in detail: "She looked at them and said, 'Wow, you know these are amazing. These look right. Where are you getting these?'" In her opinion, the paintings were "of the period. Physically they look dead right."[2]

Feeling charged by this report, Ron and Roger closely followed the postings of the Aachen seller. Every few weeks, he would put four or five new items up for auction. The brothers tried to win these works while keeping their bids under one thousand dollars per painting; [Figs. 12–13] they were outbid in about half of the auctions. During this time, Ron sought out as much information as he could about the possible origins of the paintings. A friend of his, a former airline steward who had traveled periodically to Saint Petersburg, had once had the opportunity to tour the storage rooms of the State Hermitage Museum during the Cold War and told Ron about seeing hundreds of Russian modern paintings there, stacked on top of each other, unprotected and uncataloged. Ron knew that after Stalin's suppression of this style of art in the 1920s, it had never regained its credibility. It seemed plausible

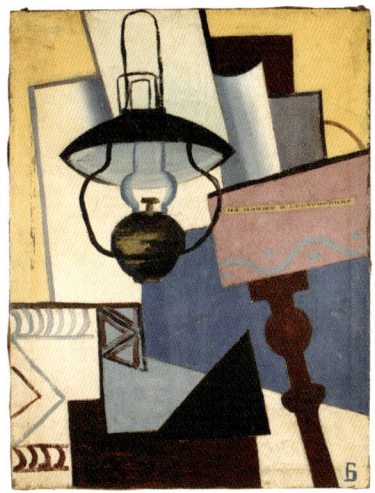 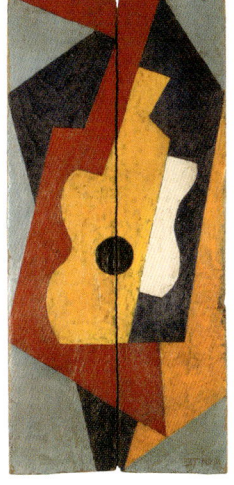

Fig. 14
Ron and Roger noticed similarities between this work and the paintings of the lesser-known Russian avant-garde artist Ivan Puni.

Fig. 15
This painting on wood from Ron's collection seemed authentic to the brothers, because several Russian avant-garde artists painted on wood to comment on the physical nature of their works.

that, after the fall of the Soviet Union, corrupt museum employees or government workers could have gotten their hands on these all-but-forgotten paintings and sold them on the black market.

After a monthlong absence from eBay, the mysterious German put up a new selection of paintings. Ron and Roger decided to contact him off-line and offered to purchase the works directly. After corresponding with someone who appeared to be the business partner of the original seller, the brothers eventually bought some of the paintings through eBay and others directly from the sellers, spending a total of ten thousand dollars and acquiring five more paintings. [Figs. 14–15, 21, 46, 72]

The brothers were hooked. They realized that what they had acquired was only a small part of a large collection of seemingly authentic avant-garde paintings, but they couldn't afford to continue to buy all of the works themselves. They decided to ask others to get involved, including their friend Brad Gessner, an epidemiologist in Alaska, who had kayaked with Roger and who collected art made in Alaskan villages. When Roger asked him if he was interested in purchasing some of the eBay paintings, Brad was somewhat reluctant, but he eventually bid on a painting that he won for about two thousand dollars. [Fig. 23]

For the next few weeks, Ron and Roger and some of their friends continued to buy paintings through a combination of online auctions and direct purchases from the sellers. Within four months from

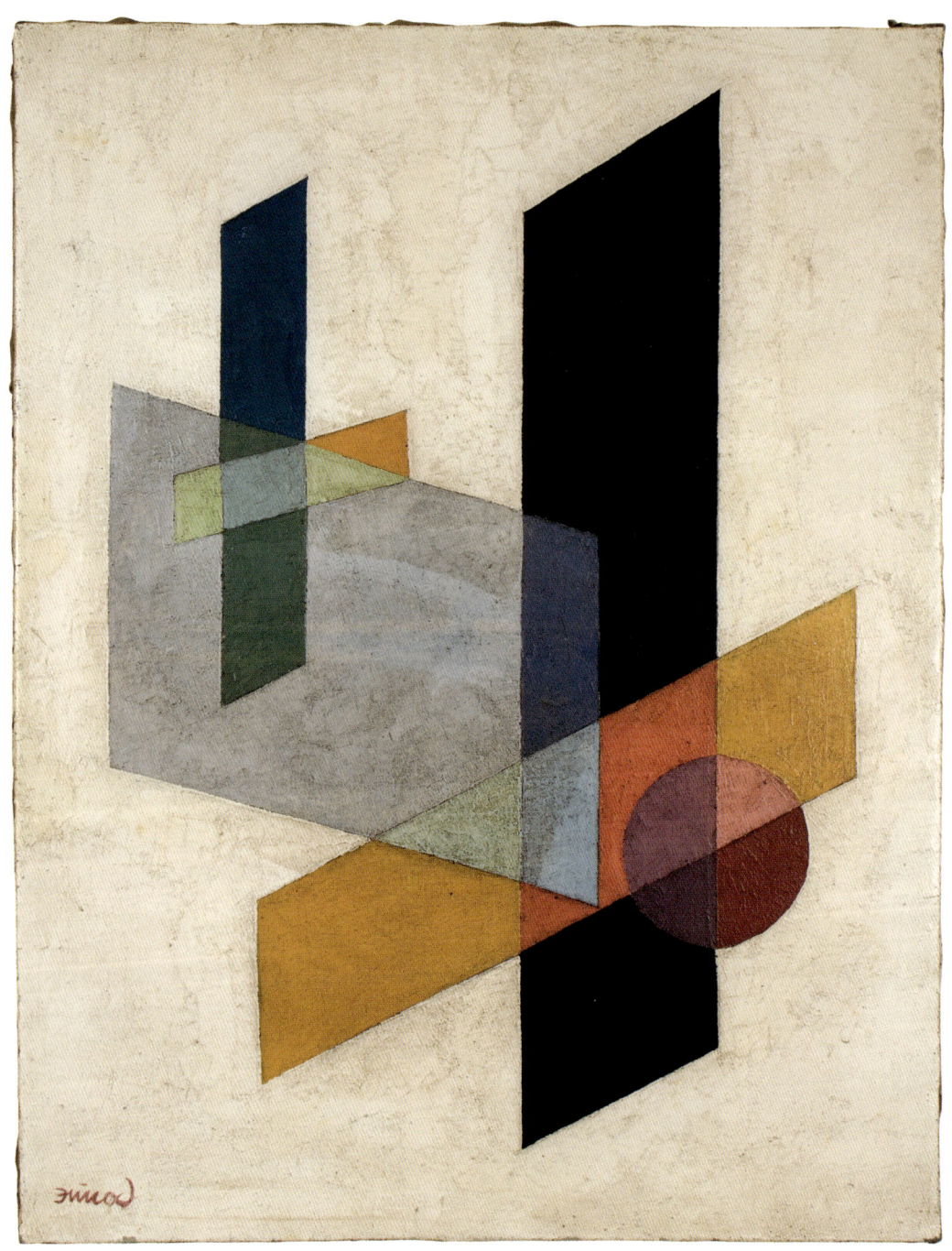

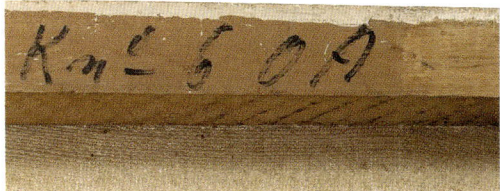

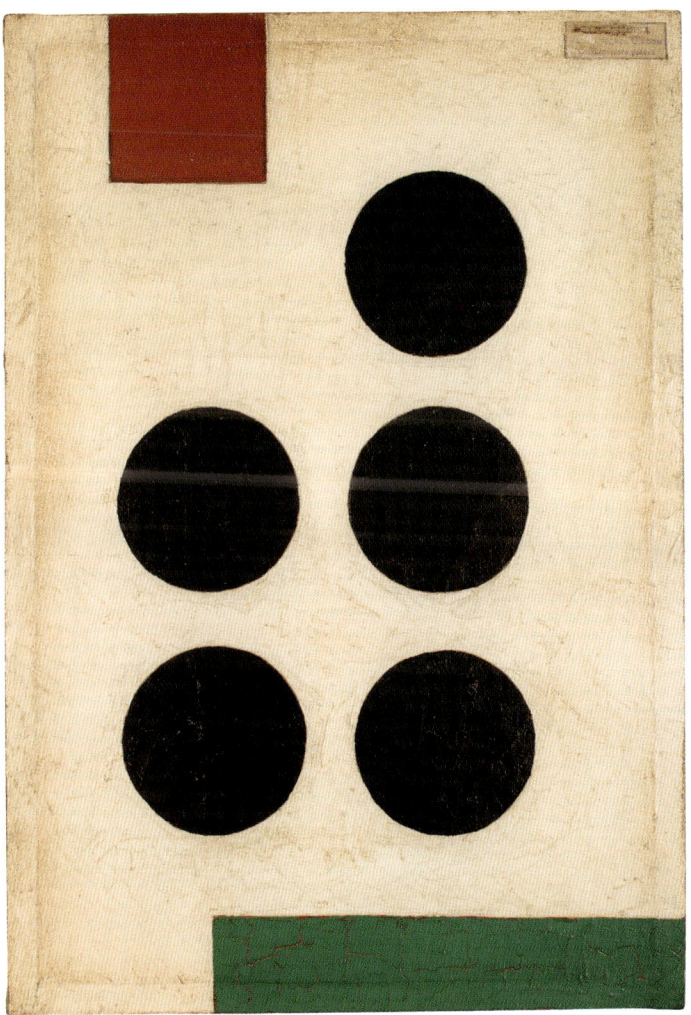

Fig. 16 (opposite)
The oblique parallelograms
in this painting are
suggestive of the works of
László Moholy-Nagy. The
text in the lower left corner
translates to "study."

Figs. 17–20
Many paintings from the
Aachen sellers—including
this one—cannot be tied to a
specific Russian avant-
garde artist, but have the
pared-down elegance of the
best works of the period.
In order to sell directly to
Ron and Roger, the sellers
ended the auction with only
a minor misrepresentation.
The label on the image's
upper right is obscured but
appears to read, "Library,
School # 20, Borough of
Sverdlovsky." The number
inscribed on the stretcher
bar looks like an inventory
number.

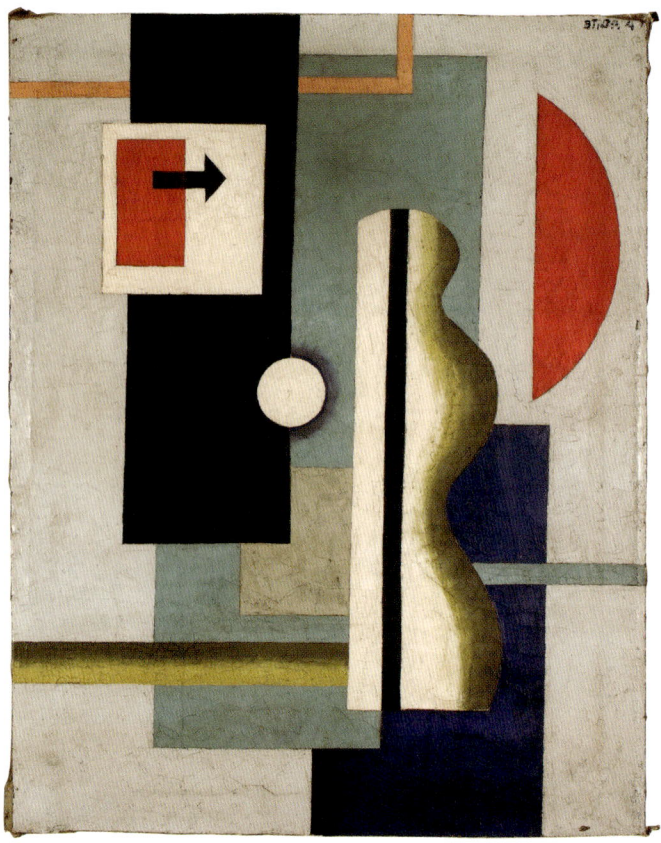

Figs. 21–22

When Roger asked the seller if he could buy this painting from him directly, the seller said that he could not stop an auction that already had bidders. Roger won the painting on eBay after an aggressive bidding war, paying at least three times more than the typical amount. In retrospect, he believes that the seller probably had a shill bidding against him.

Fig. 23 (opposite)

This painting purchased by Brad has a strong resemblance to the works of El Lissitzky.

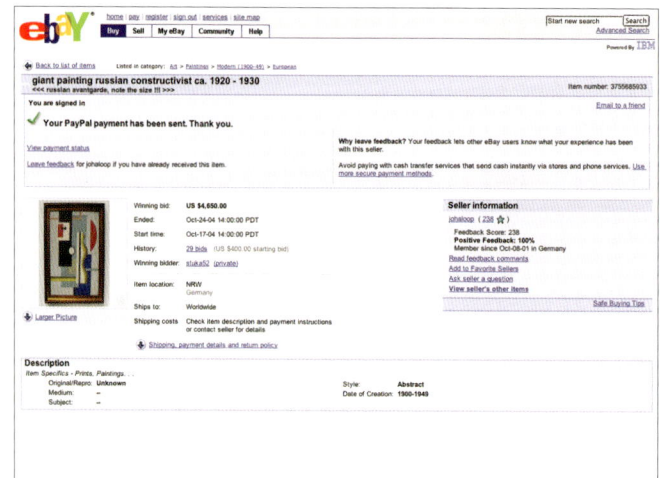

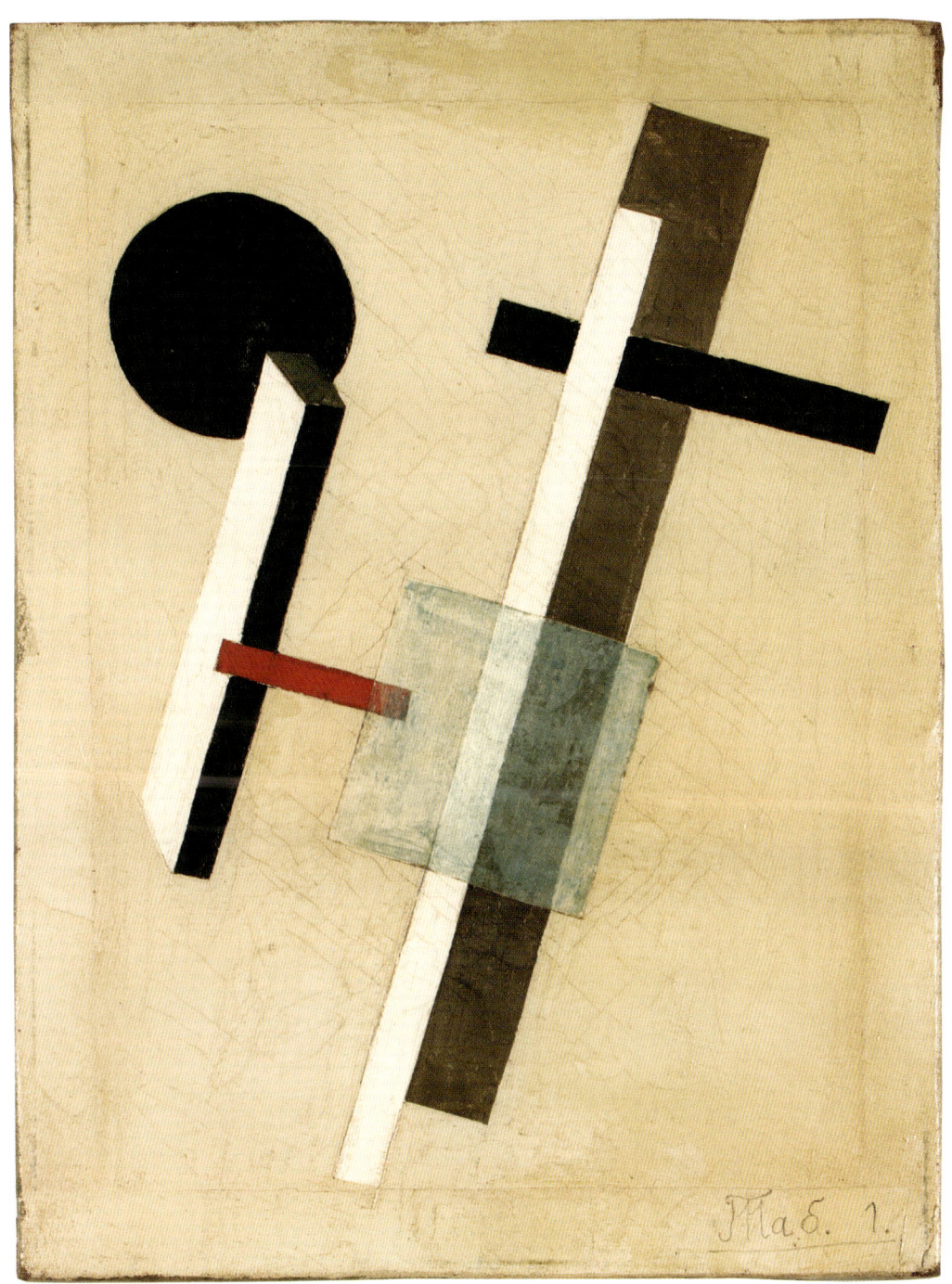

Figs. 24–25
A painting sold directly to Ron and Roger that, with its subtle play of flatness and dimensionality, was executed in the style of **Liubov Popova. The** inscription in the lower left corner is the letter "yat" in the old **C**yrillic alphabet.

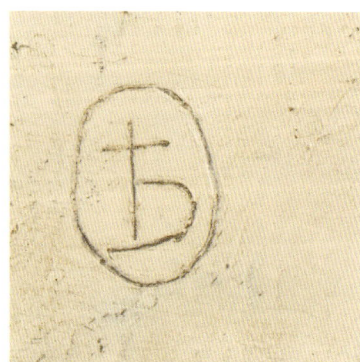

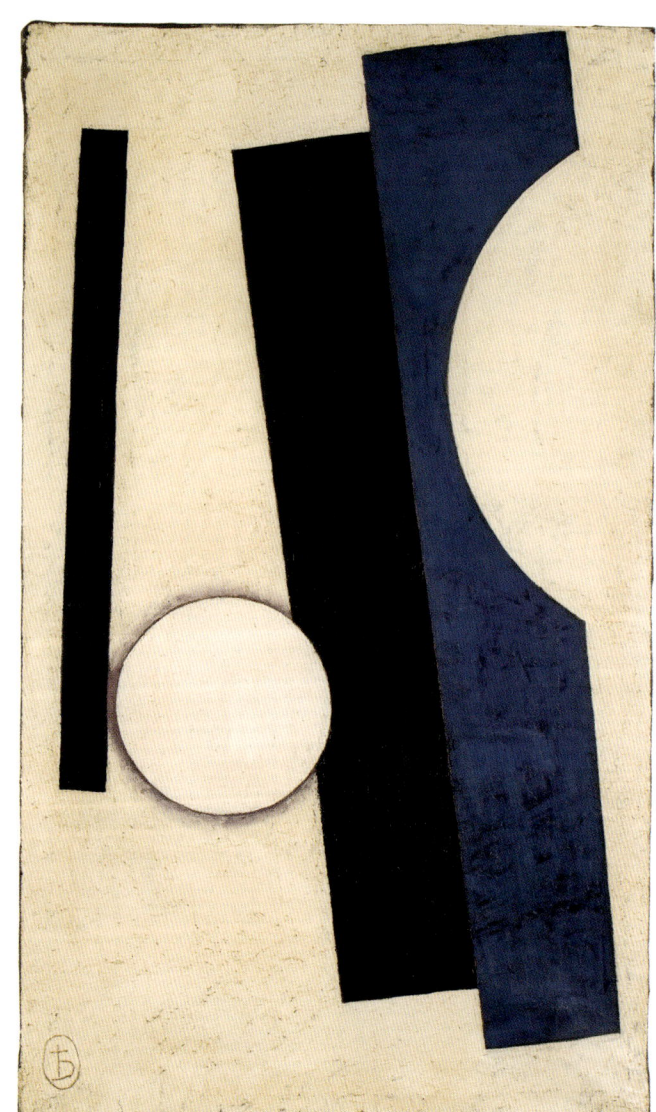

when they saw the first painting from the German seller on eBay, the brothers had acquired thirty paintings, and Brad and other friends had bought about a dozen more. [Figs. 17–25] Ron and Roger alone spent about forty thousand dollars.

Convinced that they had authentic Russian masterpieces in hand, Ron hired an appraiser who had been a curator at a local museum for thirteen years and an independent consultant for almost twenty years. For a fee of ten thousand dollars she spent three months inspecting the works and another month researching the market, examining auction results in Moscow, London, New York, Berlin, and elsewhere. In the end, she produced a 111-page report with the following assessment: "Based on a reasonable degree of appraisal probability, it is my opinion that the total fair market value for the 30 paintings is $50,101,909."[3]

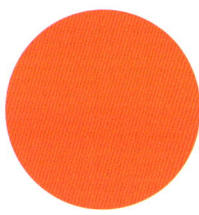

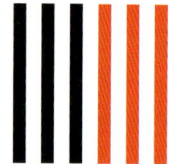

THE RUSSIAN
AVANT-GARDE

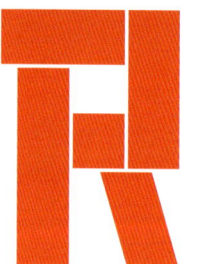on's fascination with the art of the Russian avant-garde, which began long before he knew of its astronomical market value, is understandable given the rich philosophical, artistic, and political issues at play around the time of the Russian Revolution. The story of the Russian avant-garde begins about a decade before the revolution, when a group of Russian artists attempted to surpass the achievements of their peers to the west. Trying to transform the advances of the cubists in France and the futurists in Italy into a new movement entirely their own, the Russians ended up following two different paths—or rather, they discovered two sides of the same coin.

These two sides were already a point of discussion within Marxist philosophy, which became influential in Russia around the same time. When Karl Marx and Friedrich Engels wrote, "In direct contrast to German philosophy, which descends from heaven to earth, here we ascend from earth to heaven," they underscored that Marxism prioritized work over thought, seeing the material conditions of life as the hidden source for the lofty ideas born in the minds of philosophers.[1] The Russian avant-garde movement in art took up this question, but where Marxism focused on materialism, the Russian artists of this period were continually divided between the physical reality of work and the sublime ideals of art.

Oversimplifying matters for the moment, the duality of the Russian avant-garde is neatly symbolized by the titan figures of Vladimir Tatlin and Kazimir Malevich. The two artists settled into their opposing paths in the 1910s, even before the revolution amplified the fervor of their ideological differences. Tatlin stood for what was real, believing that art was the manipulation of the cold, hard materials that make up the modern world. As he put it, art was a simple matter of the "shaping of material in space."[2] Malevich, on the other hand, believed that artists embody the "purity of human creative life," and saw the miraculous in the simple human capacity for invention.[3]

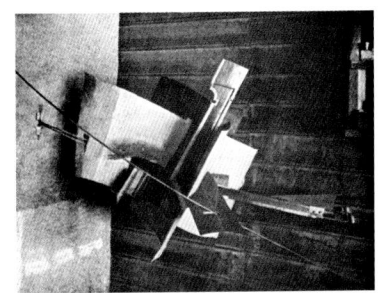

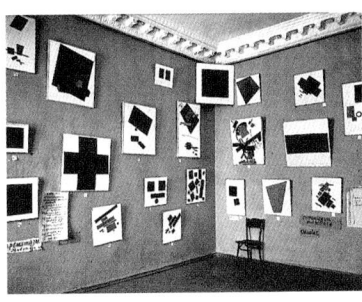

Fig. 26
Vladimir Tatlin's *Corner Counter Relief*, 1914–15, at the 0.10 exhibition. Whereabouts unknown.

Fig. 27
Malevich's suprematist paintings at the 0.10 exhibition

The conflict between these two approaches came to the fore at the exhibition 0.10: The Last Futurist Exhibition of Paintings, held in Petrograd in 1915. At 0.10 (pronounced "zero-ten"), Tatlin presented cubist-derived assemblages of industrial materials, reliefs that protruded off the wall and hung from cables pulled taut across the corner of the room. [Fig. 26] While Tatlin's works in the exhibit bore the weight of industry, Malevich's pieces seemed to hover in space. In a groundbreaking body of work that he called suprematism, he produced paintings containing sharp-edged shapes. Neither landscapes nor portraits nor still lifes, the canvases offered an ideal white space on which rectangles, rods, and other geometric forms floated. The most famous of these paintings—*Black Square*, consisting of a black square on a white ground—hung high in a corner of his room in the exhibition. [Fig. 27] According to Malevich, the square is the "zero form," the emptiness at the very center of things.[4]

Tatlin's work for 0.10 involved pounding, cutting, balancing, and welding. He was a sailor before becoming an artist, and his approach to art making was that of the worker harnessing materials and natural

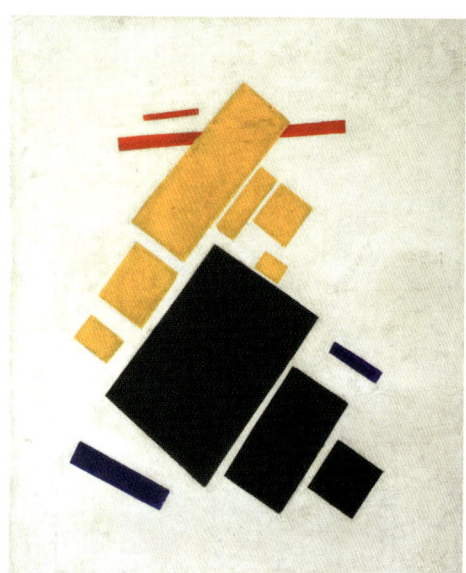

forces. Malevich, on the other hand, painted shapes that were removed from the recognizable world. He gave the subtitle *Airplane Flying* to one of his suprematist paintings that consists of geometric shapes traveling in loose formation across a neutral space. [**Fig. 28**] Malevich identified with the aviator, rejoicing in the human capacity to break free from the restrictions imposed by nature. Identifying with sailor and aviator, respectively, the two artists occupied the opposing fields of earth and sky, the dichotomy prefigured by the writings of Marx and Engels.

Despite the differences in their approaches, Tatlin was paranoid that Malevich would steal his ideas. He even went so far as to build a kind of tent inside his studio and kept his current work locked inside it.[5] In the months leading up to the 0.10 exhibit, the two artists worked in absolute secret, only installing their works in the gallery on its opening day. At the opening itself, they supposedly got into a fistfight.[6] This shift from a conflict of ideas to a contest of physical strength might serve as a metaphor for the movement as a whole, which seemed to turn on a dime between the metaphysical and the physical. At Malevich's funeral, in 1935, Tatlin looked at the corpse and said, "He's faking." [7] It is possible to see this as more than just a cheeky insult—the continuation of a rivalry into death. Since nothing is more real than a corpse, Tatlin's comment reads like the materialist's final dig at the idealist for refusing to traffic in reality.

After the Bolshevik Revolution, Tatlin began to use the language of the revolution in his art. Rather than talking about the manipulation of materials, he spoke of art in terms of its utility for society. He became one of the founders of the constructivist movement, which eschewed the idea of individual expression in art and denounced artists like Wassily Kandinsky for their subjectivity and mysticism. Espousing the constructivist idea that art should merge with life, Tatlin designed pots, pans, overcoats, and stoves.[8] Fellow constructivists Liubov Popova

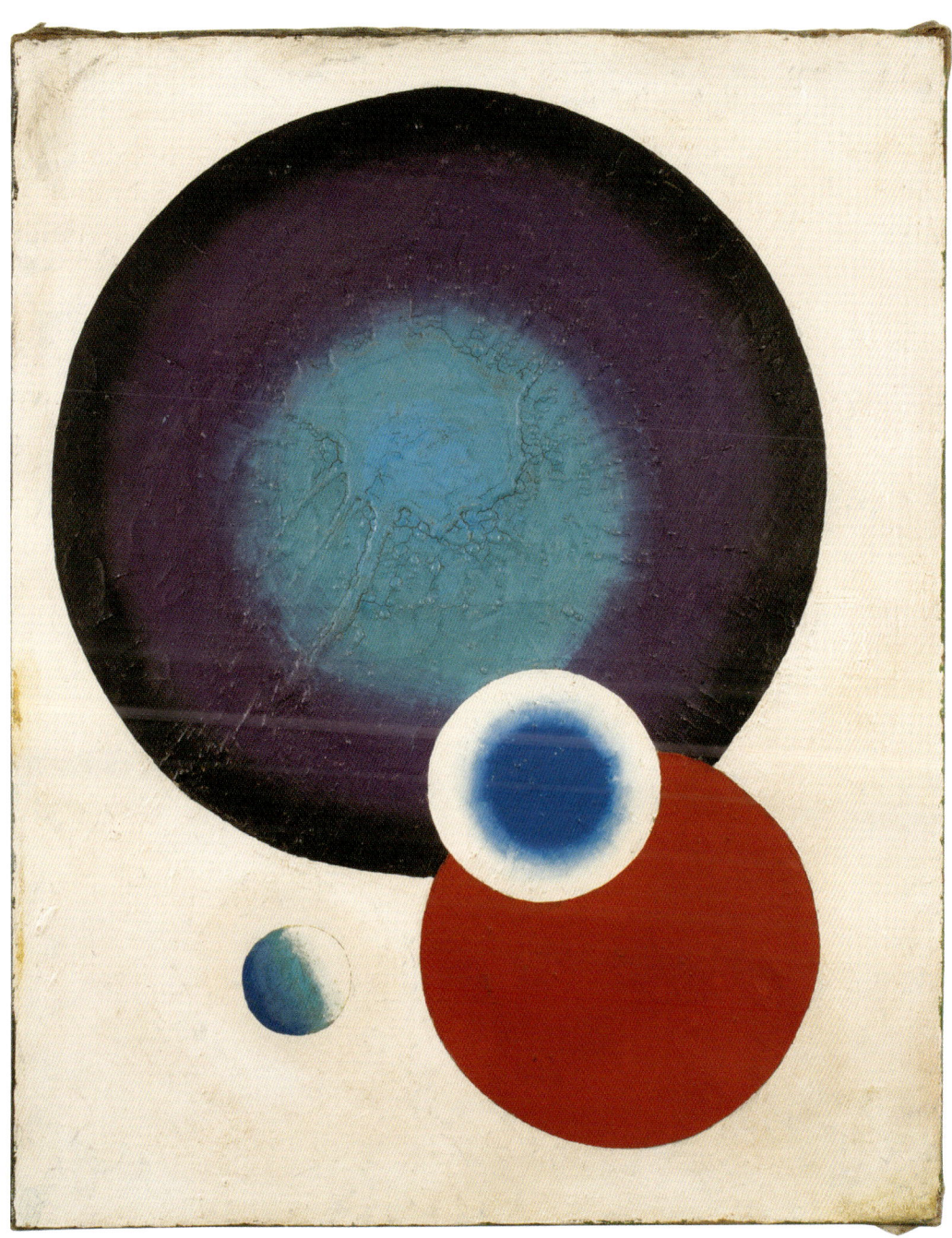

Fig. 30
This painting in the collection is similar to Popova's constructivist works.

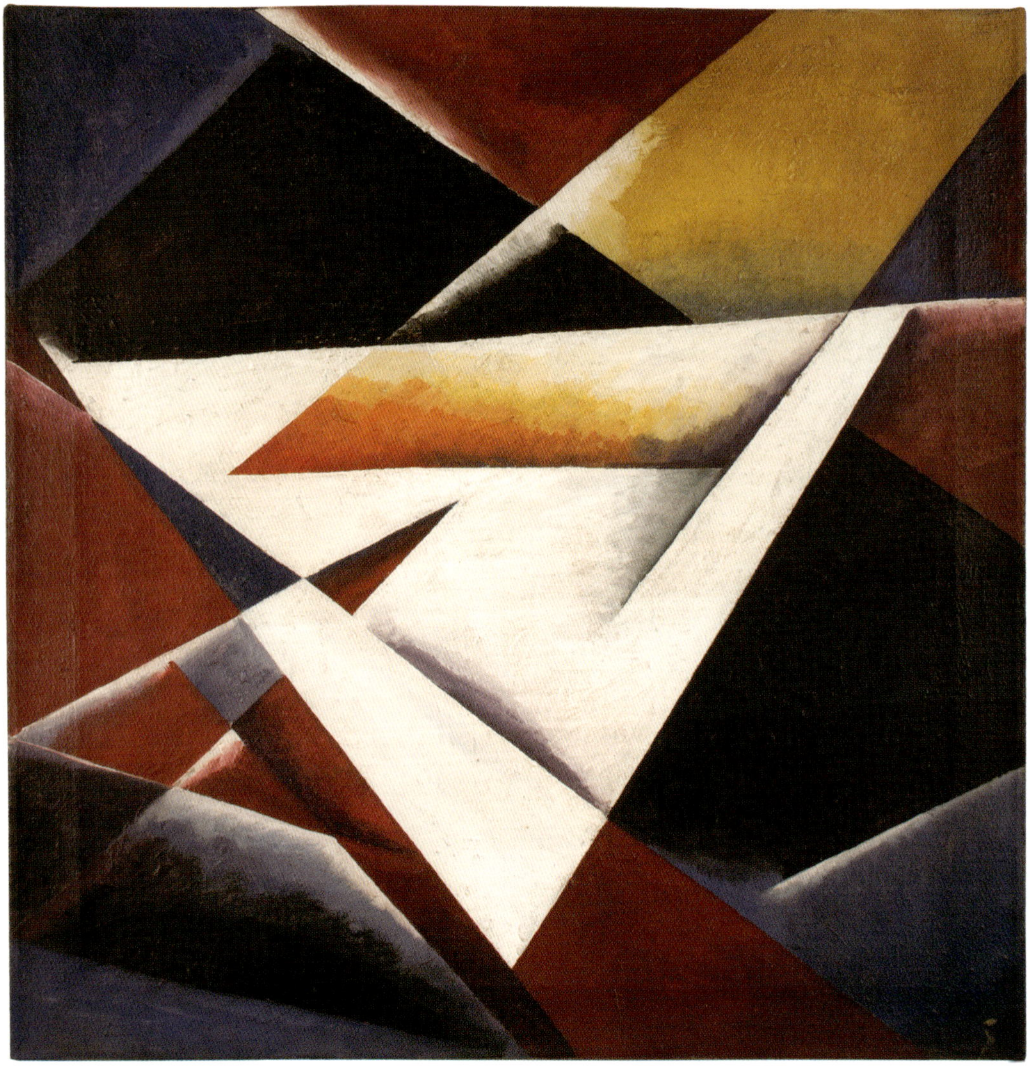

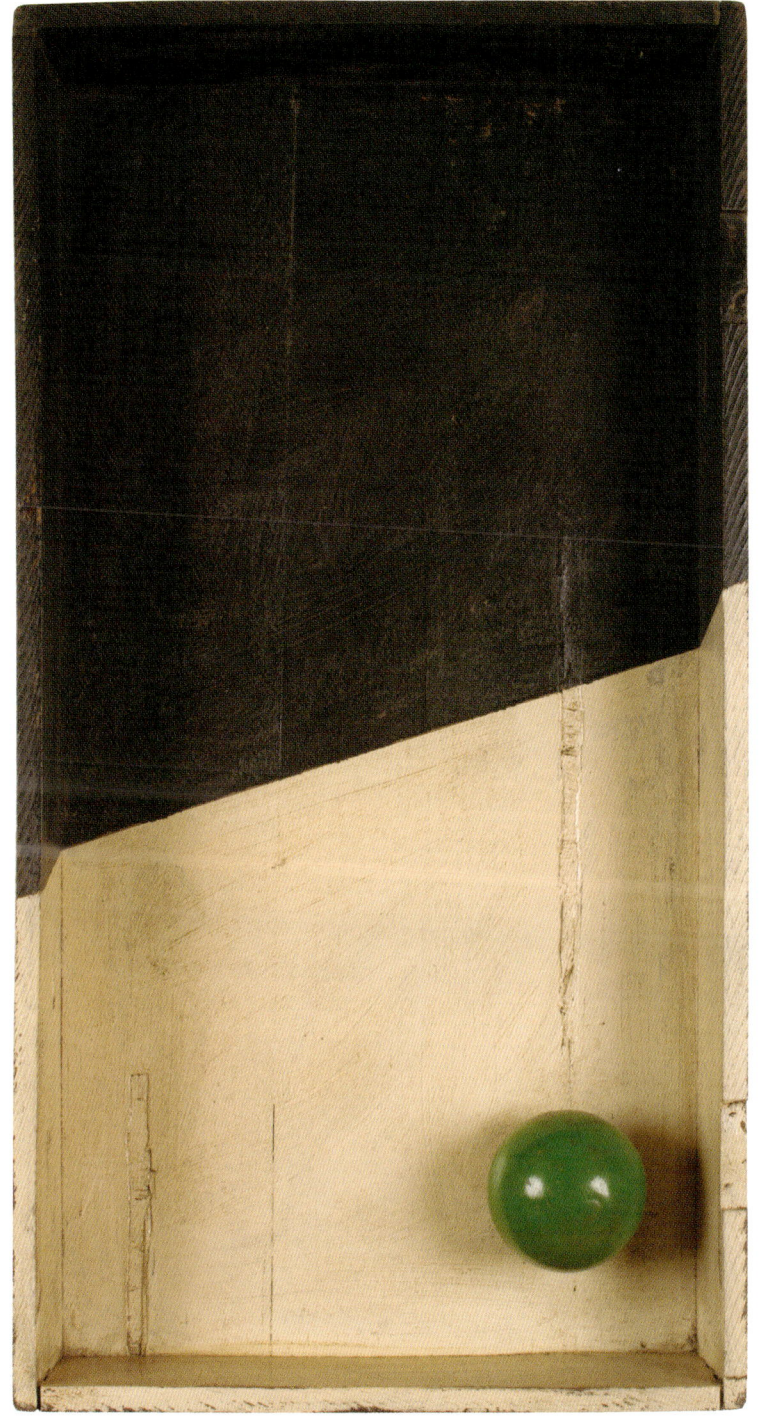

Fig. 31
An assemblage reminiscent
of the works of Ivan Puni

and Varvara Stepanova designed clothing and mass-produced textiles, while Aleksandr Rodchenko created packaging and advertising for Soviet state-owned businesses.[9] These endeavors emphasized the utility of art, integrating it into a new visual vocabulary for Communist society.

Tatlin and Malevich make easy caricatures for the two sides of a conflict, but their ideological differences cannot be summed up as a clear-cut battle between materialism and idealism. Parsing the difference between them in this way serves as shorthand for understanding the issues that ran throughout the Russian avant-garde in general, but the artists did not always partition so smoothly. For example, constructivist art was not entirely oriented toward mass production and industry. Through 1921 Popova and Rodchenko made paintings and sculptures in dialogue with the purely aesthetic impulses explored by both Tatlin and Malevich before the revolution. Several of the early works that Ron and Roger purchased bore a resemblance to Popova's and Rodchenko's experiments with technical and geometric elements in painting. [Figs 11 + 25] Even as these artists formulated ideas about the practical purposes of art, their works spoke directly to the movement's earlier experiments with nonobjective forms, the detachment of art from objects of nature.

Ron and Roger collected paintings suggestive of both sides of the divide represented by Tatlin and Malevich, with works in the style of both constructivist and suprematist schools. [Figs. 29-32] However, the figure of Malevich looms over the collection more prominently than any other artist. This is partly because the works attributed to him made up the majority of the fifty-million-dollar appraisal and partly because he was predominantly a painter, while many of the other artists worked in sculpture and other media. But Malevich's story also speaks to the issues surrounding the paintings in the bank vault. Like Ron's unauthenticated

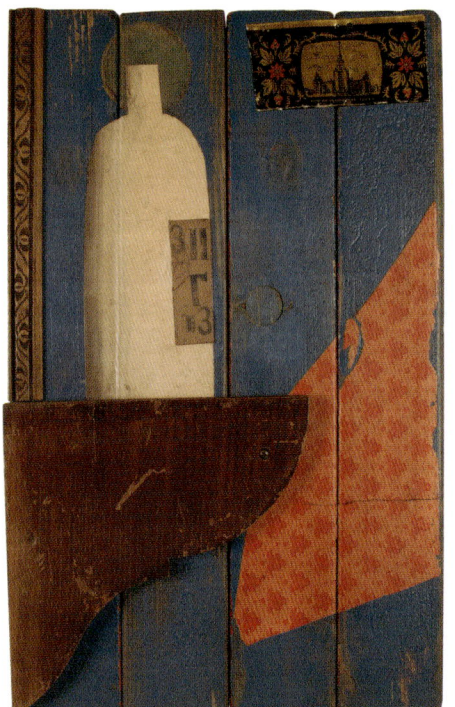

Fig. 32
Constructivist artists made paintings out of nontraditional materials—similar to this work—to emphasize their connection to everyday life.

paintings, Malevich's works vacillate between being objects with simple, physical properties and works of cosmic significance. [Figs. 36–37]

Recent research by scholar Aleksandra Shatskikh in her book *Vitebsk: The Life of Art* paints a picture of Malevich as an artist whose desire to create ideal art was continually in conflict with his interest in material conditions. For example, in 1919, when he decided to leave a teaching position in Moscow and accept one at the provincial Vitebsk School, he wrote the following announcement:

> In spite of my desire to continue working here I have been compelled, in the absence of an apartment (I'm living in a cold dacha), firewood, or electricity, to accept the offer made by the Vitebsk studios, which will provide me with the necessary working and living conditions, and to leave Moscow. — K. Malevich [10]

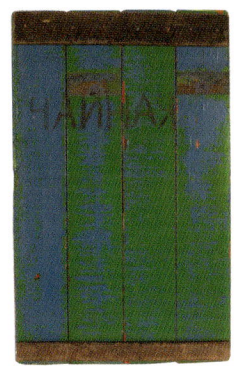

Fig. 33
Reverse of Fig. 32. The inscription translates to "Tearoom."

After such a baldly physical proclamation Malevich arrived in Vitebsk and presented himself before the student body as if he were a mythical figure. He appeared at the top of the university's main hall, in front of the entire school assembled below, and then slowly descended the steps while continually waving his arms in giant circles. He then continued this motion at the podium. Though he created a lasting impression on many students, none of them was able to remember if he spoke any words on that occasion. [11] Malevich was enacting the suprematist principles of his art in this performance, embodying a form of movement that did not correspond to any found in society or nature.

Fig. 34
Malevich's original *Black Square* painting was lost. He created this later version in 1923. (State Russian Museum, Saint Petersburg)

Though Malevich was fervently pursuing abstraction, or non-objectivity, in his paintings from this time, it would not be unreasonable to see his circular arm motions as being suggestive of the propellers of an airplane, given that the airplane was such an important symbol for him. In his 1926 manifesto, *The Non-Objective World*, he referred to suprematism as being "aeronautical," because he saw his art as being detached from the modern, industrial vision of the city that inspired the cubists and futurists. [12] Talking about the inspiration for his art in the manifesto, he describes a view of Earth from an ascending airplane: "The familiar recedes ever further and further into the background.... The contours of the objective world fade more and more and so it goes,

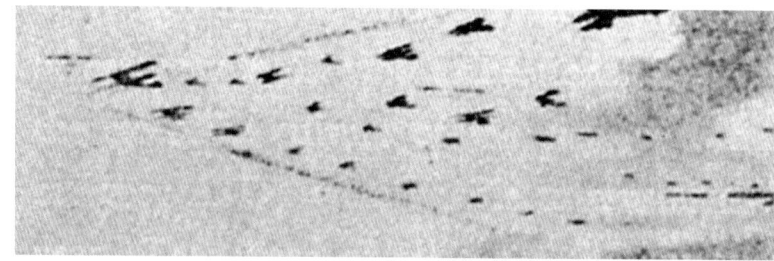

Fig. 35
Airplane flight was a source of inspiration for Malevich's suprematist ideas. This photograph appeared in Malevich's major treatise *The Non-Objective World: The Manifesto of Suprematism*, 1926.

step by step, until finally the world—'everything we loved and by which we have lived'—becomes lost to sight."[13] In flight, the airplane allows for a metaphysical perspective, a pure place from which to grasp the presence of the world without having to see any one thing in particular. [Fig. 35]

Though the image of the airplane in flight suggests a sense of detachment from the life of the city, Malevich was surprisingly invested in the dissemination of suprematism in public life. In Vitebsk he worked with his closest associate, Lazar Lissitzky [Fig. 38], to create suprematist decorations throughout the city. They adorned factories, stores, homes, and other buildings with panels of floating geometric shapes on white backgrounds.[14] This public display was consistent with the growing theatricality of Malevich's leadership at the school. The artist became the leader of a new association at the school—called Exponents of the New Art, or Unovis—and wore a white gown and hat to symbolize the group's belief in "the purity of human creative life."[15] In a gesture that combined elements of both religion and politics, he asked his students to "Wear the Black Square as a Sign of the Economy of the World."[16] Lissitzky adopted the forename "El" based on the hymn of the Unovis group, which derived from a nonsensical line in an earlier poem by Malevich: "U-EL-EL'-UL-TE-KA."[17] Malevich even named his daughter, Una, after Unovis.[18] All this suggests that, as much as Malevich thought that he was representing the pure act of human creation, he spent a great deal of time in Vitebsk not creating but promoting. Instead of locking himself away in a studio, he made art a part of the real activities of life.

As Malevich adopted a quasi-political role in advocating for his particular approach to art, it is not surprising that his historical reputation was heavily affected by real political conditions. In 1924 he began

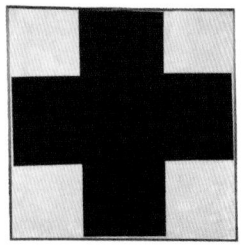

Fig. 36
Malevich's cross paintings—including this 1923 work, *Black Cross*—generally showed the same width for the vertical and horizontal axes of the cross. Though not interested in religion, Malevich imbued his works with a deeply spiritual impulse. (State Russian Museum, Saint Petersburg)

Fig. 37 (opposite)
This white cross on a black background is stylistically similar to Malevich's suprematist work.

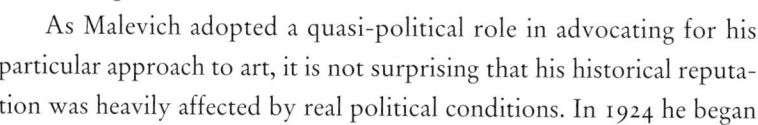

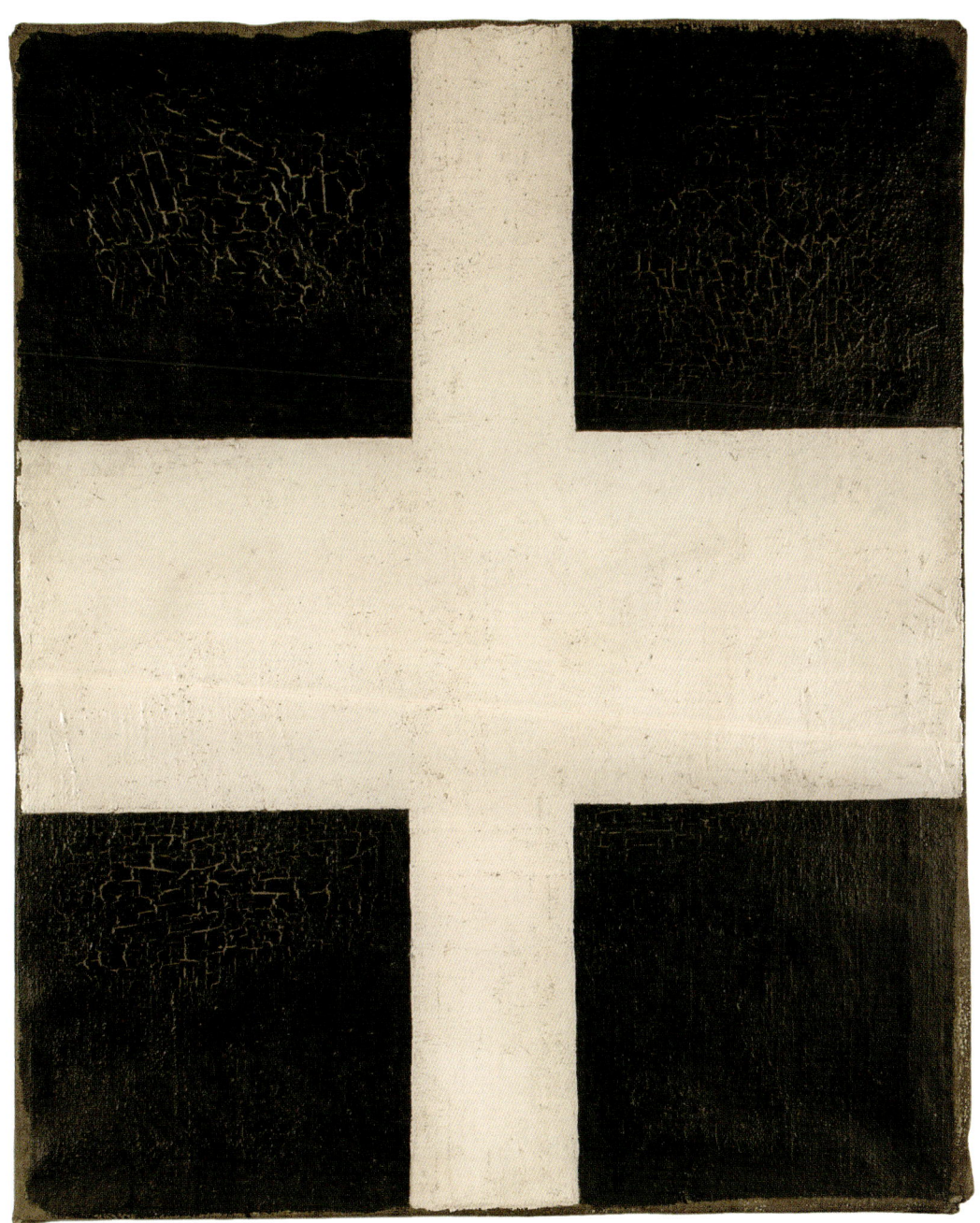

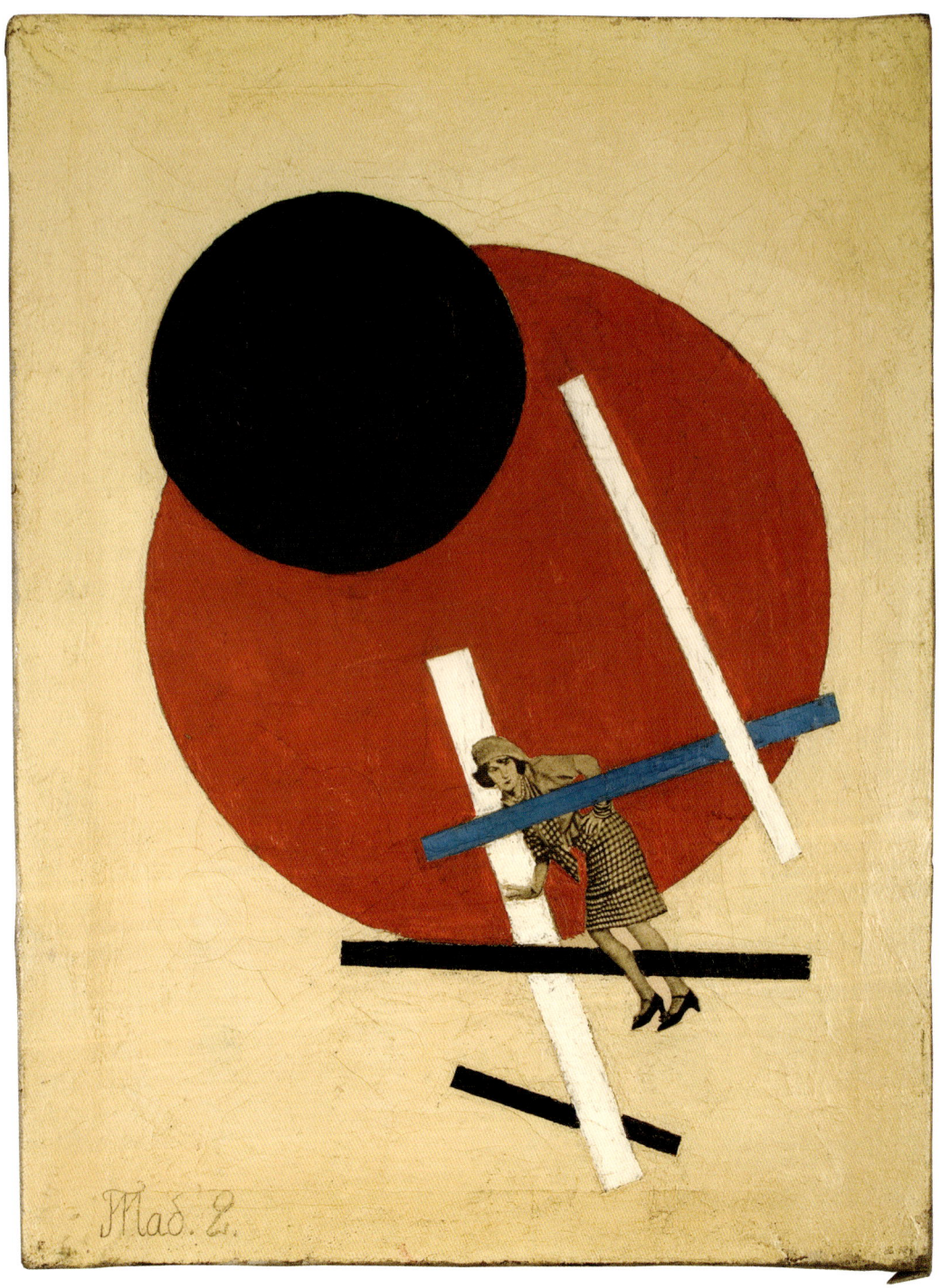

petitioning the government to allow him to travel abroad, and in 1927 he was able to leave the country and mount a major survey exhibition of approximately seventy of his works at the Great Berlin Art Exhibition. Malevich left Germany four months before the exhibition closed to return to the State Institute for the History of Art in Leningrad, where he was based at the time, leaving his works in the care of architect Hugo Häring, who had organized the exhibition.[19]

By this time the political climate in Russia had shifted against the avant-garde, and the artist was concerned enough about his fate and that of his works to draw up a will in case of his untimely death. Within a few years, Malevich was fired from his post at the institute in Leningrad, and his department was dismantled. He wrote to a friend, "I am left without a piece of bread....The last fighter for new forms has fallen down."[20] The government, which now favored the new socialist realist style, accused Malevich of making art "not for serving society but only for the sake of form." He was jailed for a time amid accusations that he was practicing "formalism."[21] His later requests to travel abroad were denied, and when he died in 1935 at age fifty-seven, many of his works were still in Germany.

The year of Malevich's death Alfred Barr—then director of New York's Museum of Modern Art (MoMA)—traveled to Germany and selected twenty-one works by the artist to bring back to New York. To get them out of the country, he rolled four paintings up in his umbrella and shipped the remaining as "technical study material."[22] Most of the remainder of the works that Malevich left in Berlin were hidden away in a shipping crate to protect them from confiscation by the Nazis. Many of these were eventually acquired by the Stedelijk Museum in Amsterdam. The MoMA paintings were labeled as loans until 1963, when they were accessioned into the permanent collection.[23] All of these works were the subject of protracted negotiations and lawsuits beginning in 1993, when Malevich's heirs attempted to reclaim them after the fall of the Soviet Union. After two decades passed and many

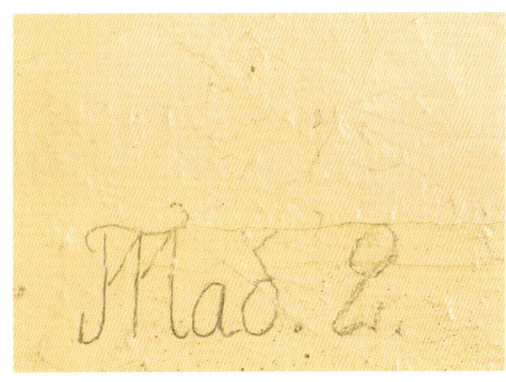

Fig. 38 (opposite)
Like his mentor Malevich, Lissitzky made art that combined architectural spaces with flat geometric shapes, similar to this work.

Fig. 39 (above)
The inscription on the lower left of figure 38 translates to "Tab.2."

millions of dollars crossed hands, the cases were resolved with the museums retaining the majority of their Malevich holdings.

Artworks that originally were put in the world amid talk of "the purity of human creative life" thus eventually became the subject of fistfights, government interrogations, and legal depositions. Paintings associated with "the emptiness at the center of things" survived confiscation because they were pliable enough to be safely wrapped around the stem of an umbrella. With this background in mind, it seems entirely appropriate that unidentified works with a possible connection to this milieu would be sold over eBay for the price of a decent sofa. These works may be icons of a glorious moment or they may just be, as Roger first intended them to be, stuff to decorate a house.

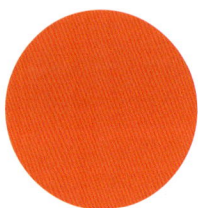

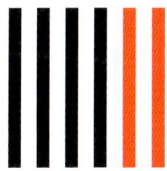

THE SEARCH FOR ORIGINS

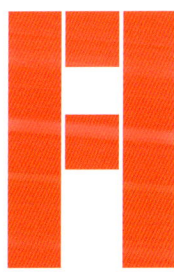fter only a few months of collecting art, Ron and Roger learned that, like the fate of Malevich's works, the destiny of their own collection would be largely determined by unsympathetic authorities. At first, they thought they might get rich from their paintings, and the fifty-million-dollar appraisal confirmed their sense of the works' worth. Then, as Roger put it, "Quickly the flame went out."[1]

Appraisals do not offer judgments about the authenticity of works of art. Rather, they assess artworks' market value assuming their authenticity. For example, to valuate a painting that looks like a work by Malevich, an appraiser would determine what buyers were paying for equivalent works by the artist. In 2000, a painting by Malevich sold for seventeen million dollars at Phillips auctioneers in New York, so Ron and Roger were not very surprised to hear that their collection, *if* it were authentic, would be worth a fortune.[2] The problem was, of course, how to get their work authenticated.

As a first step Ron and his friends tried to learn as much as they could about the paintings' sellers. Two midlevel insurance administrators living in the German city of Aachen, they were extremely responsive and accommodating and had received 100 percent positive feedback from eBay members. While they had broken eBay rules by selling some of their paintings off-line, this was not an uncommon practice. A more unusual detail perhaps was the sellers' request for payments to be sent to several different bank accounts.

When asked about the origins of the paintings, one of the sellers sent a rambling response (reproduced in Appendix B, pages 148–49), explaining that a shipping container from Russia had arrived at a German customs office in the 1980s and remained there because the shippers couldn't pay the duty. After a long time, customs officers broke open the container and found that it was filled with Russian icons and paintings. They auctioned off the contents, and a circle of antique dealers throughout Europe began to trade in Russian avant-garde art from the shipping container. Some of these works eventually made their way into the hands of the eBay sellers in Aachen. The sellers believed that the paintings were originally student works, locked away in cellars during the Stalin era when abstract art was condemned and forgotten until after the fall of the Soviet Union. At the end of his email, the seller wrote, "I hope that the message is interesting for you. You know that I won't give you the name of my 'collector-friends-dealers.'"

Though they were silent about their sources, the sellers certainly did not appear to be mastermind criminals or forgers. Three years after this exchange, Roger's friend Brad had the opportunity to meet them in person while on a trip to Europe. They agreed to connect at the Gare du Nord train station in Paris. Brad would recognize the sellers based on the following description:

> W. will wear his traditional red/orange market-success jacket from Windsurfing Chiemsee and he wears glasses. I will wear my black jacket with a small Oakley "O" icon in silver and a small backpack in blue from nitro snowboards. My hairstyle is very easy, no hairstyle! because I have nearly a bald head.

Brad later described the two men as "this large sort of enforcing looking guy and this professor looking guy." It turned out that the person that Brad thought was the enforcer was actually more of a translator. As Brad explained,

> The older guy who is really the collector was very sharp but I would say one of the things that was interesting is that he was not as knowledgeable about the avant-garde as I would have thought for somebody who has all these paintings. He didn't seem to know a lot about many of the artists or to even have heard about them. But they seemed quite open. I mean there didn't seem to be any duplicity in them. They were perfectly willing to meet.[3]

The people Brad met at the train station turned out to be a lot like him, Ron, and Roger—small-time collectors and amateur traders with an eye for novel things. In the meeting, the sellers repeated their belief that the paintings were probably student works that ended up in Europe in an unclaimed shipping container.

Several elements of the sellers' story about the paintings are dubious, however. There is something overly cinematic about customs agents breaking open an abandoned shipping container and finding a treasure trove of art. It is also too convenient an explanation for why the works have no history of ownership. Based on the sellers' story, Ron and his fellow painting owners would have no way to trace the works' provenances back to a caretaker in Russia, let alone to their original makers.

Some parts of the sellers' story seemed plausible enough, though. It made sense that, given the relatively low price of the works, they would move through a network of antique dealers rather than art galleries. The sellers' theory that the paintings were made by students also made sense, as most of the major figures of the Russian avant-garde surrounded themselves with students. Malevich had the loyalty of nearly an entire school at Vitebsk. It was common practice for students to adopt the approach of a single teacher with whom they aligned, and students would often copy the works of their teachers in order to master the techniques of the great artists. Many of Malevich's

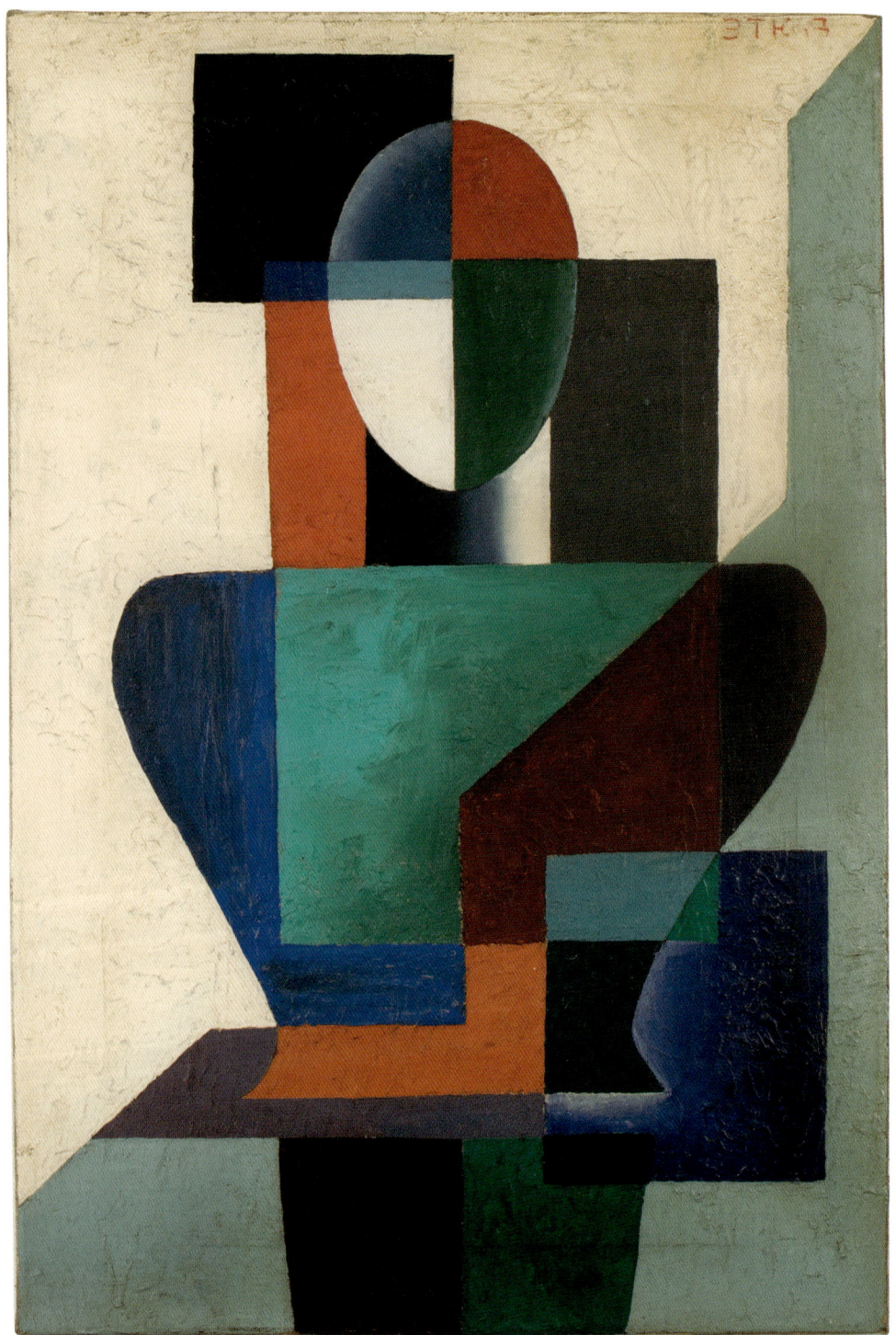

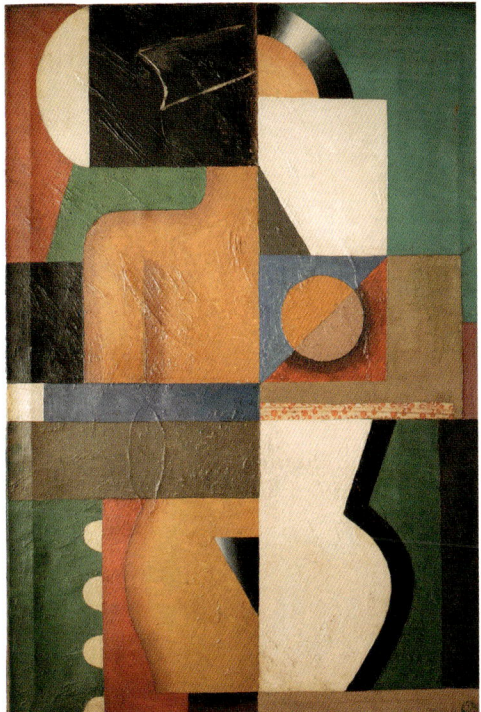 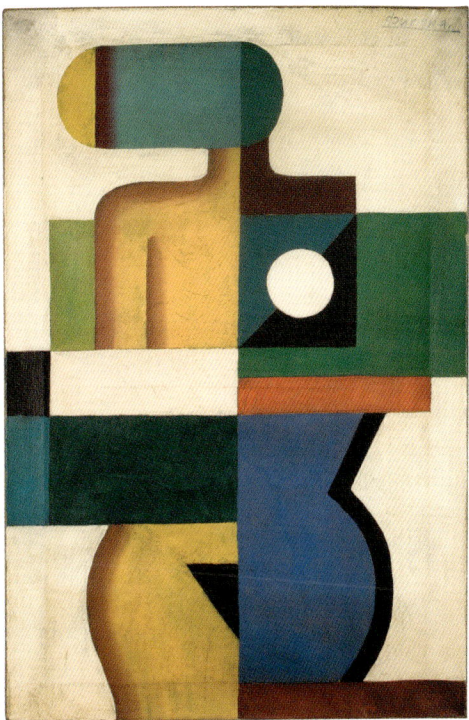

students and others imitated his style in their own works—a practice that he encouraged.[4] This would explain the existence of many older, unsigned works in the style of the Russian avant-garde masters.[5] [Figs. 40–46]

Though Ron and his friends had initially hoped that their purchases would make them rich, they were not entirely adverse to the idea that their paintings might be student works. Ron, in particular, holds an intuitive belief that the works were made by the masters of the Russian avant-garde, but their value to him would not change greatly if he found out that they were painted by the masters' students instead. Having the mentality of a collector of antiques, rather than art, he thinks of authenticity primarily in relation to a particular time period, not a particular person. Even if the paintings turned out to be student works, they would still be the products of an exciting moment in art history and be authentic works of the Russian avant-garde. Unfortunately, even this basic information could not be known for certain.

Figs. 40–46 (opposite, above, overleaf) These works, which appear to have been painted by different artists, all depict a human body defined by simple geometric shapes that extend to the edge of the canvas, with a strong vertical division in their center. The existence of so many similar works suggests that they were made following a teacher's assignment.

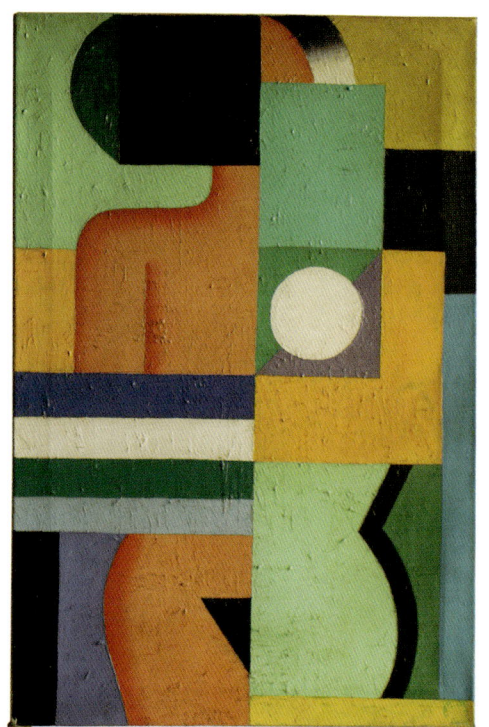

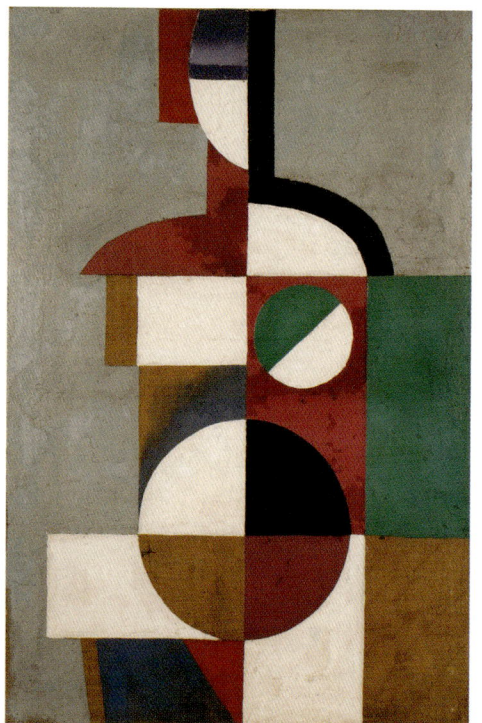

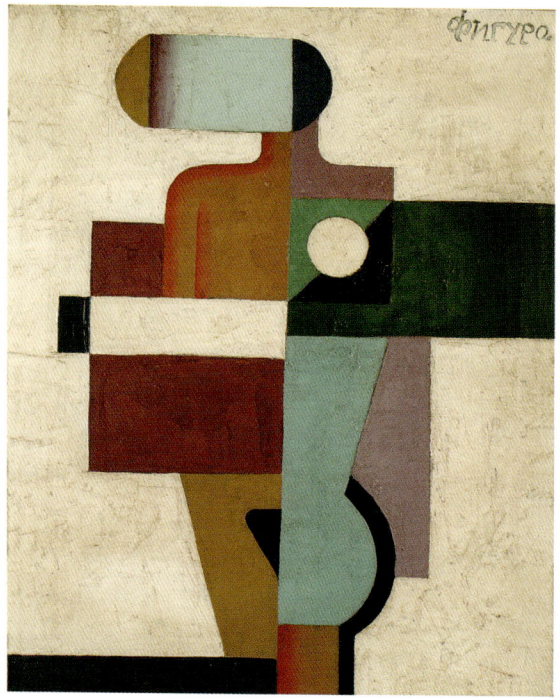

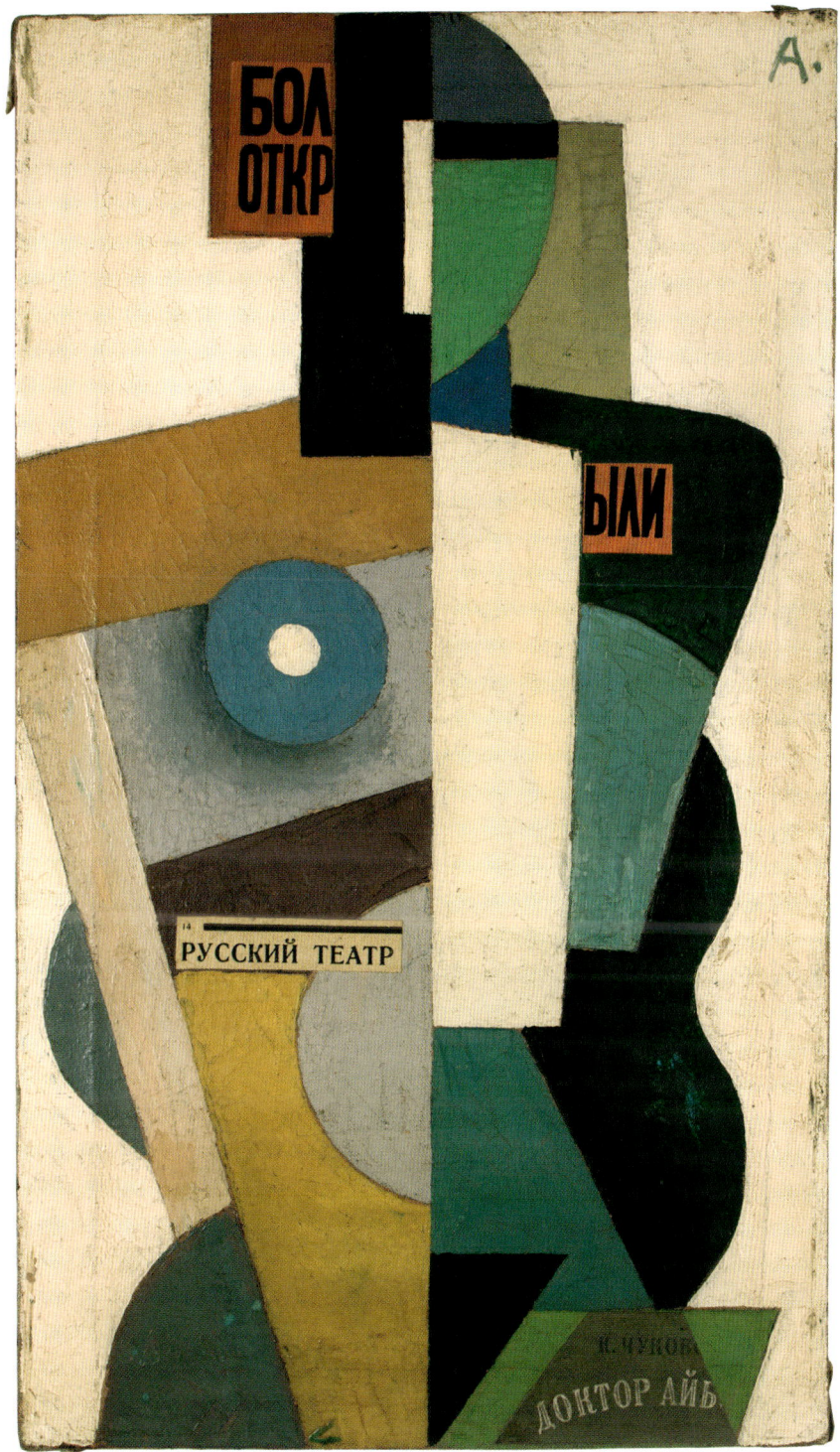

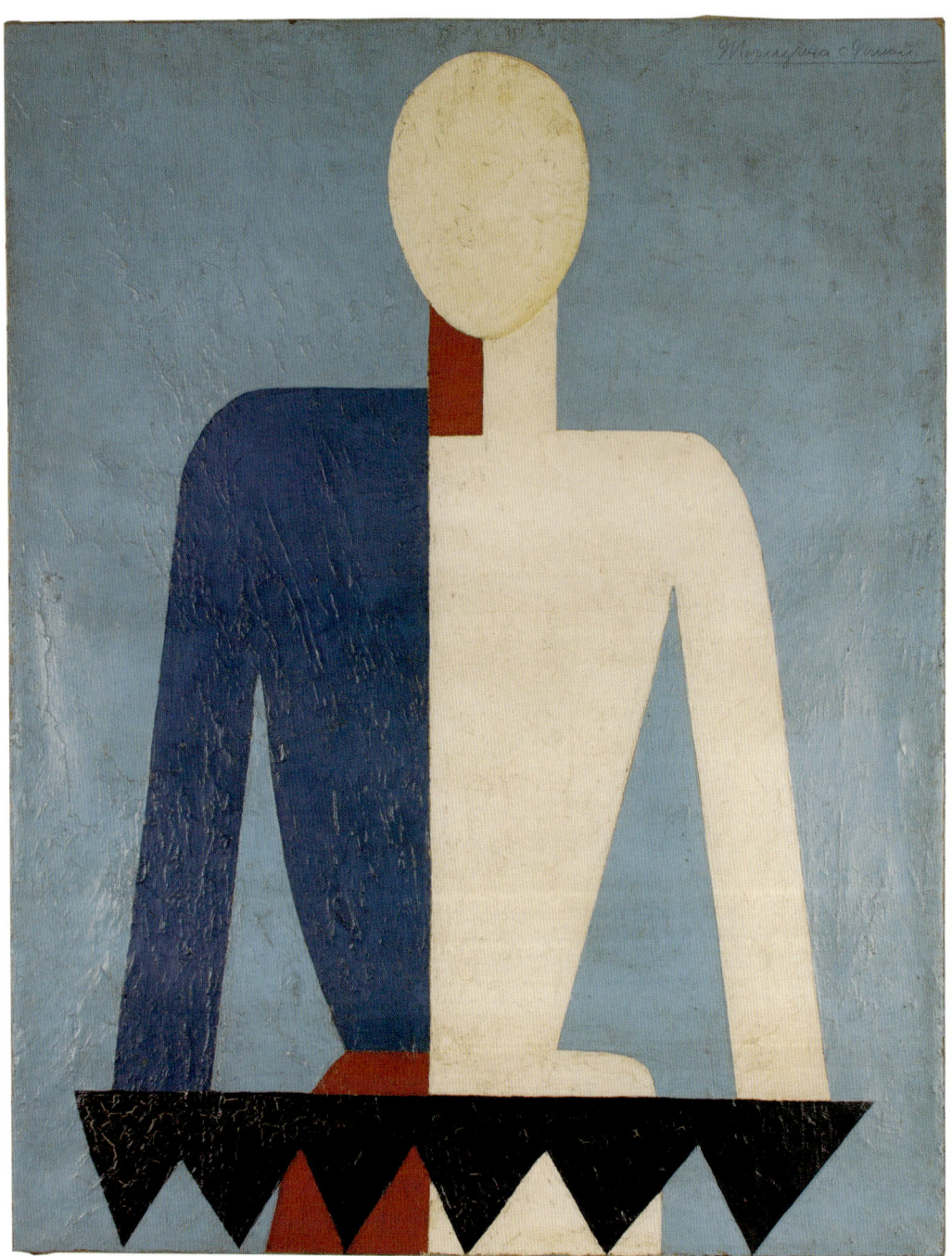

Since the sellers' story about the paintings' provenance did not open any avenues for research, Ron decided he would have to seek out the evidence of their origins from the works themselves. He contacted a forensic handwriting analyst to find out whether the handwriting on some of the pictures matched that of one of the Russian avant-garde artists. In particular, he sent her a photograph of an inscription that was lightly penciled on the upper-right corner of one of the paintings that looked nearly identical to a work by Malevich found in the State Russian Museum. Both works depict sparsely outlined torsos, and the unauthenticated painting also has what looks like a saw—an object that Malevich included in some of his earlier works—on the bottom of its canvas. [Figs. 47–48] The Malevich painting in the museum has the initials "K. M." on it, but there is no signature on the unauthenticated work, just a Cyrillic inscription in a corner that translates to "Woman with a Saw." [Fig. 49]

The handwriting analyst compared the inscription on Ron's painting to several documents that Malevich is known to have written, including his journals. After completing her analysis, she reported that there were "similarities in word spacing, initial and terminal strokes, letter connections, upper and lower connections, angular and rounded letter styles," and other characteristics. She concluded that there was a "high probability" that the two texts "were authored by one and the same writer." [6] This analyst had thirty-eight years of experience in handwriting identification and often serves as a qualified expert witness in federal courts. Her testimonials are used to put people in jail. She had no financial stake in her findings on the painting, one way or the other.

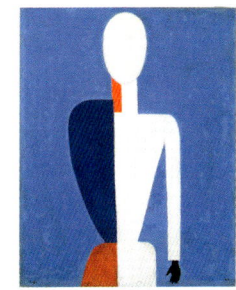

Fig. 47 (opposite)
Ron suspected this painting, which is very similar to Malevich's *Torso, Transformation to a New Shape,* **to be by the same artist.**

Fig. 48
Malevich painted *Torso, Transformation to a New Shape* **between 1928 and 1932, a period when he was interested in archetypal human figures. (State Russian Museum, Saint Petersburg)**

Fig. 49
A close-up of the Cyrillic inscription on the upper-right corner of the painting

Fig. 50
Text known to have been written by Malevich

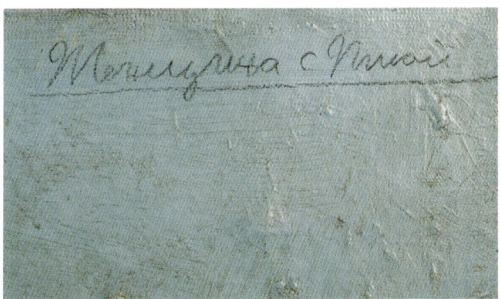

When Ron and Roger learned of the apparently perfect handwriting match, they became increasingly certain that they possessed an authentic Malevich. Why would someone have forged the words "Woman with a Saw"? Why would someone with the ability to imitate Malevich's handwriting perfectly enough to fool a professional handwriting analyst not simply forge the artist's signature or even just his initials on the painting? Only two letters, not an entire phrase, would have been needed to make the artwork look convincingly authentic. A forger with a great sense of subtlety would have had to make the work. Why would such a talented forger be willing to sell his or her paintings for so little money? After all, if the sellers in Aachen were willing to sell the works on eBay for as low as six hundred dollars, they themselves could not have paid more than two or three hundred dollars per painting. It wasn't just the opinion of an expert but also the application of simple logic that suggested that the work was genuine.

Ron, Roger, and their friends were encouraged by the report from the handwriting analyst and continued to buy paintings from the Germans. However, this apparent confirmation of the works' authenticity brought up other issues. Ron began to think of the risks associated with possessing important paintings acquired through such suspicious circumstances. If the works were indeed genuine, he imagined that something horrible must have happened to separate them from the families that owned them. They could have been illegally confiscated during Stalin's purges in the 1930s, or the Nazis could have seized the paintings from the homes of collectors during World War II. Issues of cultural patrimony were potentially at stake.

Ron decided to hire a lawyer to find out more about these matters. He wanted to protect himself, his brother, and his friends if they ever sold any of the works and it was discovered that they were originally acquired illegally. When Ron showed the lawyer the paintings' fifty-million-dollar appraisal report, he quickly recommended adding a co-counsel who specialized in offshore asset protection. Even though anyone in the art world would have considered the works' appraisal useless because they have not been authenticated, the lawyers took it to be a meaningful assessment of value. After hearing Ron's story, the co-counsel recommended that Ron inform the Federal Bureau of

Investigation about the collection before selling any of the paintings to make sure that they were not stolen property.

An FBI agent in Salt Lake City spoke to Ron, Roger, and the two lawyers for almost an hour, gathering the facts about the purchases and discussing the collectors' options and the associated risks. After this initial discussion, the agent began working with Interpol to determine if any of the eBay paintings had been reported as being stolen. (Incidentally, before obtaining any findings, the FBI agent contacted one of Ron's lawyers to ask if the brothers would be willing to participate in a sting operation, possibly to nab Russian mobsters who were trafficking in stolen artworks. The lawyer rejected the agent's request on his clients' behalf.)

While waiting to hear back from the FBI agent, Ron decided to try another method of authenticating the paintings. By this time, he and his fellow buyers had acquired approximately seventy-five artworks from the Aachen sellers. A pigment analysis would determine if the chemical composition of the works' paint was consistent with the types of paint that were used in the second and third decades of the twentieth century. Unfortunately, no scientific analysis exists that can determine if artworks are in fact from a certain time, and it is common for forgers to acquire old canvases and paint over them with old paints. The best that a laboratory can do is look for elements that could not have existed at the time that a painting was supposedly made to offer evidence that a work was created later than originally suspected. Therefore, a laboratory cannot prove that a work is authentic but only provide evidence that a work is inauthentic, if it contains elements that are too new for its alleged date of origination.

Ron sent one of his works—the painting of the white cross [Fig. 37]—to a lab in Chicago, informing the head microscopist that he suspected that Malevich had painted it in 1915, the year of the famous 0.10 exhibition. Based on its appearance alone, the microscopist initially told Ron that the painting he had sent seemed to check out with his story.[7] A few days later, though, he told Ron that they had found titanium in the work's white paint. Titanium white pigment was first invented in 1916, but experts believe that it was not used in paintings until many years later.[8] Responding to Ron's initial direction, the report concluded that the painting could not have been painted in 1915.

This was devastating news for Ron and his cohorts, who had been fairly certain that the paintings were authentic works of the period. They began to find flaws in the lab's analysis. Brad questioned the expertise of the scientist who conducted the analysis, writing in an email to Ron and Roger, "What is the predictive value positive of his tests (see if he knows the term predictive value positive)?"[9] Ron conducted his own quasi-scientific analysis, asking a different lab to test the titanium levels of regular house paint. He concluded that, by comparison, the titanium in his unauthenticated painting was miniscule. Ron and his fellow painting owners performed their own research on the use of paints around the time of the Russian avant-garde art movement. Roger found a reproduction of a chart published in a 1932 issue of the *Journal of the Royal Society of Arts* indicating the dates of introduction of various "inorganic derivatives of metals."[10] This chart stated that titanium white was introduced in 1920 and thus could have been used by Malevich. After their own investigations, Ron, Roger, and their friends remained unconvinced of the value of the professional pigment analysis.

While the collectors were determined to disprove the results of the lab, its analysis did not actually entirely rule out the possibility that Malevich had painted the white cross. Ron had asked the lab to test whether it had been painted in 1915—the year of Malevich's breakout exhibition of suprematist works, which included a black cross painting. The lab's official report specified that the painting was "most likely created shortly before or, more likely, after 1924, and, even more likely, after 1938."[11] The painting could not have been painted in 1915, but when Ron submitted the painting to the lab, he did not know that Malevich made cross paintings and drawings through the late 1920s. According to Malevich's catalogue raisonné—usually accepted as the definitive source of an artist's work—he even made a large black cross painting as late as 1924.[12] While this fact does not authenticate Ron's white cross painting or even prove that it was made in Malevich's lifetime, it does keep the door to those possibilities open a crack.

As another step in finding out more about the paintings, Ron photographed them in front of a light box—a low-tech substitute for X-ray

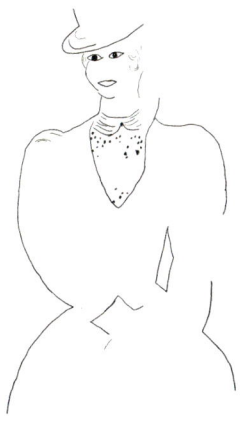
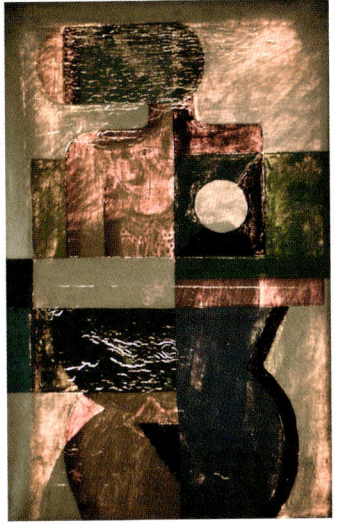
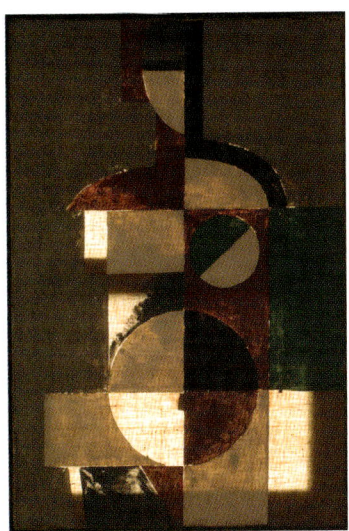

photography—to reveal any underpainting. While the resulting images showed that some of the canvases had been painted over, their analysis did not reveal anything about the identity of the artists. [Figs. 51–52]

In the meantime the FBI agent in Salt Lake City had checked with Interpol and other stolen art registers and had found no record that any of the works bought by Ron and the others had been reported stolen. As strange as it seems, the friends might have preferred a different report. If the paintings had been found to be stolen, Ron and his fellow collectors would have returned them to their rightful owners and, so they imagined, have received a finder's fee for their efforts. This outcome would also have brought some certainty to the origins of the paintings.

Attempting to add his own interpretation to the case, the FBI agent waxed philosophical about art, telling the brothers, "What one person values, another person could care less for. One person may pay a million bucks for something another person wouldn't pay ten cents." [13] He assumed that if someone was willing to pay a fortune for something, this reflected what they saw in the work. But the agent did not quite grasp that the situation was different in the high-dollar modern art world, where monetary value has little to do with what works are worth to anyone personally. An artwork's value is in fact almost completely determined by objective factors that have nothing to do with

Figs. 51–52
In one of Ron's light-box photographs, the face of a woman is visible under the red paint in the torso of the surface.

Fig. 53
The results of Ron's light-transmission images are often striking photographs, even if they do not reveal any underpainting.

Fig. 54 (opposite)
**The painting in Ron's
collection that a leading
expert on Malevich
dismissed as inauthentic**

the eye of the beholder. A guarantee of authenticity, a legalistic deter-
mination by a recognized authority, affects the price of a work by
powers of ten.

Understanding the system, Ron knew that he needed the approval
of elite figures in the commercial art world in order to have the collection authenticated. He decided to engage his friend Michel Pariseau, a
project manager at a Connecticut architecture firm, to help him make
connections with the New York art world. Michel became a partner in
Ron's endeavor, negotiating a percentage of the paintings' future sale
prices in exchange for his assistance in bringing the works to market.

Soon after he became involved, Michel contacted a fairly well-
connected art dealer in Connecticut who tried to show the works to
various people in New York City's art world. She approached a major
gallery that deals in modern art, but their blunt response to the paintings' story was, "If they are not fake, they're stolen."[14] The art dealer
had better luck with one of the top auctioneers in New York, who
examined a book of photographs of the collection and agreed to meet
with Michel. While he told him directly that the works looked great,
he also let him know that without a convincing record of the paintings'
ownership, there was nothing to be done with them.

Michel eventually hired a person referred to here as Susan, an expert
with many years of experience in conducting art-authentication research,
for a fee of three hundred dollars an hour. According to Susan's detailed
invoice, she began by conducting "Internet research on Museum websites Met, Guggenheim, MoMA" (see Appendix C on pages 150–51 for
a reproduction of her invoice). She flew out to Denver to look at Ron's
painting collection and agreed to contact a specialist on Russian avant-
garde art on the brothers' behalf.

A few months later, Susan met with a leading scholar on
Malevich, referred to here as Alexis. This scholar regularly provides
opinions on questions of authenticity, making determinations on
whether works are worthless fakes or treasured masterpieces. Alexis
looked at photographs of four of Ron's paintings that resembled
works by Malevich. According to Susan, after studying the painting shown on page 57 [Fig. 54]—a complex composition of rods and
other geometric shapes that Ron believed was painted around 1915—

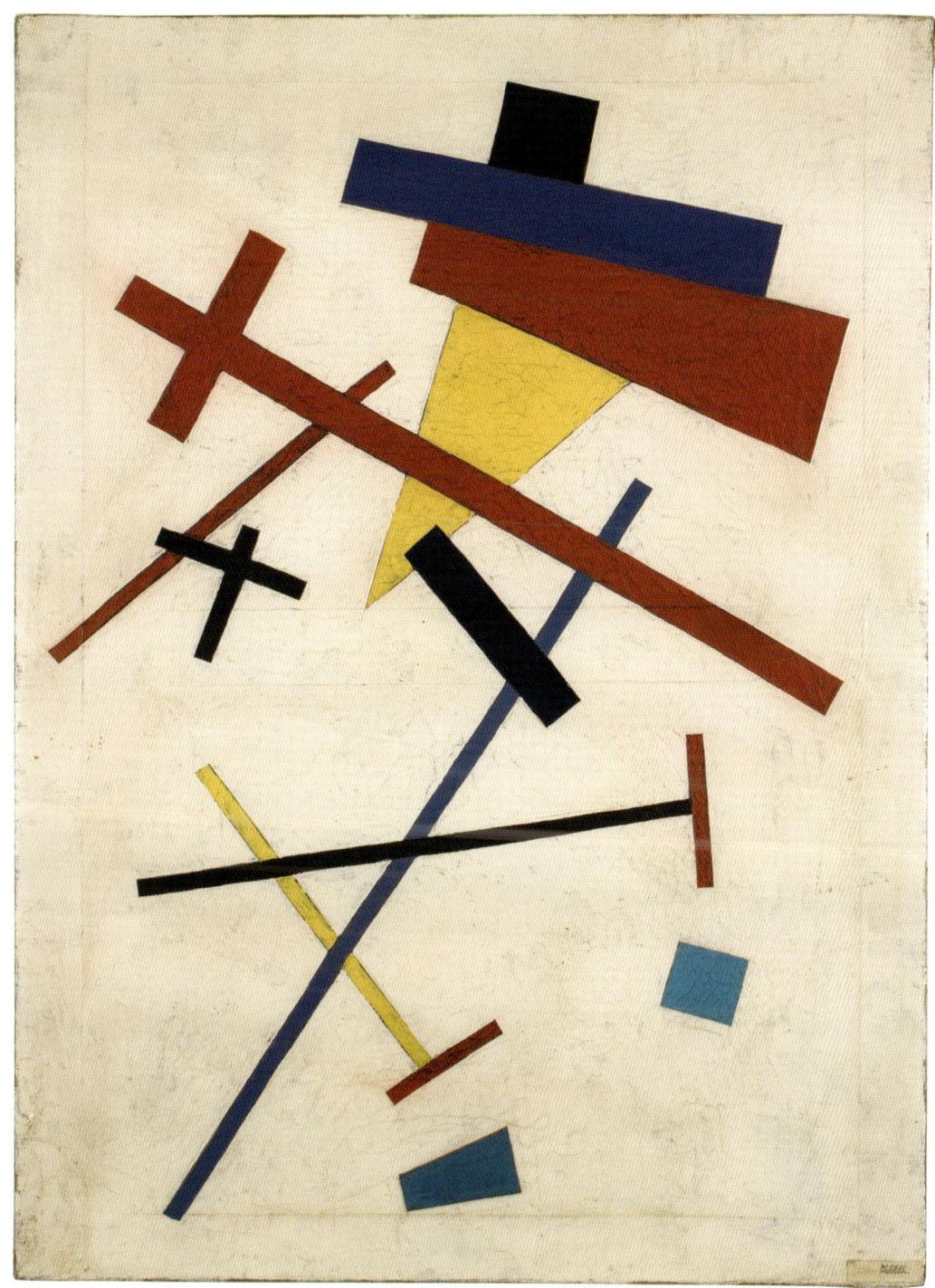

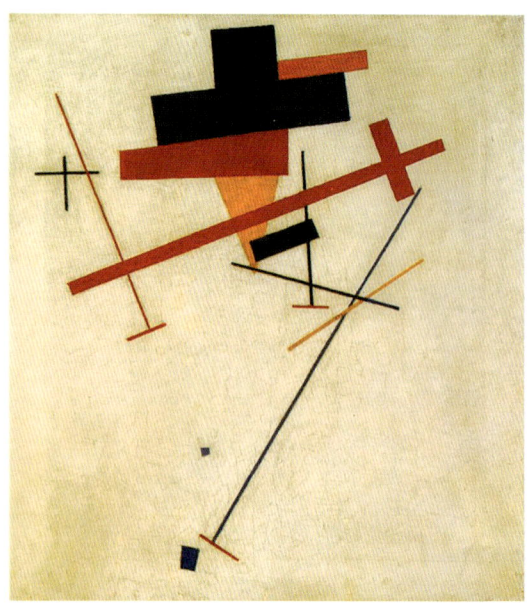

Alexis "did not recognize the mind or the process of Malevich" in the work.[15] Susan went on to report that Alexis was especially suspicious of the dark red cross in the upper part of the painting because she believed that "the cross shape as a motif did not enter Malevich's vocabulary until fifteen years after the style that this painting is imitating and could not appear in a Malevich of this period of his work."[16] Since the suprematist style that the painting is "imitating" emerged in 1915, according to the scholar, Malevich would not have used the cross shape until 1930.

The scholar's assertion that Malevich did not incorporate the cross motif in his suprematist-style paintings of the 1910s is peculiar, to say the least. A nearly identical cross appears in a very similar painting by Malevich, dated 1915–16, in the collection of the Wilhelm-Hack-Museum in Germany.[17] [Fig. 55] As there are only about 350 authentic Malevich paintings in existence, clearly the scholar would have known of the painting in the museum's collection. In fact, the cross motif appears in some of the artist's most iconic works from the 1910s and 1920s.[18] The scholar's argument that crosses did not appear in Malevich's works until the 1930s—fifteen years after Ron's painting was supposed to have been created—is equally curious. This period was likely the only time in Malevich's postsuprematist career that he *did not* use the cross motif, because in the 1930s he was painting portraits and other figurative works.[19]

How could such a respected Malevich scholar make such glaring mistakes? One explanation could be that Susan accidentally misrepresented Alexis's words. This seems unlikely, though, as Susan transcribed her notes from the meeting word for word in her invoice to Ron. If Susan did in fact accurately record the scholar's words in her transcription, it is possible that Alexis may not have taken the interview seriously. However, this is also unlikely. A serious scholar would

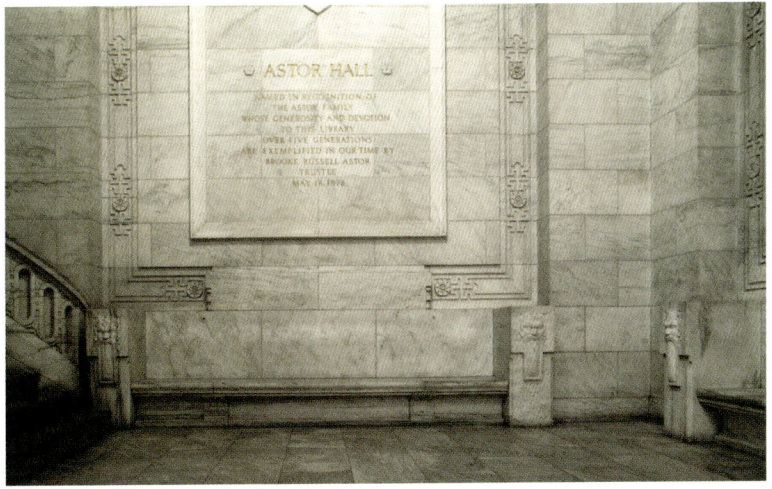

presumably avoid stating gross factual errors, even in off-the-cuff remarks in an informal interview.

There is, in fact, something suspicious about Susan's account of the interview with Alexis. The report begins:

> 11:27 — I met [Alexis] in the entrance lobby of the New York Public Library at 42nd Street, where there are some marble benches halfway up the side staircases. [Fig. 56]

Why did Susan indicate the meeting time up to the minute? In other reports, she approximated the time or omitted it entirely. And why mention the precise location of the bench? It seems that Susan wanted no one to doubt that an interview with Alexis had occurred. Is it possible that Susan faked the meeting to placate her client?

Before Susan's meeting with Alexis, Ron had requested that she ask where the scholar thought the paintings might have originated from if she thought that the works were fakes. According to Susan, Alexis said that the paintings were likely created in Leningrad in the 1970s for Jewish émigrés who were leaving the Soviet Union around this time. These refuseniks were not allowed to take currency with them, only property. Some believe that a small industry arose in Leningrad of made-for-export copies of Russian avant-garde art for Jews to sell in their adopted country.[20] It makes sense that these emigrants would have tried to find alternative currencies, and rolled-up canvases would be easy to stow in luggage.

The refusenik hypothesis is commonly used to explain the large number of Russian avant-garde fakes in existence. Susan herself suggested to Ron that his collection might consist of fakes made for Jewish émigrés when she first saw the paintings in Denver. Though this theory is unproven, Ron was intrigued by the idea that the entire collection of paintings might have been created as a form of international currency for struggling immigrants.

After five years of researching the origins of their works, Ron, Roger, and their friends were left with only a few clues and wild hypotheses. They still believed that the works were genuine, and the handwriting match on just one of the paintings seemed to confirm that many of their works could be legitimately from the period. They believed against all reality that they might be able to persuade an authority to endorse their beliefs. This task would have been difficult enough for amateur collectors in any area of art history but in the case of the Russian avant-garde, the issue of authority is a minefield.

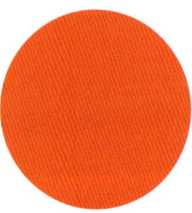

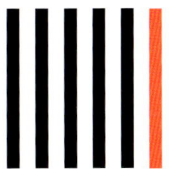

WHOM DO YOU TRUST?

on, Roger, and their friends are not unique in finding themselves with Russian avant-garde art whose status is uncertain. A 2009 article in *ARTnews*, a widely read art magazine, reported that "the number of Russian avant-garde fakes on the market is so high that they far outnumber the authentic works."[1] But even this assertion is misleading, because it implies there is certainty on such matters in the field. It suggests that there is common agreement on which works are fake and which authentic.[2] In fact, no major forgers of Russian avant-garde art have been arrested and their works uncovered in the way that forgers of other styles of art have.[3] There may be many fakes, but the bigger issue is that the status of numerous works is unknown or contested. The problem is that so many of these works lack provenance, a clear record of who owned them over time, which makes it impossible to authenticate them.

Many of the provenance issues for artworks of the Russian avant-garde stem from the fact that when the movement's artists died—and many of them died young—there was no accurate public account of

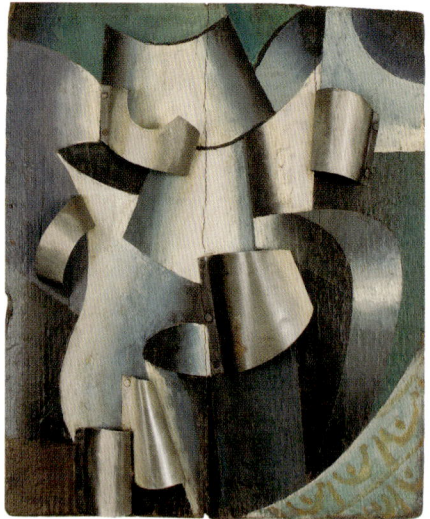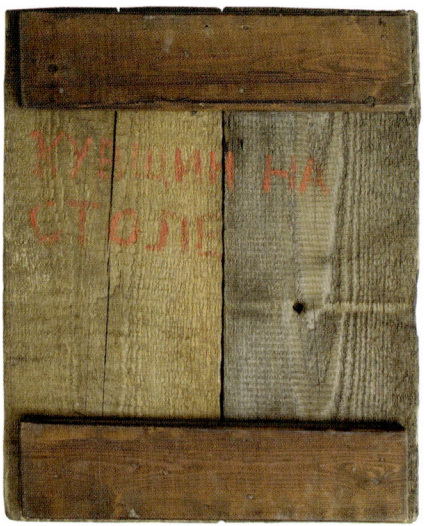

Fig. 57
A painting on wood in the style of Popova's works from 1915

Fig. 58
Reverse of Figure 57, with the inscription "Water on a Table"

the works they left behind. Because the style fell out of favor with the Soviet government, the works were often scattered and unaccounted for. Their owners attributed no value to them and took little care to preserve them. During the Cold War, Western scholars who were interested in this material had limited access to it. And after the fall of the Soviet Union, corruption posed a challenge to the careful inventory of art from the period.

Illustrating the problem is an account by George Costakis, one of the great early collectors of Russian avant-garde art, who worked as an administrative clerk in the Canadian embassy in Moscow from the 1940s through the 1970s. Trying to find paintings by Liubov Popova during his time in Russia, he visited the home of Popova's nephew [Figs. 57–58]:

> I found a village house, a big garden. I came just at blossom time; everything was in bloom, apple trees and cherries. They received me warmly. The first thing I noticed, going up the stairs to the second floor, was a Popova painting on plywood being used to support the trough where they did their laundry. Anyway, they showed me many Popovas, gouaches, drawings. Then we went for a walk around the garden. We went past the barn. I noticed that one of the windows was covered with a piece of plywood, and on the plywood was a number, then another

number, then the name "Popova."
I went inside, and on the inside of
the plywood was a splendid painting. I said, "I'll take this one too."
"No, he replied, "This one I can't sell.
It will rain, and everything will get
wet. Bring me another piece of plywood, and then I'll give it to you." So
I had to go back to Moscow to look
for a piece of plywood.[4]

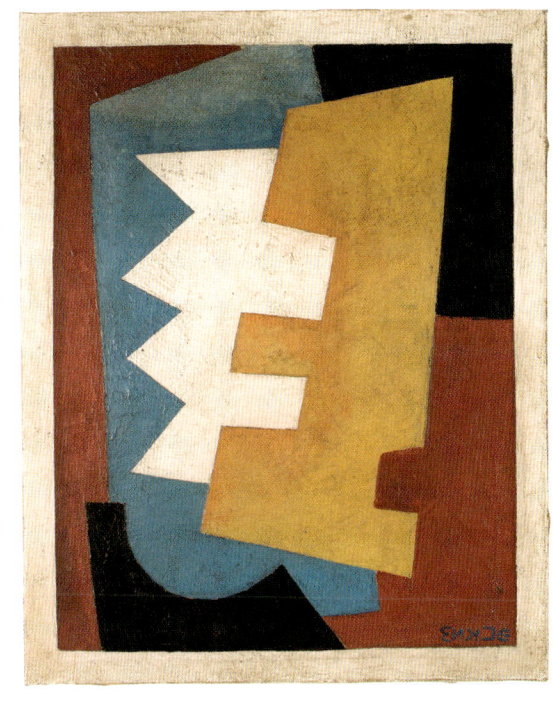

Costakis's story makes one wonder how many other paintings in the
Soviet Union were used to protect
houses from the rain. Once the art
was devalued, it became just property
to be passed along, or not, through
generations.

Fig. 59
**A painting in the style
of Alexandra Exter that is
similar to the works that
French police confiscated
from the exhibition in
Tours, France**

In light of these particular circumstances surrounding the Russian
avant-garde movement, it can be difficult even for well-intentioned collectors, art dealers, or museum directors to decide what is an authentic
work and to know whom they can trust. The previously mentioned
ARTnews article appeared a few months after the *Art Newspaper*
reported that French police had closed down and confiscated an entire
exhibition devoted to Russian avant-garde artist Alexandra Exter at
the Château Museum in Tours. The police seized the works following a complaint by the renowned Russian avant-garde expert Andrei
Nakov, who believed that the works were fakes. Nakov told the *Art
Newspaper* that only one of the 180 works was genuine.[5] [**Fig. 59**]

Nakov, who studied art history at the University of Paris's Institut
d'Art et d'Archéologie and the Ecole des Hautes Etudes, is the author
of a Malevich catalogue raisonné. He organized an exhibition of the
artist's works at the Tate Gallery in London in 1976 and he has written countless essays, books, and exhibition catalogs featuring other
Russian avant-garde artists, including four thematic books on the
movement.[6] According to Nakov's biography in his four-volume set

of books on the art of Malevich, he is "the leading world expert on the work of Kazimir Malevich and the Russian avant-garde."[7]

The exhibition that the scholar condemned was organized by art dealer Jean Chauvelin. Chauvelin studied ballet with a Russian instructor in the 1950s, which is how he made the connections that allowed him to acquire art of the Russian avant-garde. Though he does not have a formal education in art history, Chauvelin has "dedicated his life to the work of Exter."[8] Galerie Jean Chauvelin has been exhibiting Russian avant-garde artists since 1969 and presented a solo exhibition of Exter's work in 1972, along with a catalog written by Nakov. In 2003 Chauvelin coauthored a book on Exter, and his website suggests that his catalogue raisonné for the artist is forthcoming.[9]

Nakov does not mince words in his criticism of Chauvelin. An essay published by the Alexandra Exter Association, which Nakov presides over, implies that Chauvelin relied upon a fictional provenance to establish the legitimacy of the artworks he owns.[10] According to this essay, the authenticity of this body of works hinges upon an account of a Berlin antique dealer, who allegedly brought them from Russia to Germany in the 1920s. As the essay states, there is no archival evidence that this antique dealer had any relationship to Russian avant-garde artists; Exter did not even have the dealer's address in her address book, which Nakov personally owns as part of the Exter archive.[11]

In the face of Nakov's attacks, England-based art historian Patricia Railing came to the defense of the Exter works in Chauvelin's exhibition. Challenging Nakov to a kind of scholarly duel, she engaged in an online competition to prove or disprove the authenticity of the works. In this "Alexandra Exter Tournament," she presented seven extensively researched essays (or "jousts," as she calls them) that rigorously outline a new understanding of the artist's creative achievement.[12] In response, Nakov eschewed issues of style in judging the paintings' authenticity and remained focused on the provenance of Chauvelin's works, mocking the idea that so many works by Exter could have remained undiscovered until recently. A clear victor of their duel was never publicly announced.

Railing, like Nakov, practices art history outside of an academic setting, as the president of the International Chamber of Russian

Modernism (InCoRM), which solicits opinions about paintings in question from experts and provides a written opinion if four of the experts agree. The *ARTnews* article does not go so far as to accuse InCoRM of providing false opinions, but its tone is clearly intended to cast doubt on the organization's integrity, mainly through Chauvelin's involvement in it as one of its experts.[13] For example, the article highlights a suspicious sale of Russian avant-garde art at Nagel Auktionen, an auction house in Stuttgart, Germany. Among other things, this sale included three watercolors that Chauvelin attributed to an artist whose grandson, a recognized authority, "emphatically rejected" as works executed by his grandfather.[14] Though *ARTnews* casts doubt on Chauvelin and his colleagues, it does not champion his accuser, Nakov, either. The article points out that in the 1980s, the scholar was accused of certifying more than one thousand questionable pastels and drawings by Mikhail Larionov, another master artist of the Russian avant-garde.

The disputes between Nakov, Chauvelin, and Railing suggest a radical crisis of authority. Though all of them have deep knowledge of the field, they generally do not submit articles to peer-reviewed journals or publish books with academic presses, the kinds of practices that keep scholarly communities on the same page. They also do not have to answer to professional colleagues to the degree that curators employed by museums must. Rather, these scholars participate in more informal intellectual networks, with varying levels of connection to commercial markets, often creating their own platforms by publishing with private presses and self-publishing their research on websites.

New York art dealer Ezra Chowaiki—who had a gallery in Moscow from 2006 to 2009 and has sold works by such artists as Claude Monet, Edgar Degas, and Pablo Picasso—says that he is offered fake Russian art every week.[15] Unlike Nakov or Railing, Chowaiki does not claim to be a scholar—in fact, before becoming an art dealer, he was in the ice cream import business. However, as a honest trader he wants to be certain that the works he is selling are authentic.

According to Chowaiki, when dealing with a work of art by any major artist, Russian or not, the process is always the same: "In order for a work to be bona fide—a work that you can sell, trade, or own—you need to go to the proper authority." There is always a person, foundation, or other entity that certifies whether a work is authentic; the problem with Russian avant-garde works, Chowaiki believes, is that "a lot of these authorities have been corrupted."[16] With so many corrupt, competing, or unstable authorities in this area, he and other dealers specializing in Russian avant-garde art find themselves in a situation equivalent to trading in a currency issued by a government whose legitimacy is in doubt.

Many people have echoed Chowaiki's account of untrustworthy experts. For example, it is widely believed that corrupt art historians include illustrations of forged paintings in scholarly publications in order to "launder" them. In 2006 an internal investigation at the State Tretyakov Gallery in Moscow revealed that its department of expertise had falsely authenticated ninety-six fraudulent paintings before officially ending its practice of authenticating art.[17] In turn, curators at the Tretyakov were on the other side of the table in 2011, when they condemned two new books published in France about the Russian avant-garde artist Natalia Goncharova, claiming that 25 percent of the works in one book and 60 to 70 percent of the works featured in the other book were fakes.[18]

When Railing proposed an intellectual joust to determine the authenticity of a body of art, she was being good-humored about the state of the Russian avant-garde art world. But her suggestion accurately reflects a field where everything seems to be in contest. Ron and Roger think of themselves as powerless outsiders, but in fact they are contestants just like everyone else. And for what it's worth, they succeeded better than Chauvelin in having their works on display in a museum.

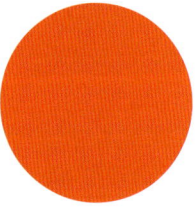

THE MERITS OF HALF-BELIEVING

In 2007, when my friend Mark Sofield told me about a guy who put together a massive collection of unauthenticated art, I had been running the Laboratory of Art and Ideas at Belmar for about two years. I created the organization, based in Lakewood, Colorado, to serve as an experimental space for investigating new approaches to art and audiences. Ron's collection was appropriate enough to what I was trying to do, but the opportunity it presented went beyond what even I was comfortable with at the time.

I was aware of the abundance of unauthenticated art of the Russian avant-garde on the market and knew that I could have curated an exhibition of unidentified Russian paintings of the period just from the current listings on eBay. So when Ron approached me with the idea of mounting an exhibition of his collection, my first reaction was not that it was too radical an idea but rather that it might be too ordinary.

I also worried about what my colleagues would think. After founding The Lab at Belmar, even though it was not technically a museum,

I was invited to join the Contemporary Art Museum Directors association, which included people like Matthew Drutt, one of the leading scholars on Kazimir Malevich in the world. Surely, the likes of Drutt and other members of the association would be appalled if a curator endorsed unauthenticated art.

I told Ron that I would need to think about his idea a little before committing to it.

In the following weeks I noticed that I was thinking about the exhibition *all the time*. I didn't believe the works were real in the sense that they were actually made by the masters of the Russian avant-garde, but I could not dismiss them either. Where did they come from? Who in the world would be knocking off masterpieces to sell for several hundred bucks each? And did it matter to me that on some basic level I felt these paintings were amazing, regardless of who painted them? My doubts prevented me from making a decision on the exhibition for a long time but in truth I was hooked from the beginning.

About a year after I first talked to Ron, I finally committed to the idea. After all, I was in a suburban shopping district where no one would care what I did. My institution wasn't even a museum. I had nothing to lose. Then, in 2009, before I had occasion to launch the exhibition, I became director of MCA Denver, which had just opened a new world-class facility in downtown Denver. Suddenly, I had something to lose.

Museums are supposed to provide expert knowledge. Visitors go to museums to see works that are authorized by people who have dedicated their careers to studying them. Museums don't just show objects they like; they show things they know about. I was worried about the damage I would do to the reputation of MCA Denver. I was afraid that people would think I was unserious if I mounted a show of unauthenticated art. I was anxious about alienating the museum's donors, who wanted their institution to be the authority on questions of art history. And I thought I might anger collectors, who were deeply invested — financially and mentally — in the mechanisms of authentication in the art world. Though I had already convinced myself to do the exhibition, my new circumstances caused me to put it off again for at least another year, while it continued to haunt me.

By the time I finally mounted the exhibition, at the end of 2010, I had grown to feel that there was something about this collection that was too important to ignore. [Fig. 60] Though it took me a long time to come to terms with it, the feelings of doubt that I felt gave this exhibition more purpose than any of the other exhibits I had been considering. I was sure about the quality of the paintings. However, I was uncertain of their status as art, which triggered in me a feeling of uncertainty about art in general: What is authenticity in art? What strange set of rules can make such delightful and vital paintings inauthentic? By provoking these questions in me, these paintings, which might all be forgeries, somehow felt more honest than anything else I had encountered.

I remember meeting a sculptor once who would create large-scale imitations of famous modern works in his backyard, simply because he enjoyed it. I remember thinking there was something so free and admirable in the fact that he was breaking all the rules for what is considered legitimate work for an artist today. I felt something similar about exhibiting Ron's collection of unauthenticated paintings, which, after all, broke the rules for what is accepted display in a museum.

Part of me wishes that I could see the works like Roger, an earthbound outsider to the art world, who only learned about it in the process of acquiring his paintings with Ron. In the beginning, Roger just wanted some artworks to decorate his house with, and the "constructivist stuff" seemed fine. When I interviewed him a few months before the exhibition opened, Roger remarked, "I find it interesting that in the art world a lot of people don't even look at the paintings. They are more into how much it is worth, where it comes from, who sold it to who, rather than just what they are."[1] I interpreted Roger's basic point to be that when someone actually looks at a painting for what it is, they are not concerned with its provenance. They see an object, and it either moves them or it does not. However, with few exceptions, the experts he encountered in relation to his Russian avant-garde paintings did not show any authentic emotional response to the works. Roger wants to simply enjoy the paintings for what they are.

Ron, by contrast, has a perspective on the paintings from up in the clouds. He *wants* to be able to see the paintings as simply beautiful

Fig. 60 (overleaf)
**Exhibition of the collection
at MCA Denver**

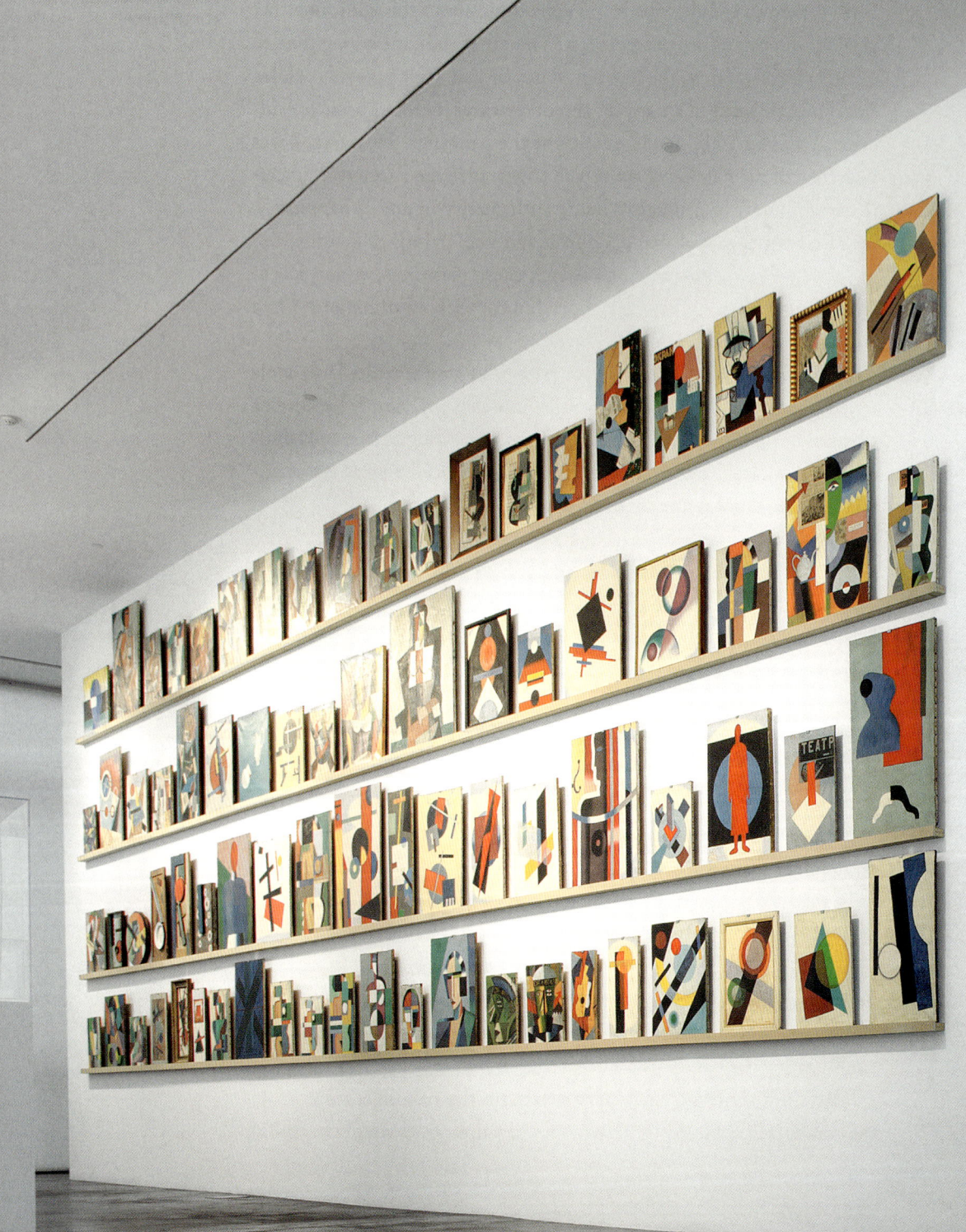

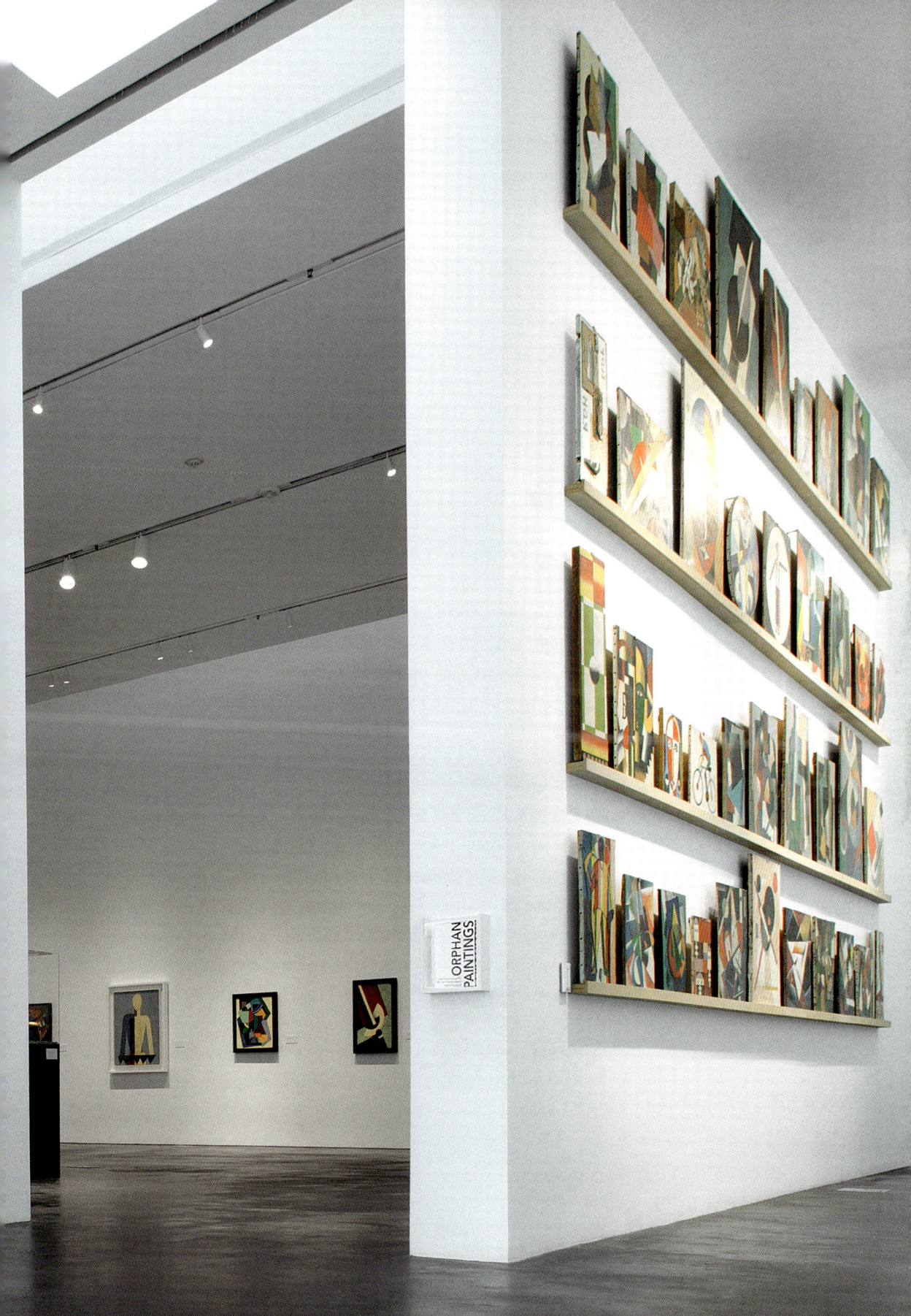

ORPHAN PAINTINGS

things but he can't help see in them something more, some connection to world history, to the great and mythical moment when Vladimir Tatlin and Malevich fought it out over the future of art. While he is affected by the possibility of getting rich, for Ron, money is mainly a sign of the magnitude of the enterprise in which he sees himself participating. He is the one who most wanted to exhibit the works in a museum and even contemplated a new museum dedicated to them.

I myself felt alternately caught between earth and sky when I saw the paintings on display at MCA Denver. It was difficult to appreciate them purely as beautiful objects because I could not look at them without seeing something bigger—or the absence of something bigger—in them. They invoked a sensory response that triggered other areas of the mind, bringing up questions such as, Why am I liking this? Is there really something here? On the walls of the museum, they looked so much like authentic works of art that their inscrutability became almost painful.

During the exhibition, it became even more clear to me that my ongoing feelings of doubt about the exhibition were part of its higher purpose. I came to understand that these works have the rare power that flows from something unknowable and provoke a sensation of drawing close to something ungraspable. Despite not being authenticated "art," the paintings in the collection accomplish what art aims for but rarely achieves: they evoke the feeling of having come from a world beyond. Authentic artworks are always absorbed within the narrative of history, but this collection remains outside of it. While even the most ephemeral works of art inevitably fall into a box labeled "Art," with a capital "A," these unauthenticated paintings are in a state of limbo. Arriving on the scene of everyday life from a realm that is unknowable, out of thin air, they are almost mythical. Art wants to be the distant light of the irrational in a rational world, but too often that light is absorbed by the system. What makes these unauthenticated paintings special is their mystery—the fact that their light stays remote and elusive.

Then again I also think that the meaning of the collection has nothing to do with art but lies in something familial and personal for Ron and Roger. I suspect the paintings help fill the gap left by the tragic loss in their childhood and are a way for the two brothers, who are very different from one another, to connect. [Fig. 61]

The lesson of the Russian avant-garde may be that the loftiest justifications for art are hinged to its most ordinary purposes. In 1929, when Stalin's edicts made it dangerous for artists to create abstract art, Tatlin occupied the bell tower of a convent in Moscow and dedicated himself to making a human-propelled flying machine that he called Letatlin. Between 1929 and 1932, he dressed as a traditional Russian craftsman and dedicated himself almost entirely to the engineless apparatus with flapping wings, a sailor's version of an airplane. He claimed that it was meant to be functional, that it would "become a part of everyday life by 1950," but he probably didn't entirely believe that.[2] I think that he half-believed in it, that he liked the idea of believing in something impossible. [Fig. 62]

This concept of "half-belief" summarizes my personal relationship to the collection that Ron, Roger, and their friends amassed. I don't know if a master artist ever touched any of the paintings, but I feel something special in them. Because they are suffused with doubt, they touch upon the possibility of belief. And the possibility of belief is the rare feeling I associate with art.

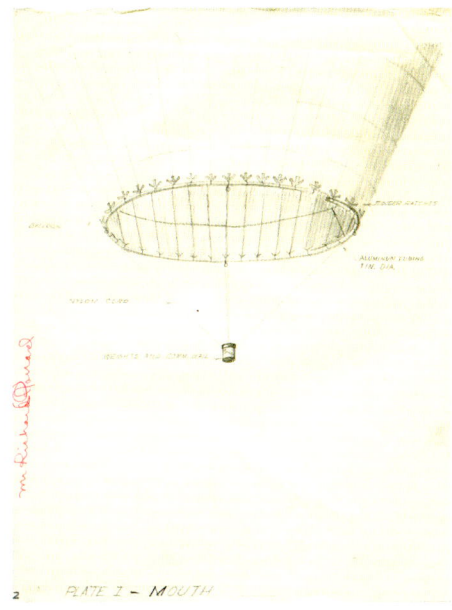

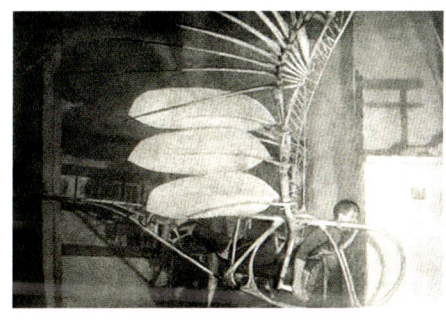

Fig. 61
Ron and Roger's older brother, Richard, made this technical drawing as a teenager, before he perished in a ballooning accident.

Fig. 62
Tatlin's human-propelled flying machine, Letatlin

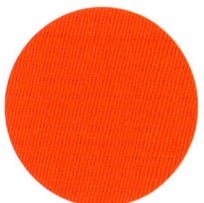

NOTES

THE BEGINNING OF THE COLLECTION

1   Recorded conference call between FBI Special Agent Bryan Stone, attorneys Mark Merric and Francis Brown, Ron Pollard, and Roger Pollard, July 29, 2005, MPEG-4 file.
2   Ron Pollard, interview with the author, Denver, August 21, 2010.
3   Appraisal for Ron Pollard, March 14, 2005, 7.

THE RUSSIAN AVANT-GARDE

1   Karl Marx, Friedrich Engels, and C. J. Arthur, *The German Ideology* (New York: International Publishers, 1972), 47.
2   Vladimir Tatlin, "Report of the Section for Material Culture's Research Work for 1924," in *Tatlin*, ed. Larissa Alekseevna Zhadova (New York: Rizzoli, 1988), 256–57.
3   Kazimir Severinovich Malevich, *Suprematism, 34 drawings* (Vitebsk: Unovis, 1920), 3, quoted in Aleksandra Shatskikh, *Vitebsk: The Life of Art*, trans. Katherine Foshko Tsan (New Haven and London: Yale University Press, 2007), 110.
4   Kazimir Severinovich Malevich, "From Cubism and Futurism to Suprematism: The New Realism in Painting," in Troels Andersen, ed., *K. S. Malevich: Essays on Art, 1915–1933*, vol. 1 (Copenhagen: Borgens Forlag, 1969), 16.
5   Vasilii Rakitin, "The Artisan and the Prophet: Marginal Notes on Two Artistic Careers," in *The Great Utopia: The Russian and Soviet Avant-Garde, 1915–1932* (New York: Solomon R. Guggenheim Museum, 1992), 29.
6   Linda S. Boersma, *0.10: The Last Futurist Exhibition of Painting* (Rotterdam: 010 Publishers, 1994), 46.
7   Nikolai Khardzhiev, who knew both Tatlin and Malevich personally, recounted this story in an interview with Ira Vrubel-Golubkina. "The Future is Now! Excerpts from an Interview with Ira Vrubel-Golubkina," in Evgeniia Petrova, ed., *A Legacy Regained: Nikolai Khardzhiev and the Russian Avant-Garde* (Saint Petersburg: Palace Editions, 2002), 25.
8   Christina Kiaer, *Imagine No Possessions: The Socialist Objects of Russian Constructivism* (Cambridge and London: MIT Press, 2005), 41–46.
9   Kiaer, *Imagine No Possessions*, 89–105, 110–17, 175–96.
10   Shatskikh, *Vitebsk: The Life of Art*, 67. This information comes from the El Lissitzky archive, RGALI, f. 680, op. 1, ed. khr. 1017, 1. 708.
11   Shatskikh, *Vitebsk: The Life of Art*, 67–68.
12   Kazimir Malevich, *The Non-Objective World: The Manifesto of Suprematism* (1926; repr., Mineola, NY: Dover Publications, 2003), 61.
13   Malevich, *The Non-Objective World*, 68. The interpretation of this passage as the view from an ascending airplane is not mine originally, but was expressed by Mark Dorrian in "The Aerial View: Notes for a Cultural History," *Strates* 13 (2007), November 5, 2008, http://strates.revues.org/5573.
14   Shatskikh, *Vitebsk: The Life of Art*, 133.
15   Malevich, *Suprematism, 34 drawings*, 3, quoted in Shatskikh, *Vitebsk: The Life of Art*, 110.
16   Shatskikh, *Vitebsk: The Life of Art*, 111.

17   Ibid., 112.
18   Ibid., 108–9.
19   Matthew Drutt, "Kazimir Malevich: Suprematism," in Matthew Drutt, ed., *Kazimir Malevich: Suprematism* (New York: Guggenheim Museum Publications, 2003), 19–21.
20   Letter from Kazimir Malevich, Leningrad, February 9, 1929, to A. Gan, New York, Howard Schickler Collection, quoted in Clemens Toussaint, "If Only Paintings Could Speak," in *Kazimir Malevich, Suprematist Composition, Circa 1919–20* (auction catalog; New York: Phillips Auctioneers, 2000), 38.
21   Quoted in Drutt, *Kazimir Malevich: Suprematism*, 21. The transcript of the OGPU (United States Political Agency) interrogation of Malevich in September 1930 is reprinted in Drutt, *Kazimir Malevich: Suprematism*, 249.
22   Joop M. Joosten, "Malevich in The Stedelijk," in W. A. L. Bareen et al., eds., *Kazimir Malevich, 1878–1935* (exhibition catalog; Leningrad: State Russian Museum; Moscow: State Tretiakov Gallery; and Amsterdam: Stedelijk Museum, 1988), 48.
23   Joosten, "Malevich in The Stedelijk," 48.

THE SEARCH FOR ORIGINS

1   Roger Pollard, Skype interview with the author, September 2, 2010.
2   Hilton Kramer, "Malevich $17 Million Sale Finally Buries Stalinism," *New York Observer*, May 22, 2000, http://observer.com/2000/05/malevich-17-million-sale-finally-buries-stalinism/.
3   Brad Gessner produced a detailed written account of the meeting with the Aachen sellers (J. and W.) for the benefit of Ron, Roger, and Michel. The account included a copy of an email by J. to Brad describing the sellers' dress and appearance. Brad Gessner, account of meeting with J. and W., January 19, 2008.
4   Nikolai Khardzhiev makes it clear that students made copies of the works of their teachers in Evgeniia Petrova, ed., *A Legacy Regained: Nikolai Khardzhiev and the Russian Avant-Garde* (Saint Petersburg: Palace Editions, 2002), 149.
5   Christina Lodder, *Russian Constructivism* (New Haven and London: Yale University Press, 1983), 111.
6   Letter from certified forensic document examiners to Ron Pollard, n.d.
7   Ron recounts the initial optimism of the microscopist (the latter was not approached for a confirmation). Ron Pollard, interview with the author, Denver, August 21, 2010.
8   The lab cited a book on paint pigments that stated that the first confirmed finding of titanium white in a painting was from around 1924. See Marilyn Laver, "Titanium Dioxide White," in Elisabeth West Hugh, ed., *Artists' Pigments: A Handbook of Their History and Characteristics*, Volume 3 (Washington, D.C.: National Gallery of Art, 1997), 340.
9   Email from Brad to Ron and Roger, October 19, 2005.
10   Noel Heaton, "The Permanence of Artist's Materials," *Journal of the Royal Society of Arts* 80, no. 4138 (March 11, 1932): 416.

11 Analysis of paintings attributed to Kazimir Malevich and other Russian Suprematist artists, November 28, 2005.

12 Andre Nakov, *Kazimir Malevich: Catalogue Raisonné* (Paris: Adam Biro, 2002).

13 Recorded conference call between FBI Special Agent Bryan Stone, attorneys Mark Merric and Francis Brown, Ron Pollard, and Roger Pollard, July 29, 2005, MPEG-4 file.

14 Quoted in Roger Pollard, *Timeline of Events*, entry for July 25, 2006.

15 See Appendix D on pages 152–53 for Susan's full transcription of her meeting with Alexis.

16 Ibid.

17 See, for example, Gerry Souter, *Malevich: Journey to Infinity* (New York: Parkstone Press International, 2008), 118–19.

18 Notably, *Black Cross*, 1915, oil on canvas, $31\frac{1}{2} \times 31\frac{1}{2}$ inches, Musée National d'art Moderne, Centre Georges Pompidou, Paris.

19 Anna Katsnelson, "My Leader, Myself? Pictorial Estrangement and Aesopian Language in the Late Work of Kazimir Malevich," *Poetics Today* 27, no. 1 (Spring 2006): 67–96.

20 Heidi Brown, "Scamsky Inc." *Forbes*, February 2, 2009, http://www.forbes.com/forbes/2009/0202/048b_2.html.

WHOM DO YOU TRUST?

1 Konstantin Akinsha and Sylvia Hochfield, "The Faking of the Russian Avant-Garde," *ARTNews*, July 1, 2009, http://www.artnews.com/2009/07/01/the-faking-of-the-russian-avant-garde/.

2 Technically, forgery refers to a copy of an authentic object made with the intention of fooling people into thinking it is authentic. A fake is a real object altered with the intention of making people think that nothing has been done to it. However, in art, it is common to refer to any inauthentic object as a fake.

3 See, for example, the 2011 case of Wolfgang Beltracchi, who claims to have forged one to two thousand old master and expressionist works. "Art Forgery Scandal: Ringleader Reveals He Faked Many More Works," *Spiegel*, March 5, 2012, http://www.spiegel.de/international/germany/art-forgery-scandal-ringleader-reveals-he-faked-many-more-works-a-819409.html.

4 Peter Roberts, *George Costakis: A Russian Life in Art* (New York: George Braziller, 1994), 66.

5 "Alexandra Exter Fakes?" *Art Newspaper* 18, no. 202 (May 2009): 11.

6 All information about Andrei Nakov is self-reported on his website, accessed February 19, 2013, http://www.andrei-nakov.org/en/nakov-biography.html.

7 Andrei B. Nakov and Kazimir Severinovich Malevich, *Malevich: Painting the Absolute* (Farnham, UK: Lund Humphries, 2010), author's biography.

8 All information about Chauvelin is self-reported on his website. "Jean Chauvelin Biography—Jean Chauvelin, Expert en avant-Garde Russe," Jean Chauvelin, Expert en avant-Garde Russe, accessed February 19, 2013, http://www.jeanchauvelin-expert.com/article-14415817.html.

9 With Nadia Filatoff, Chauvelin wrote *Alexandra Exter, Une Monographie (1882–1949)* (Paris: Max Milo Editions, 2003).

10 L'Association Alexandra Exter, "Imaginary Provenances," accessed February 19, 2013, http://www.alexandra-exter.net/en/fantasmees.php.

11 http://www.andrei-nakov.org/en/exter.html, accessed February 19, 2013.

12 Patricia Railing's "jousts" can all be downloaded from her homepage, accessed February 19, 2013, http://www.patriciarailingwrites.net/. The link for judging the tournament is now unavailable.

13 "The Faking of the Russian Avant-Garde," *ARTnews*, July 1, 2009, http://www.artnews.com/2009/07/01/the-faking-of-the-russian-avant-garde/. *ARTnews* lists Chauvelin as one of the InCoRM experts, but the InCoRM website does not include him on the list of "Specialists and Experts" on its home page, accessed February 19, 2013, http://www.incorm.eu/.

14 "The Faking of the Russian Avant-Garde."

15 Ezra Chowaiki, Skype interview with the author, October 18, 2012. Chowaiki was also quoted in Heidi Brown, "Scamsky Inc," *Forbes*, February 2, 2009, http://www.forbes.com/forbes/2009/0202/048b_2.html.

16 Chowaiki, Skype interview with the author.

17 "The Faking of the Russian Avant-Garde."

18 Konstantin Akinsha and Sylvia Hochfield, "Protecting Goncharova's Legacy," *ARTnews*, July 1, 2011, accessed February 19, 2013, http://www.artnews.com/2011/07/01/protecting-goncharovas-legacy/.

THE MERITS OF HALF-BELIEVING

1 Roger Pollard, Skype interview with the author, September 2, 2010.

2 B. Galanov, "Tainovidets lopastei," *Literaturnaia Gazeta*, February 23, 1977, in Larissa Alekseevna Zhadova, ed., *Tatlin* (New York: Rizzoli, 1988), 442.

PLATES

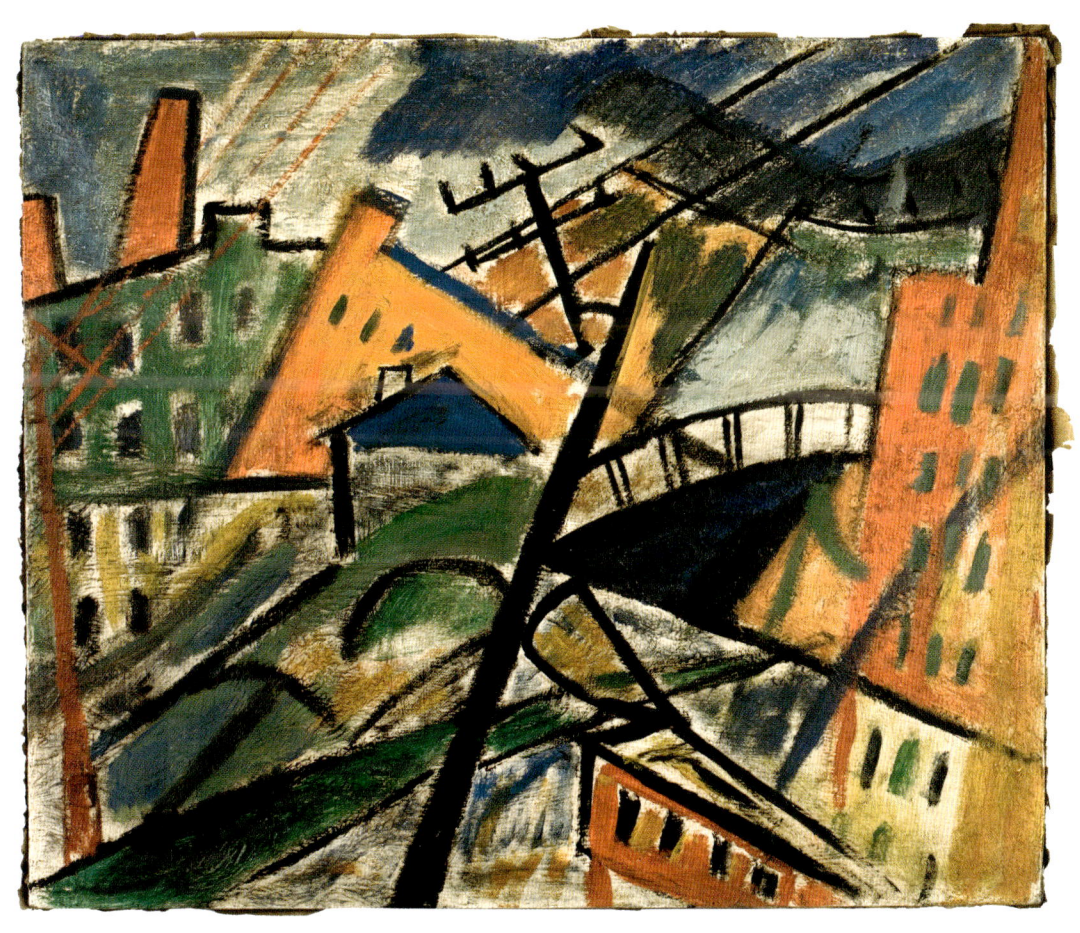

77

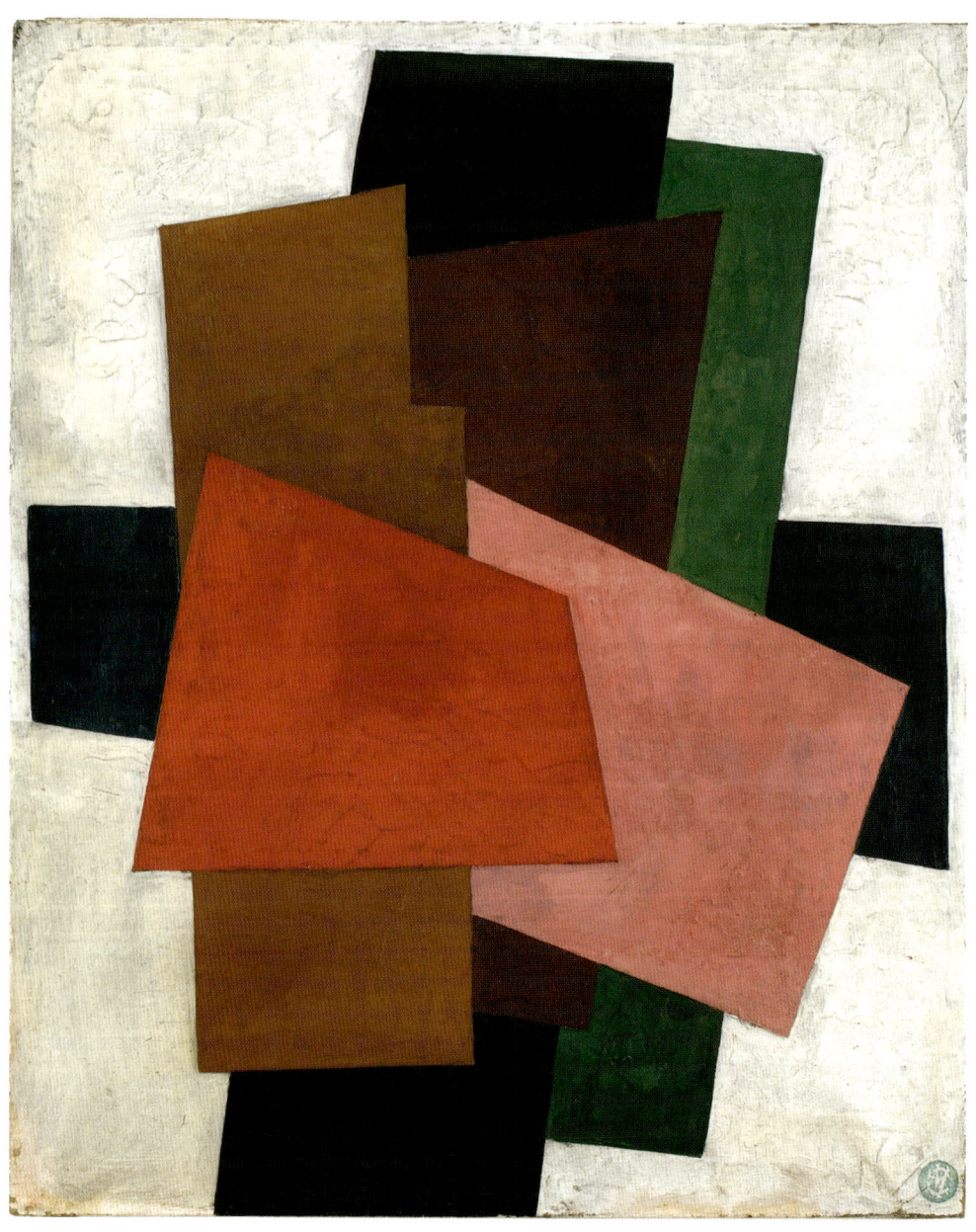

78

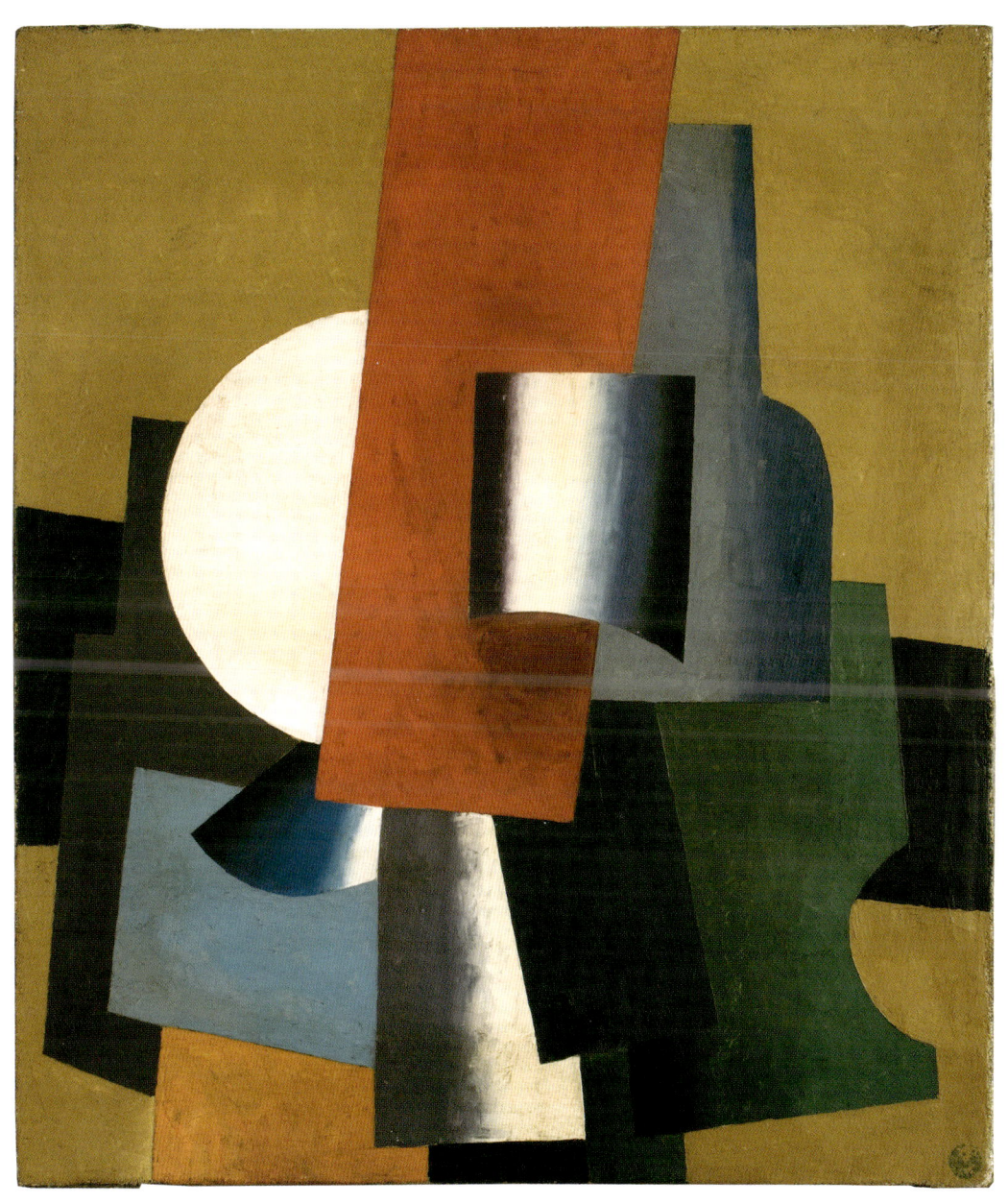

79

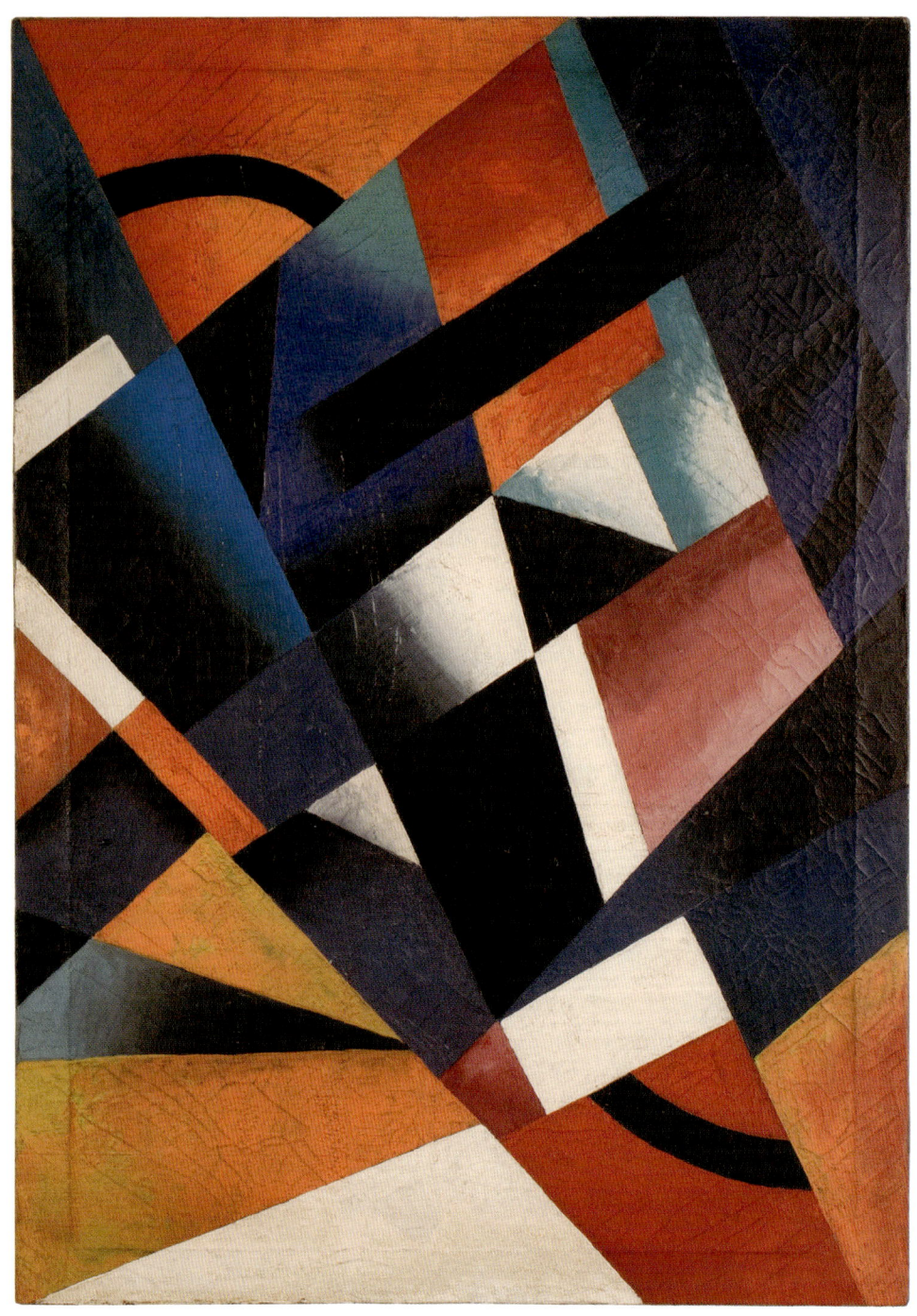

80

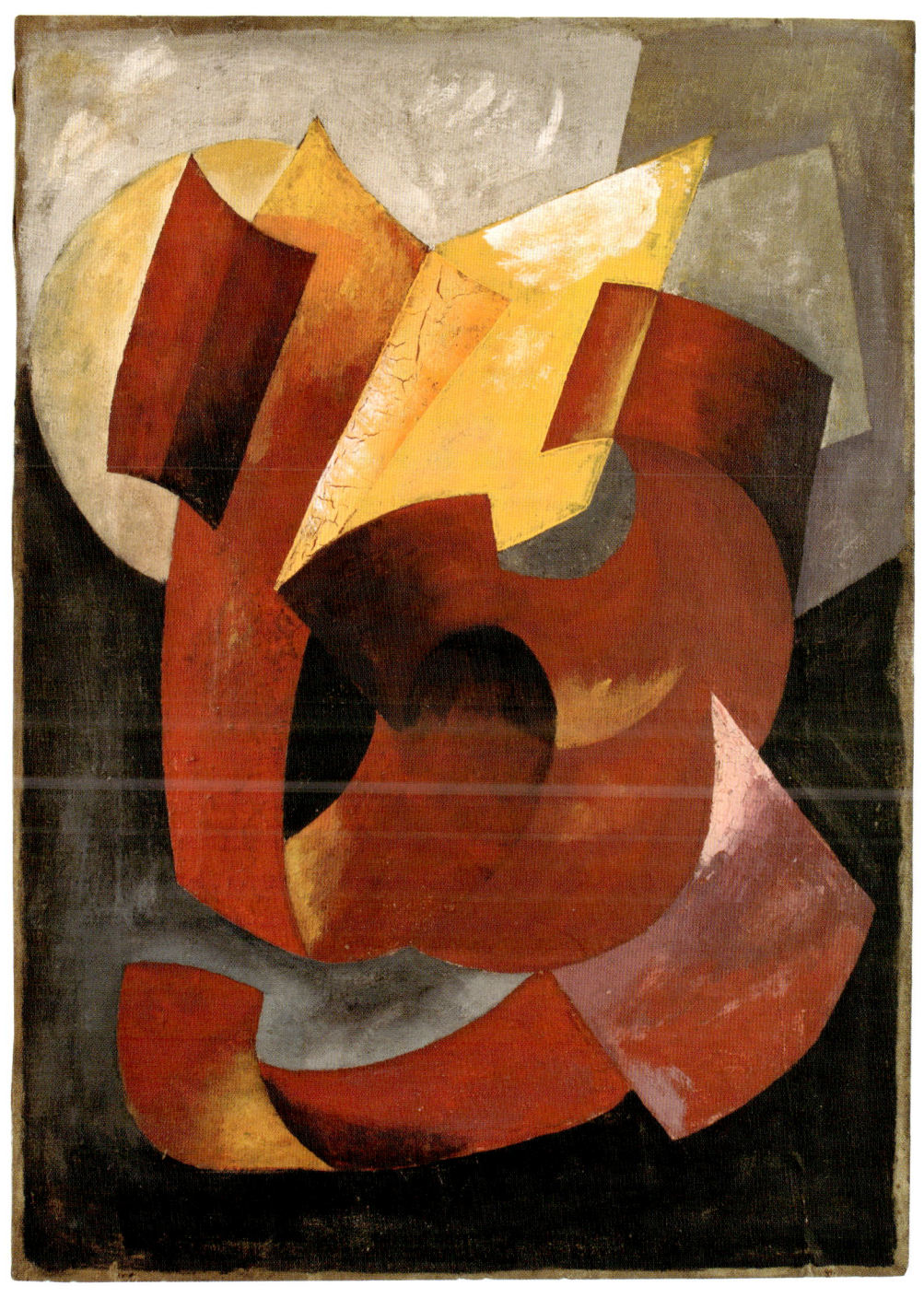

81

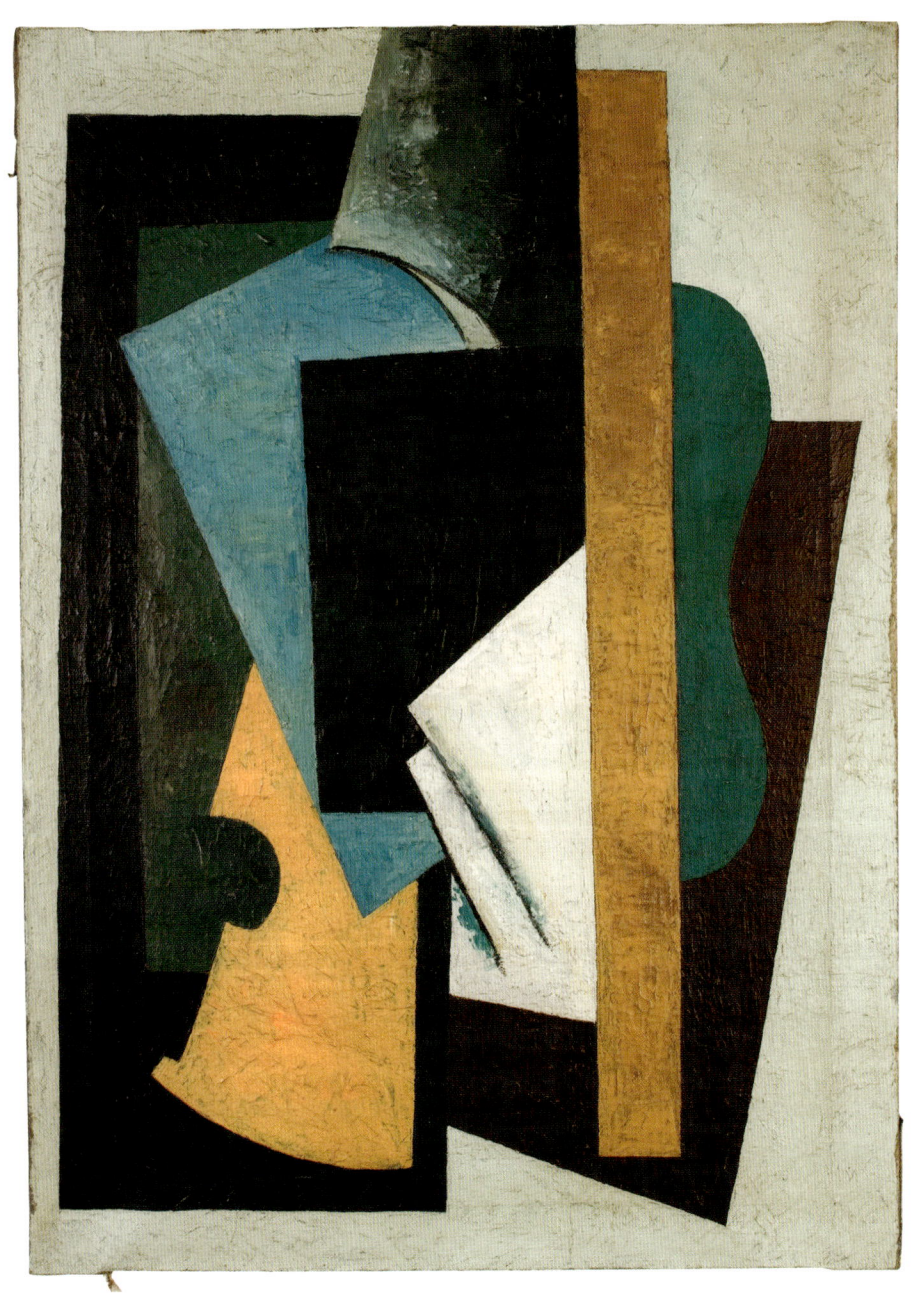

82

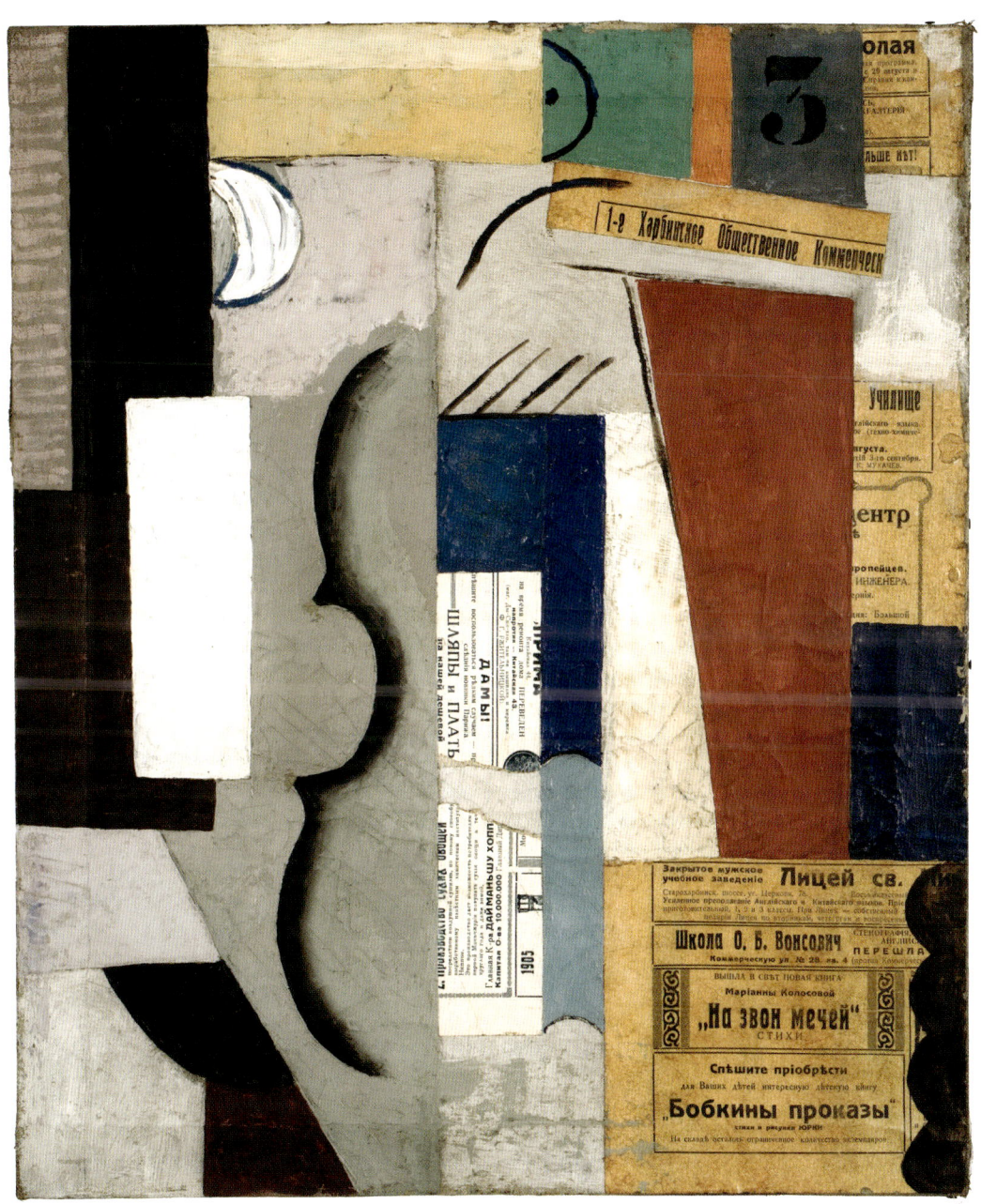

83

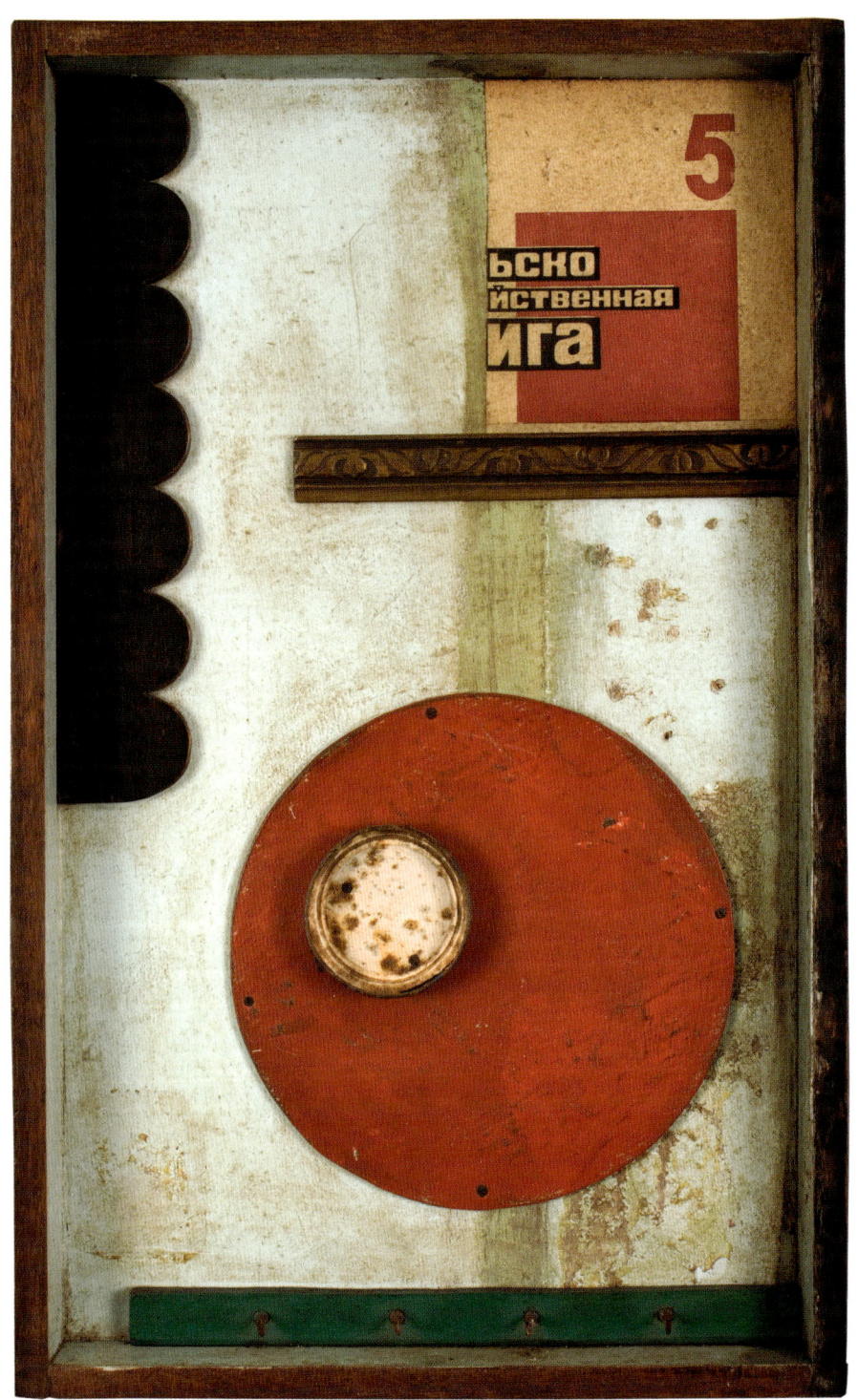

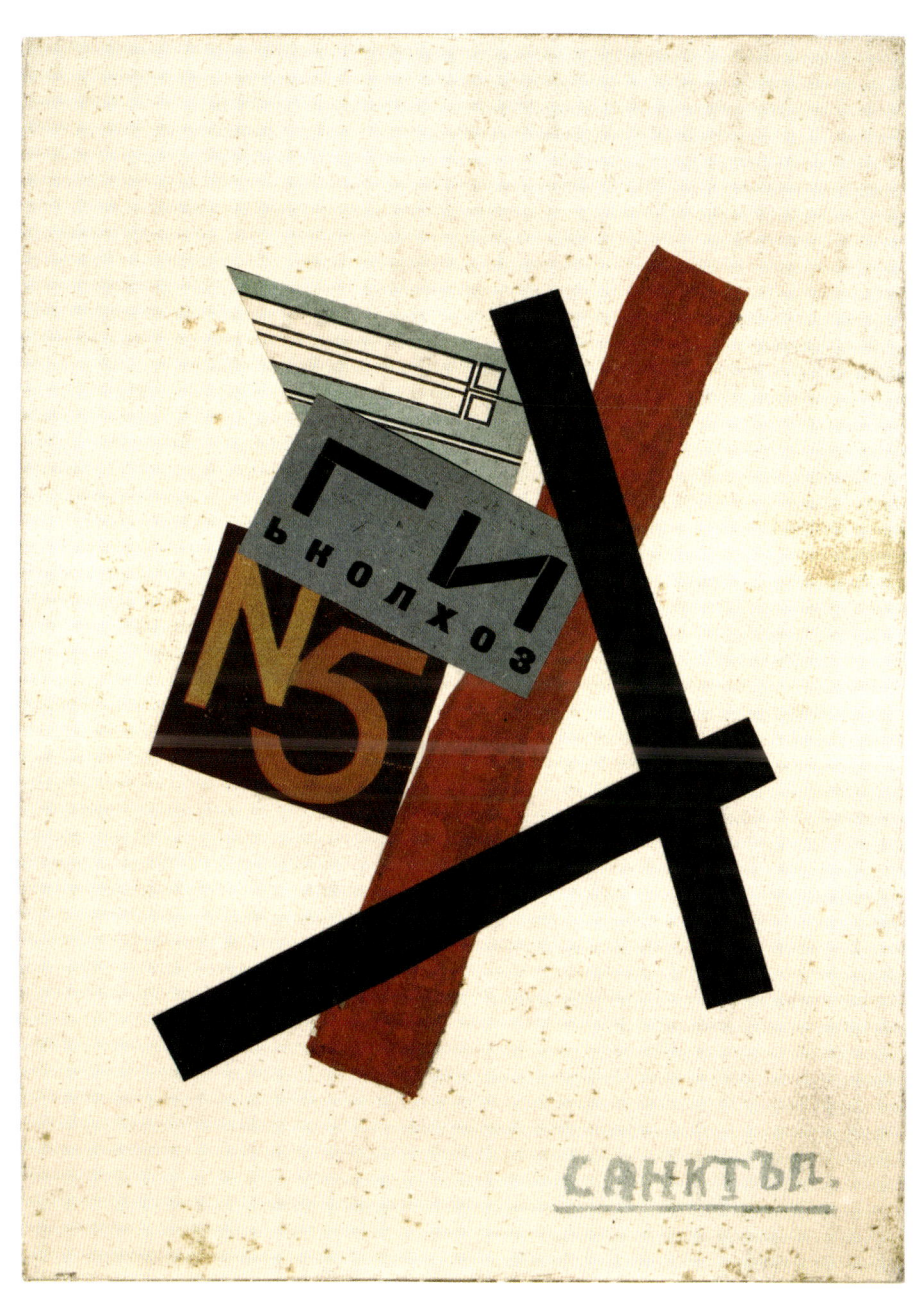

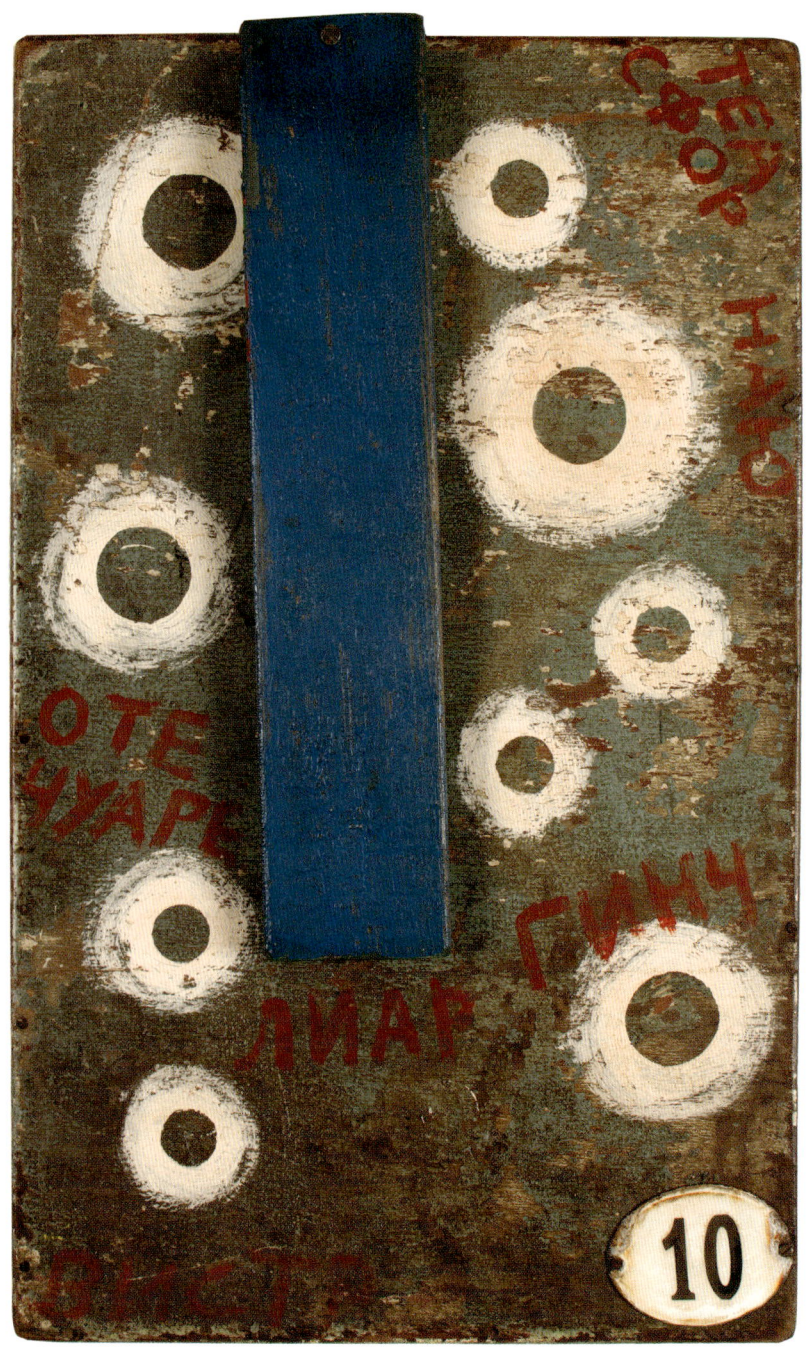

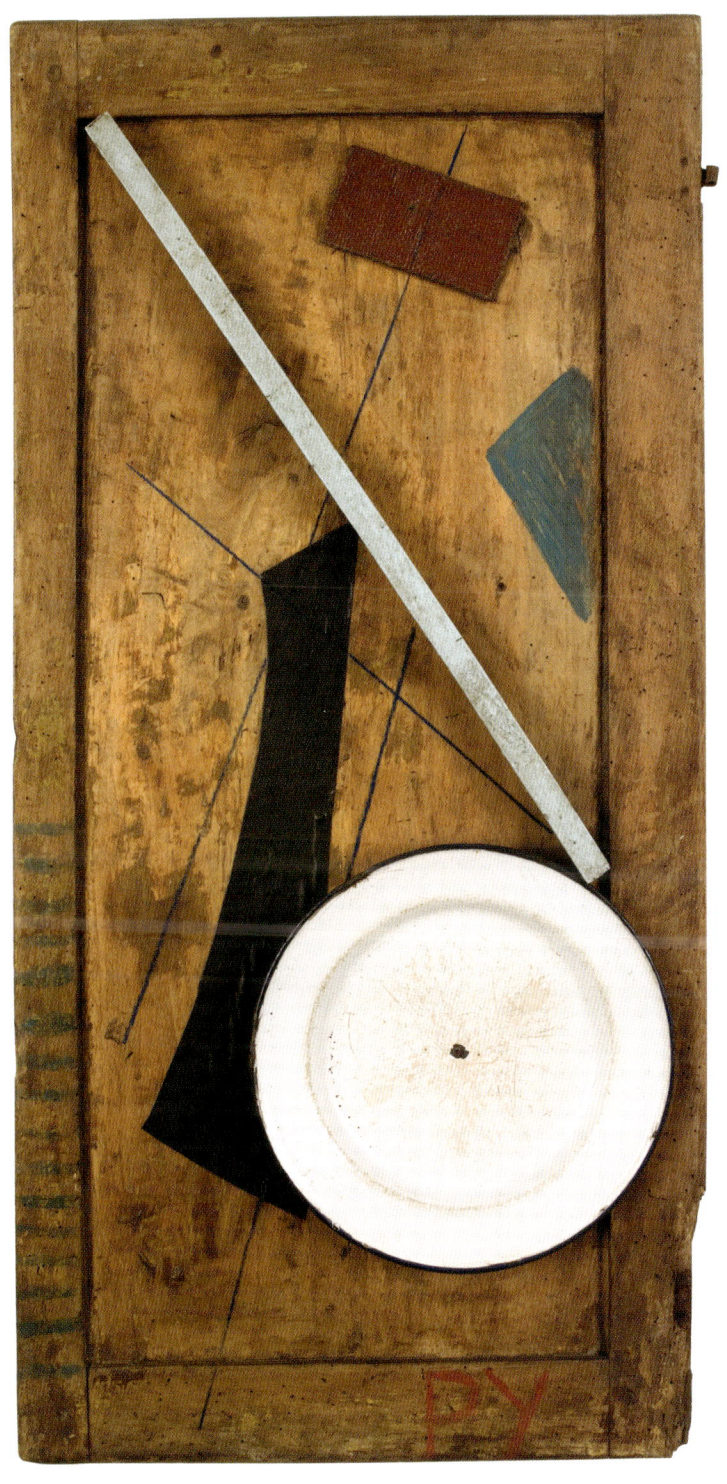

87

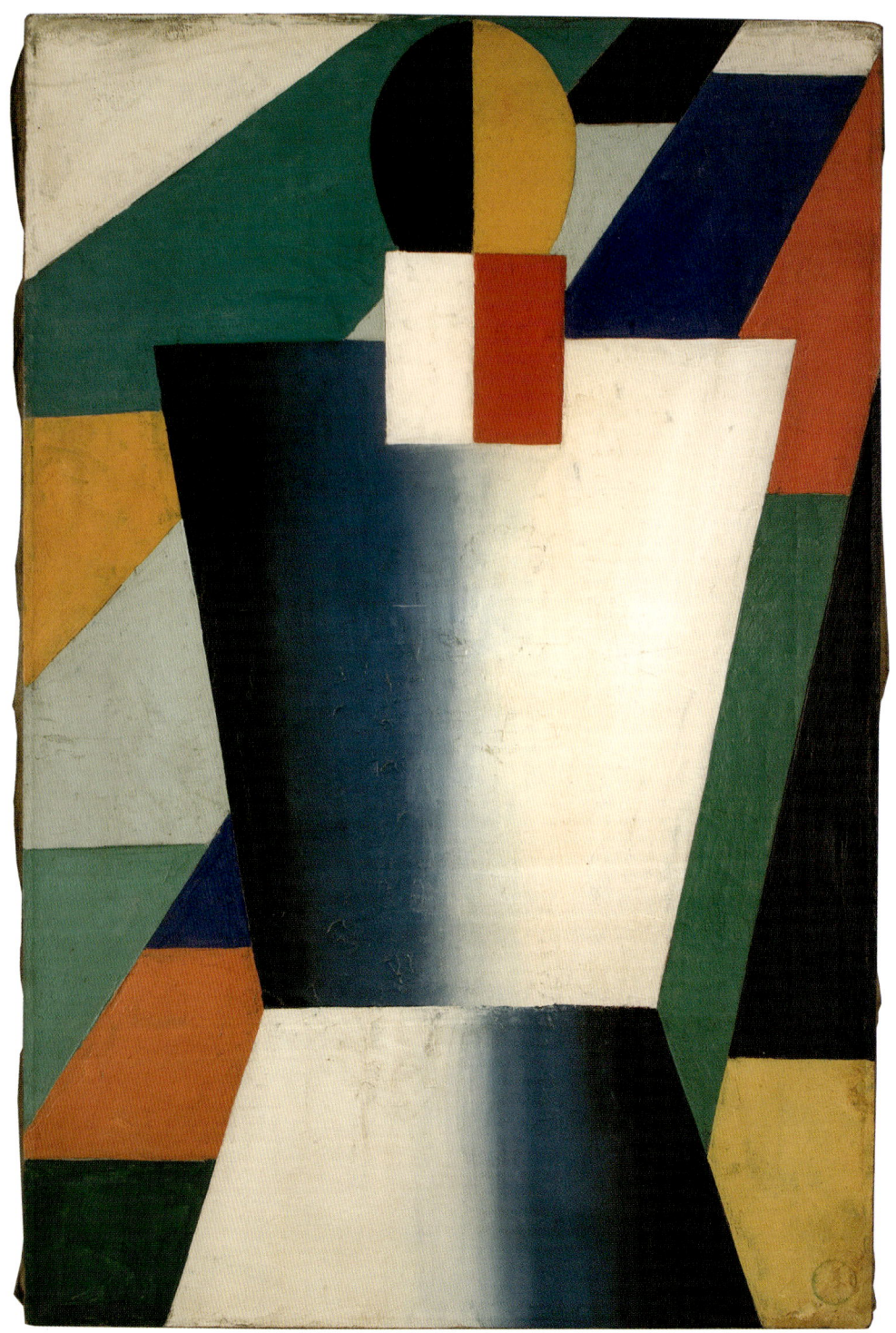

88

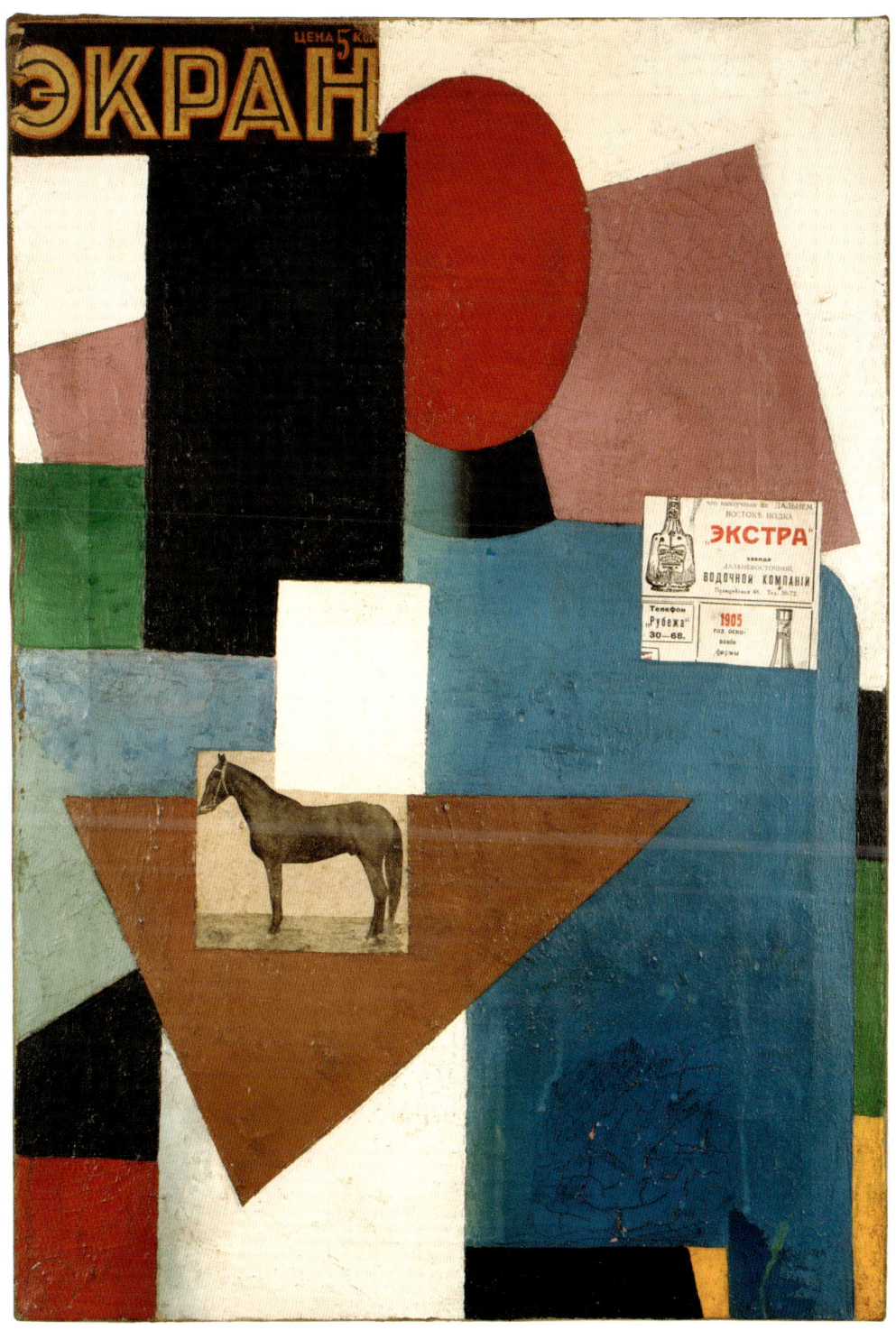

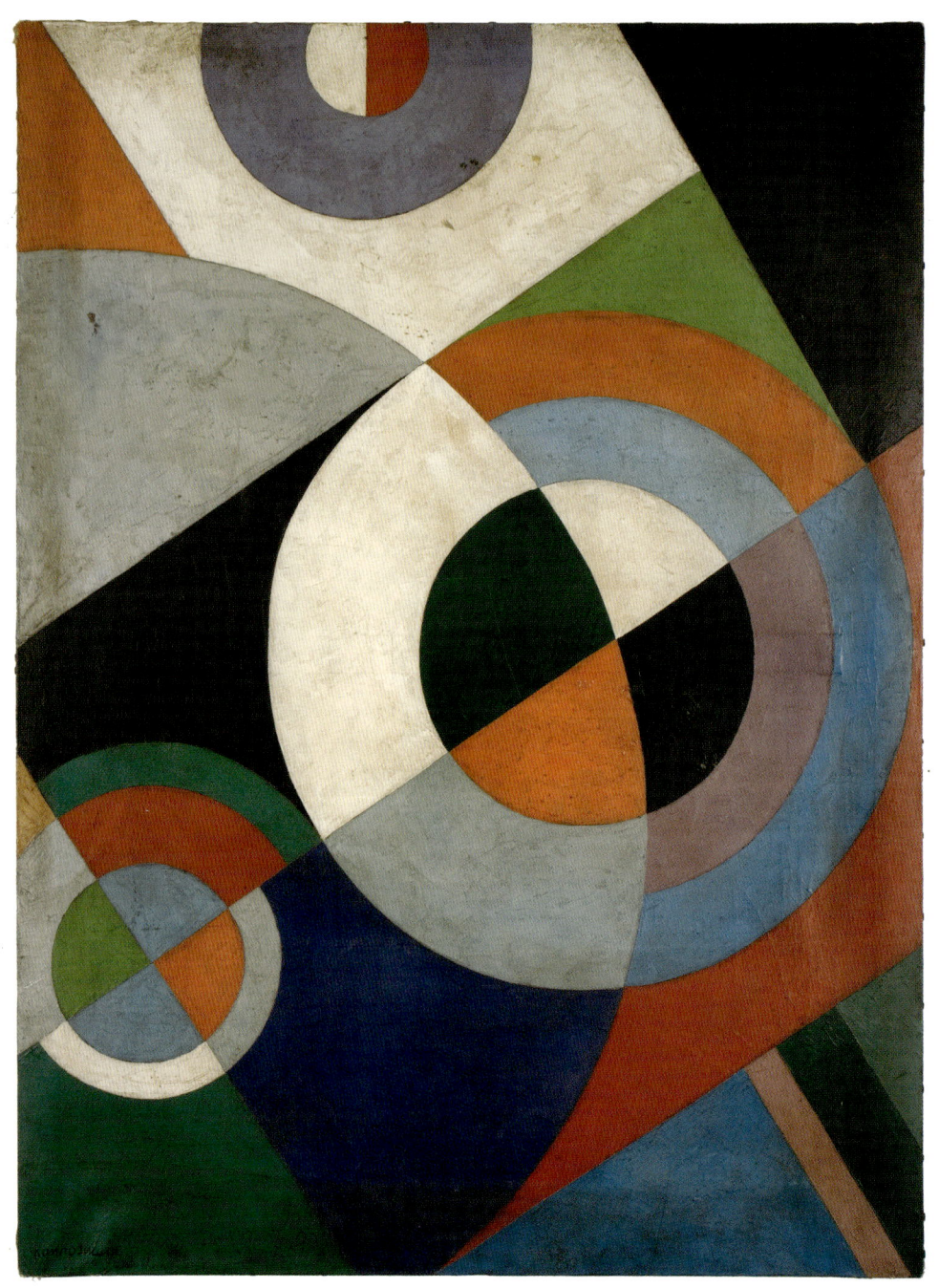

90

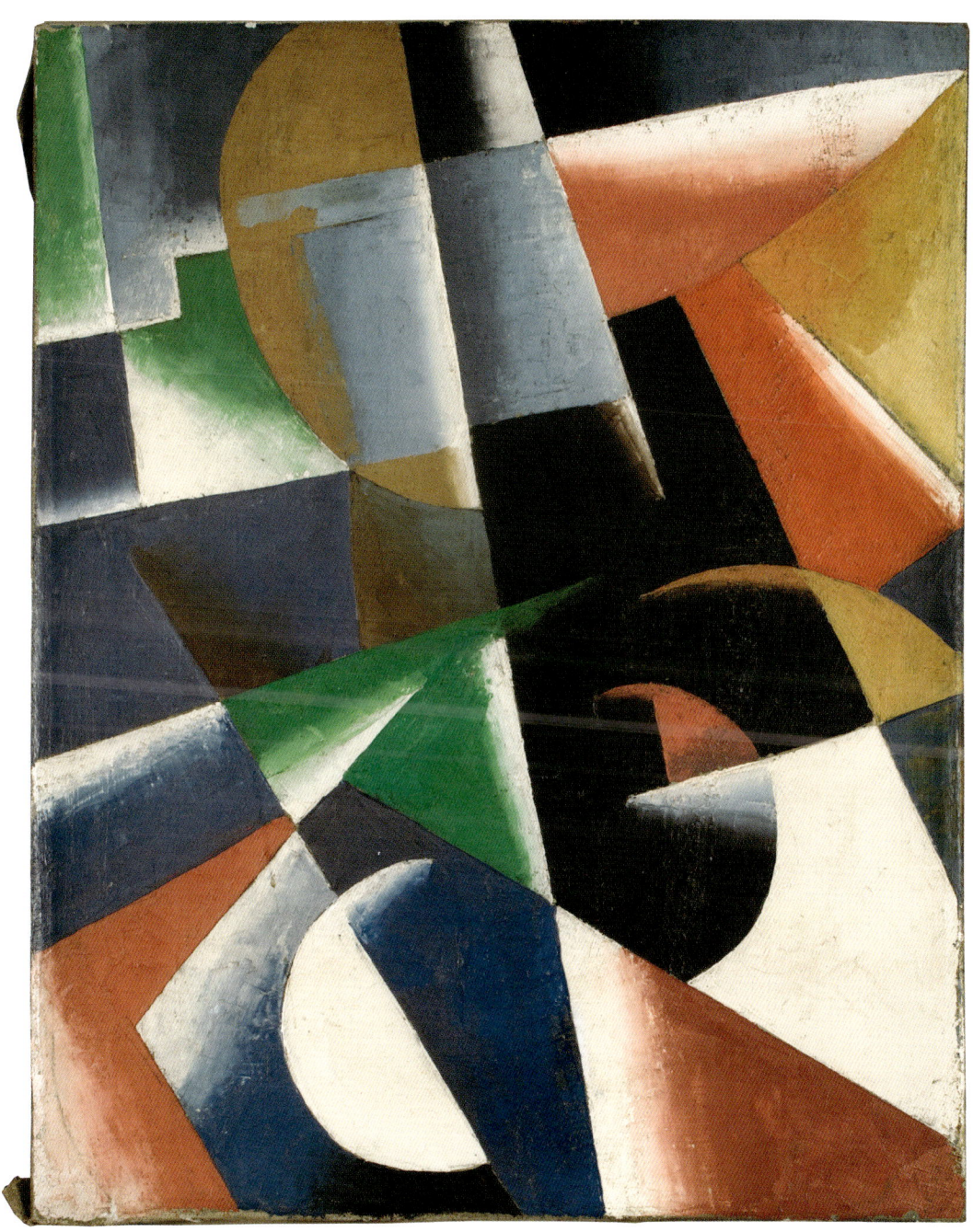

91

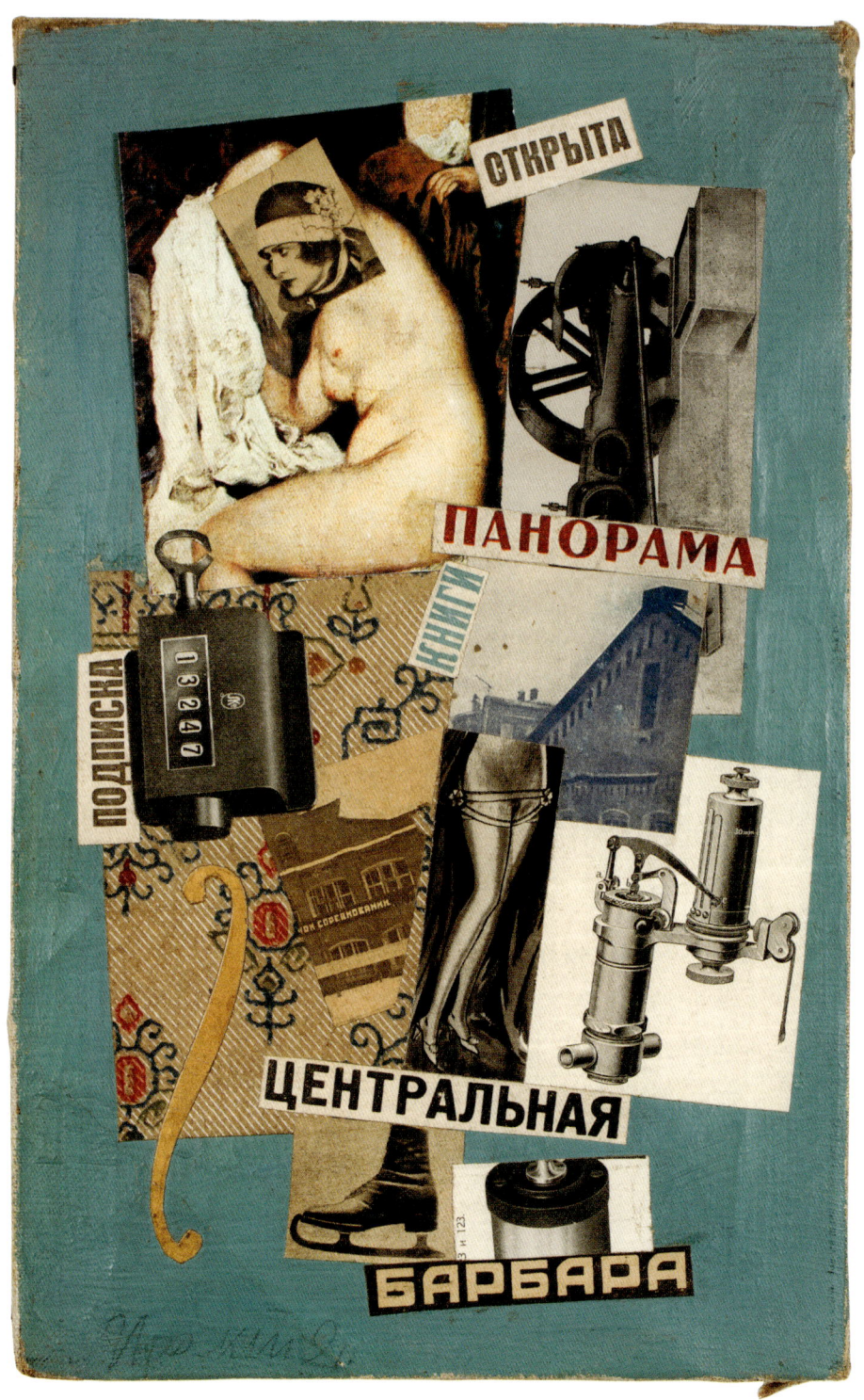

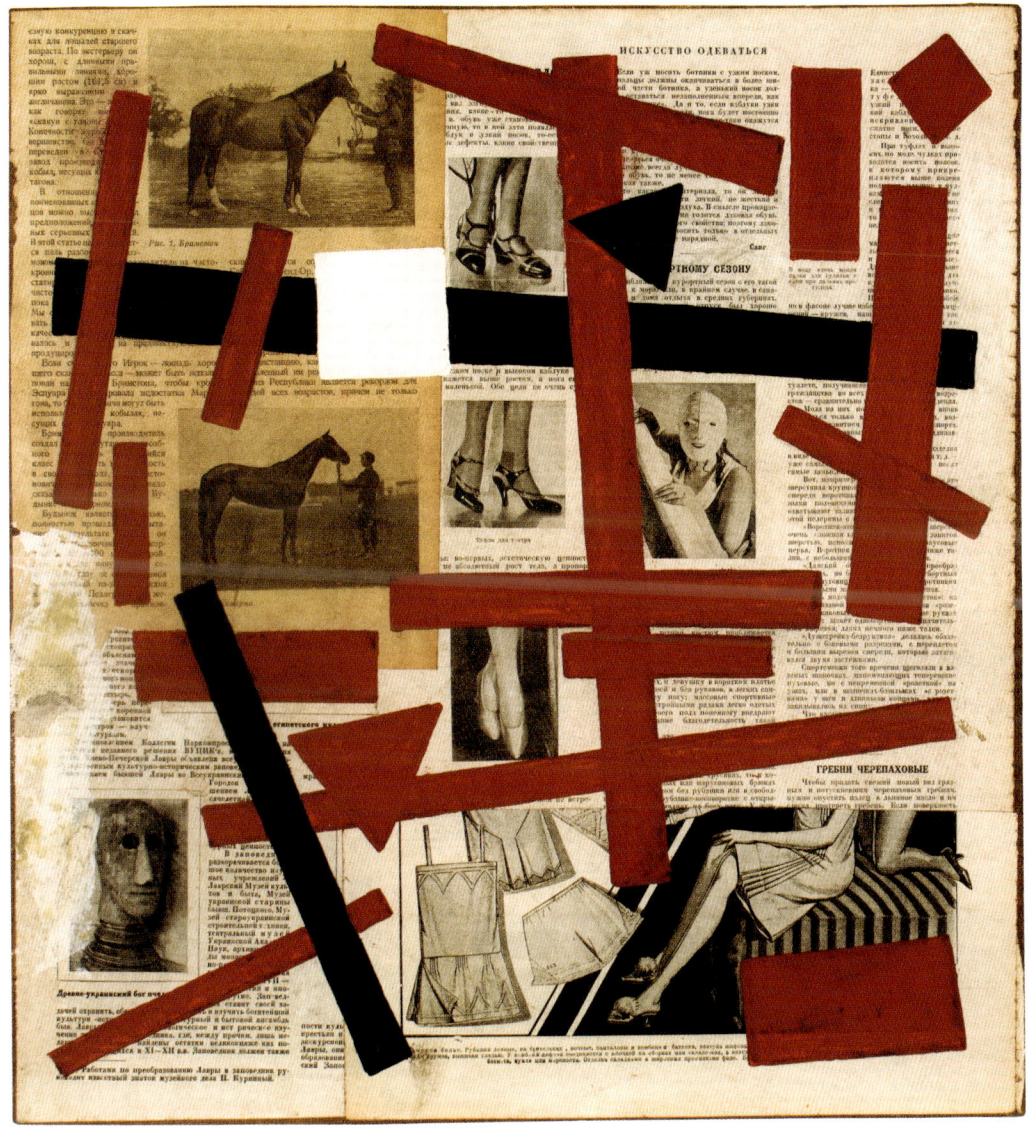

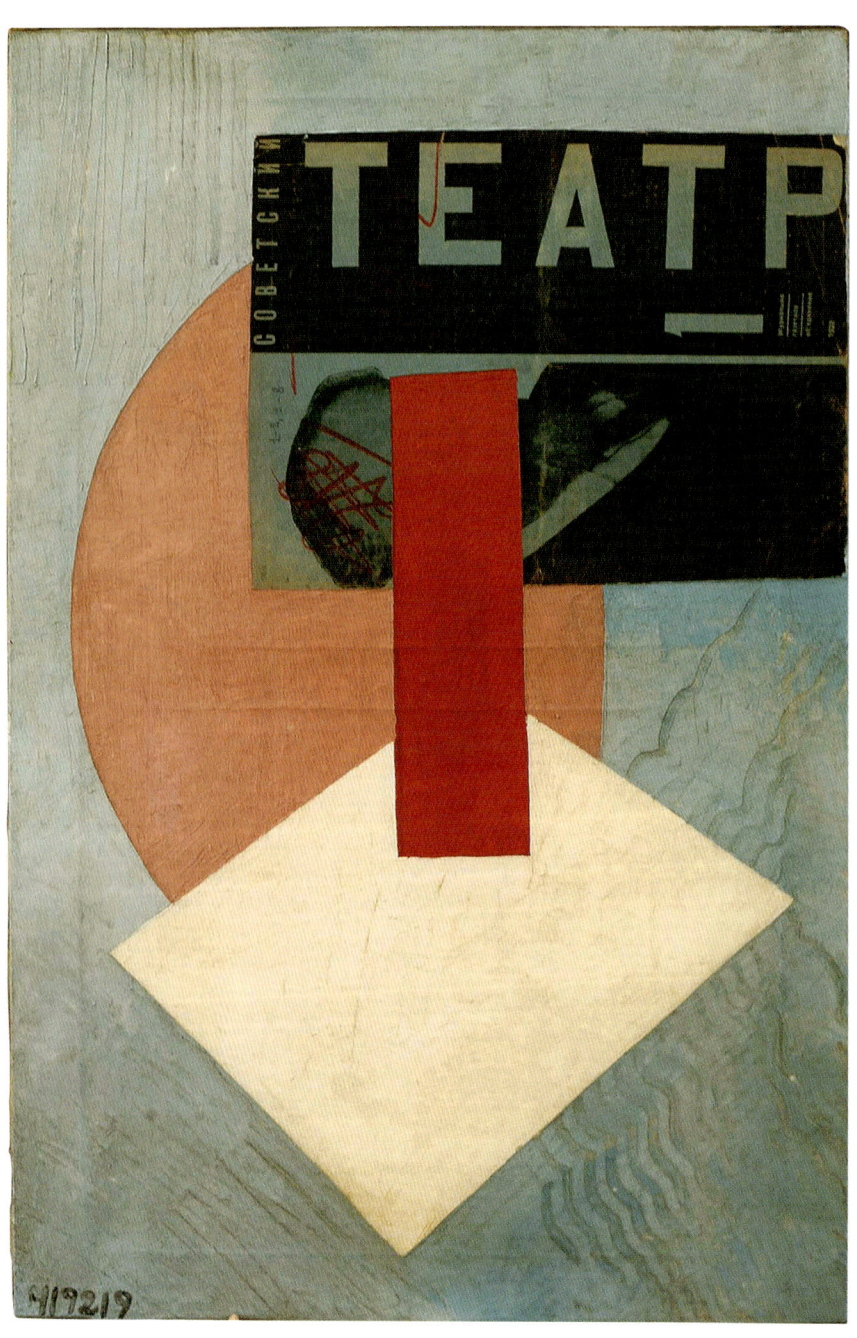

94

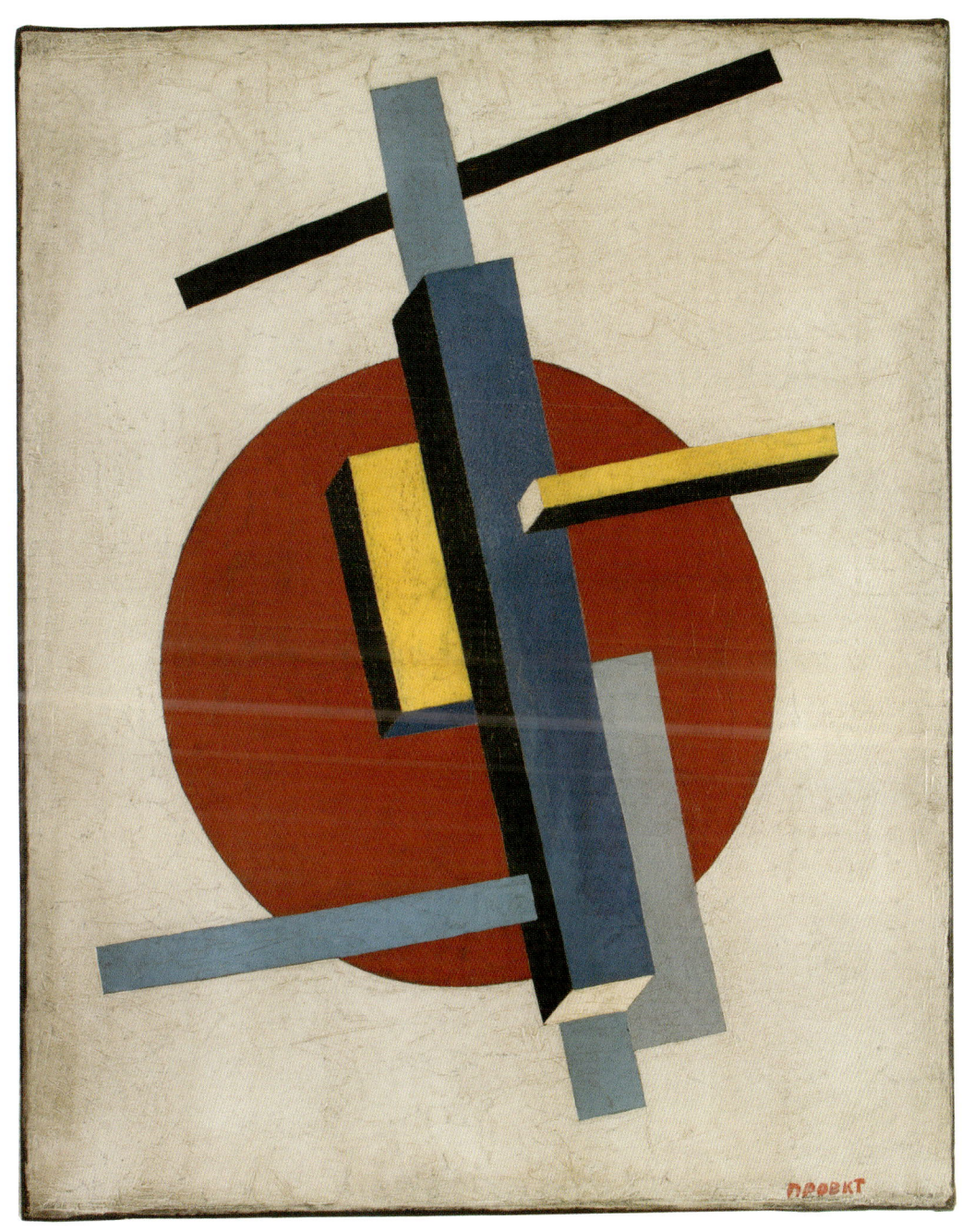

95

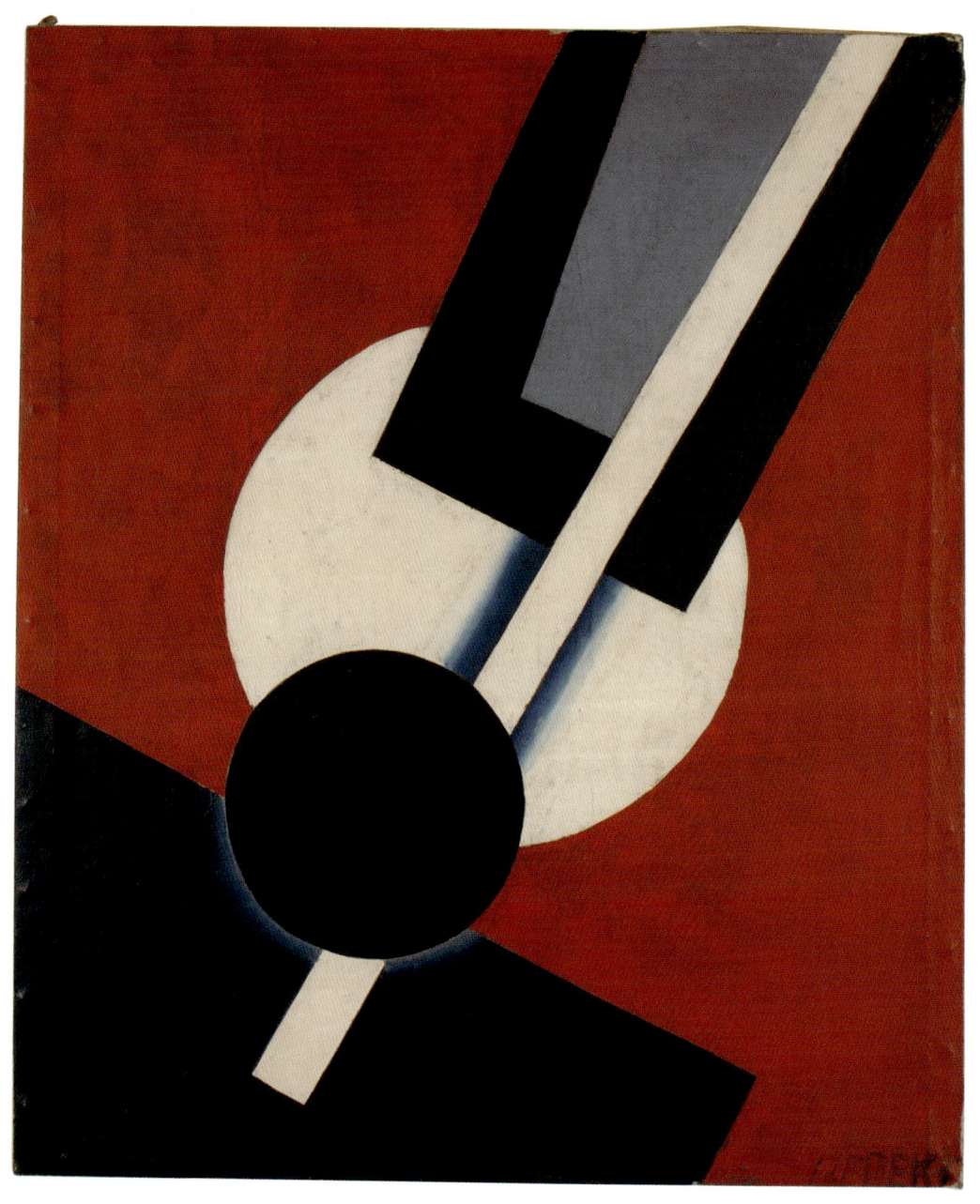

96

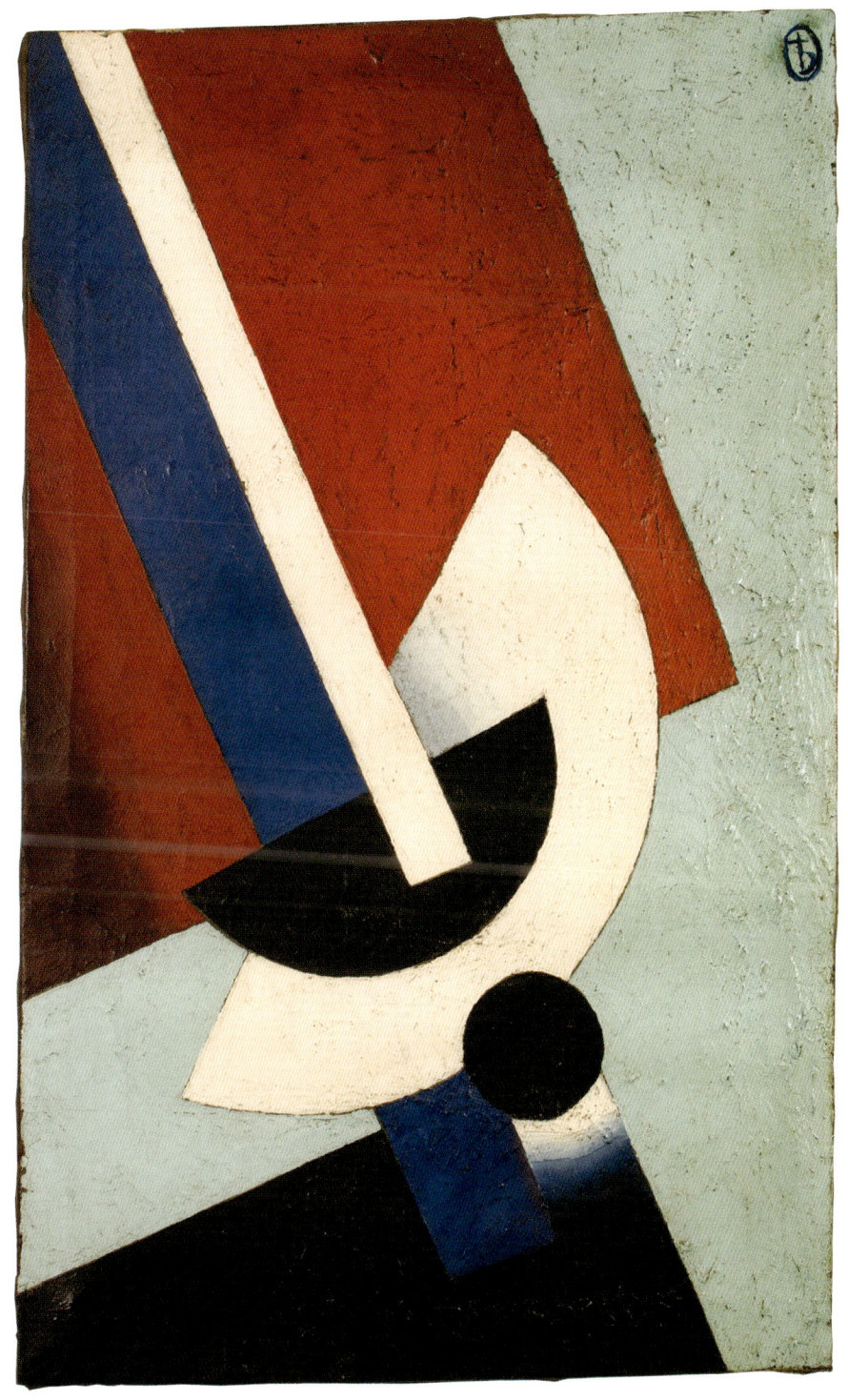

97

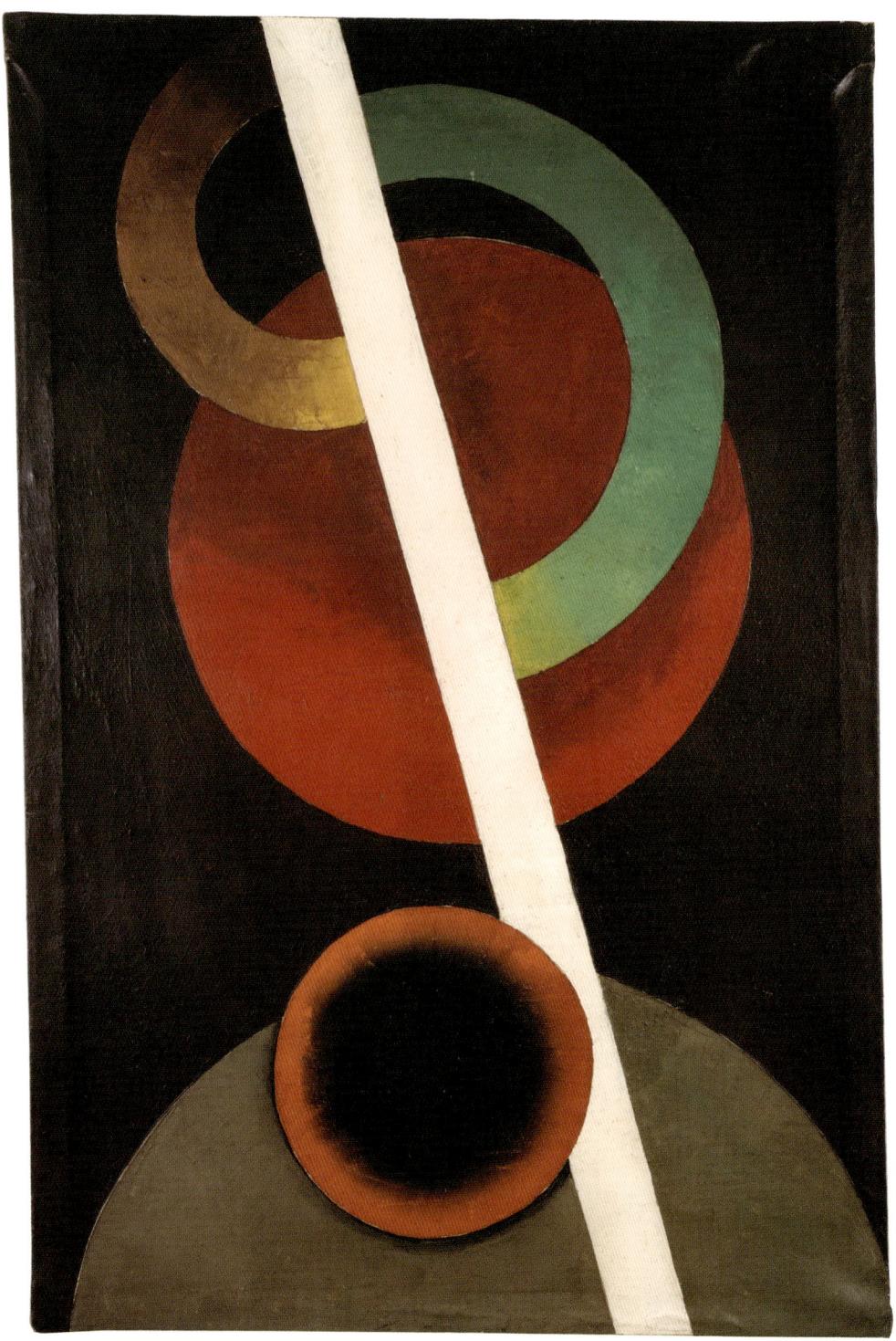

98

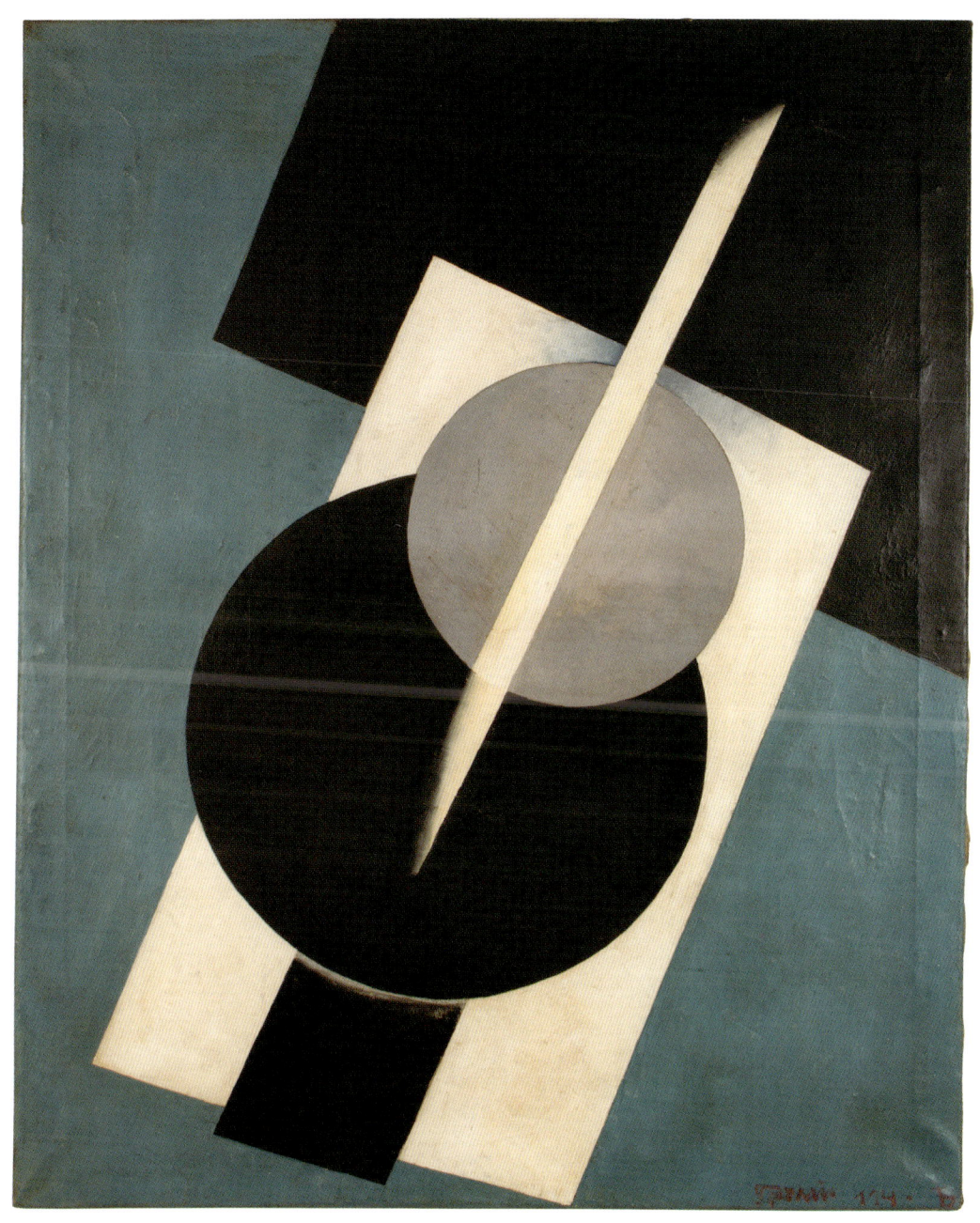

99

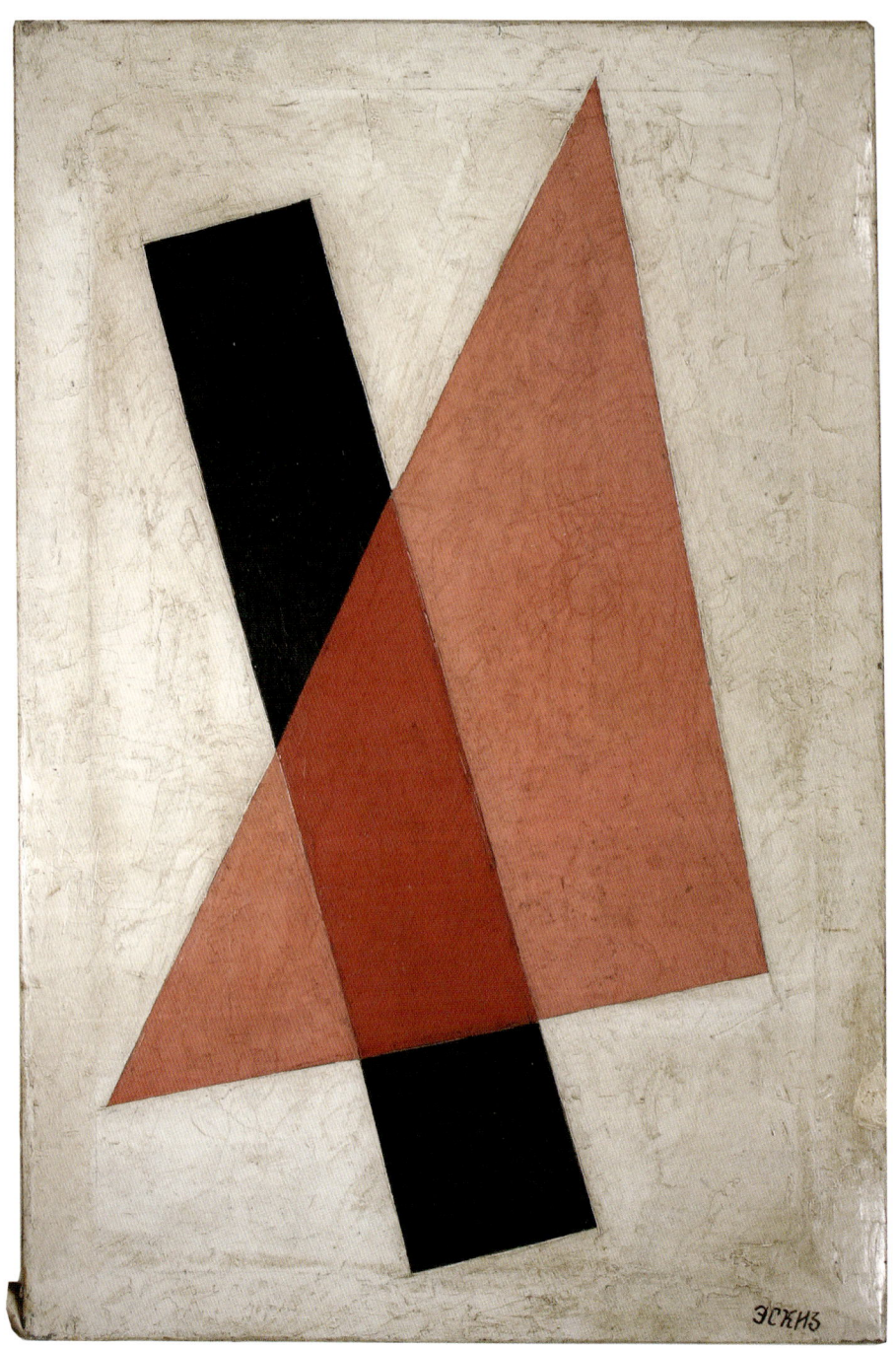

100

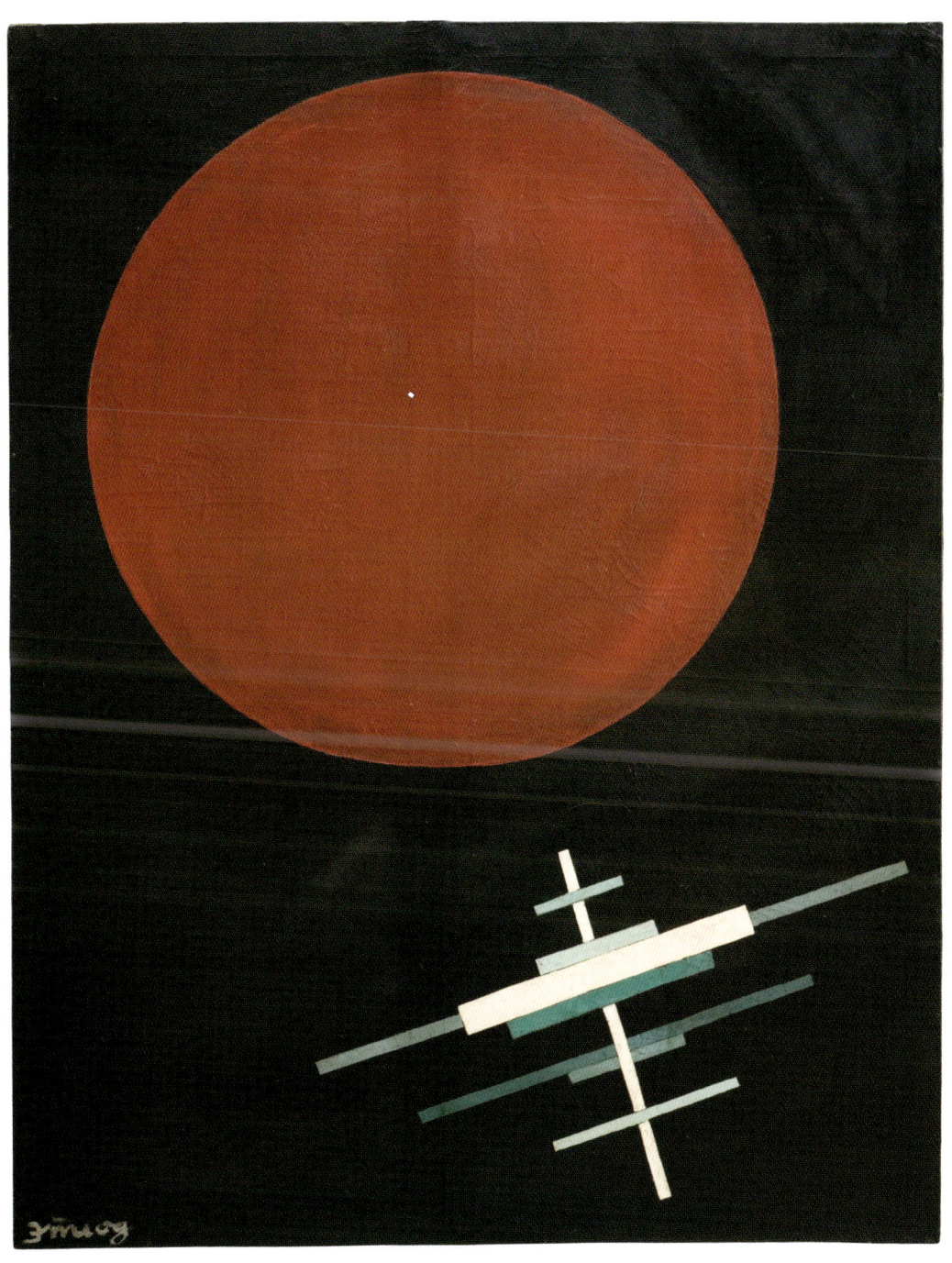

101

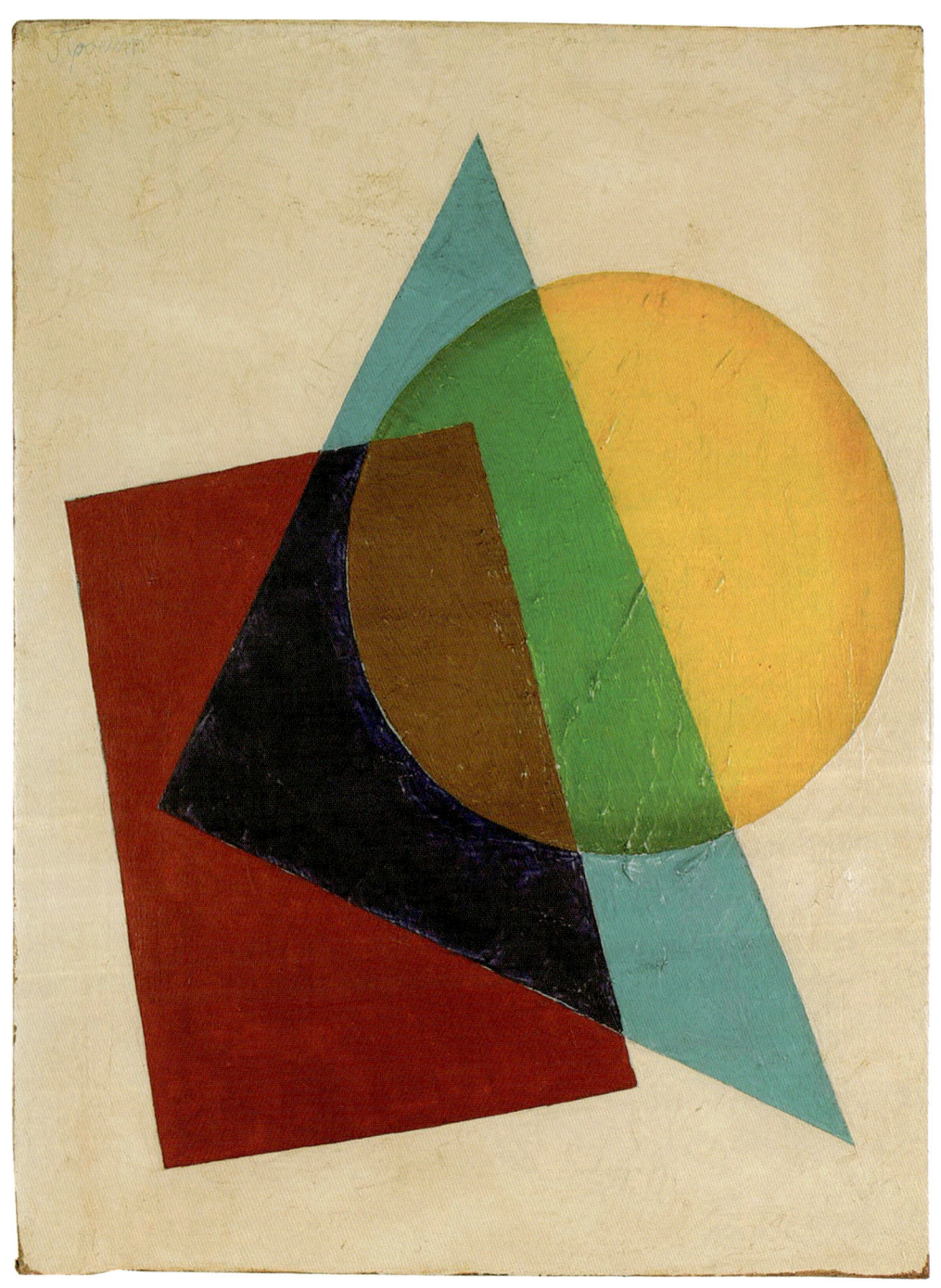

102

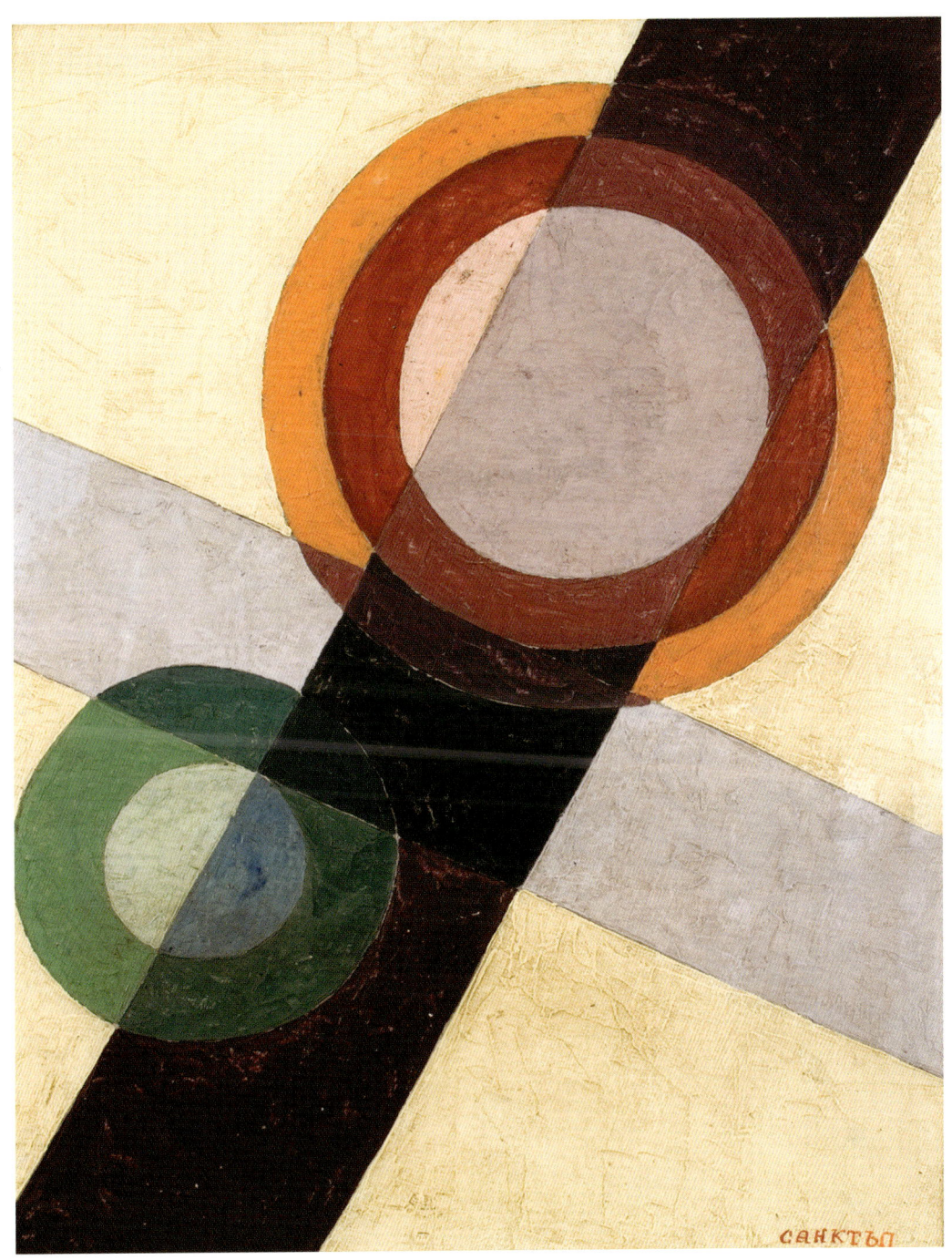

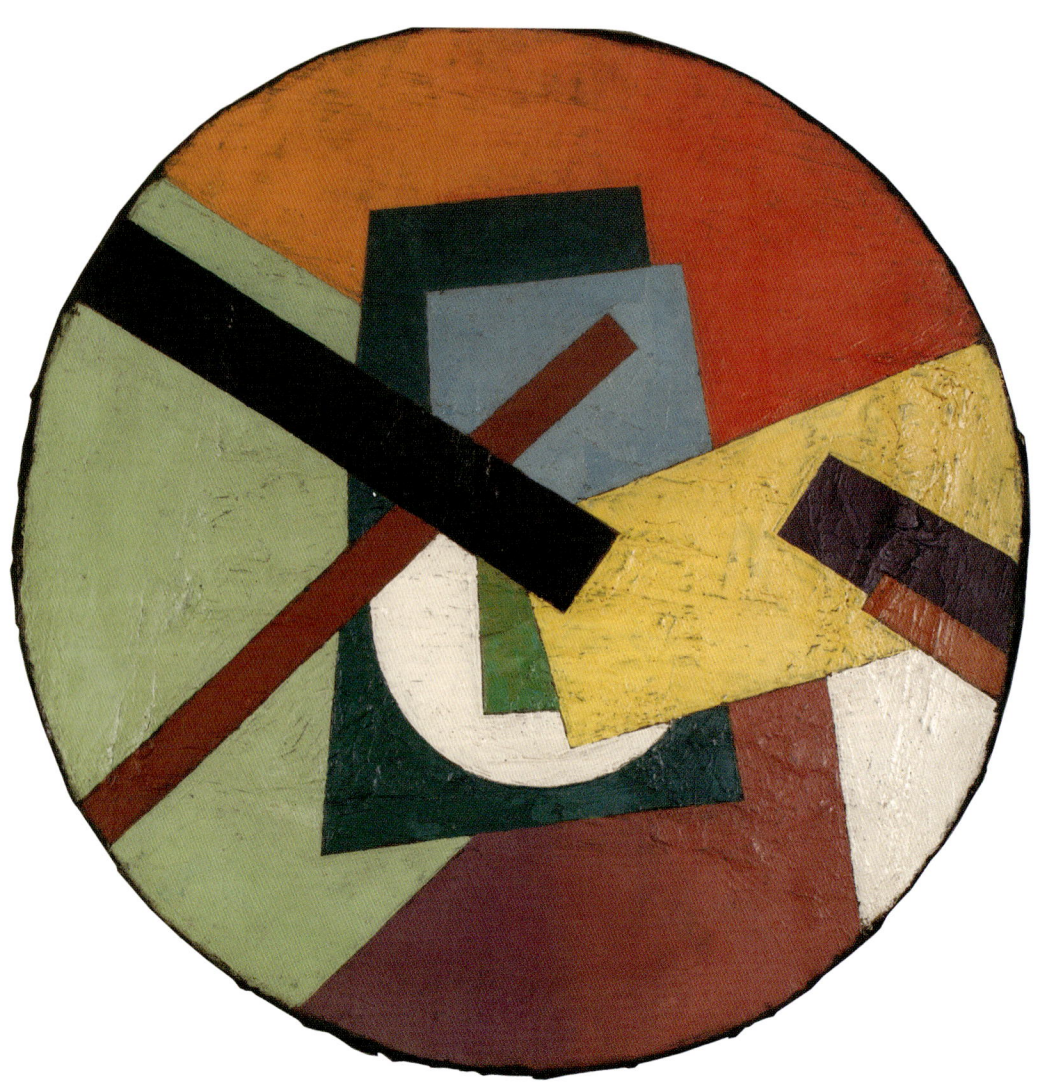

104

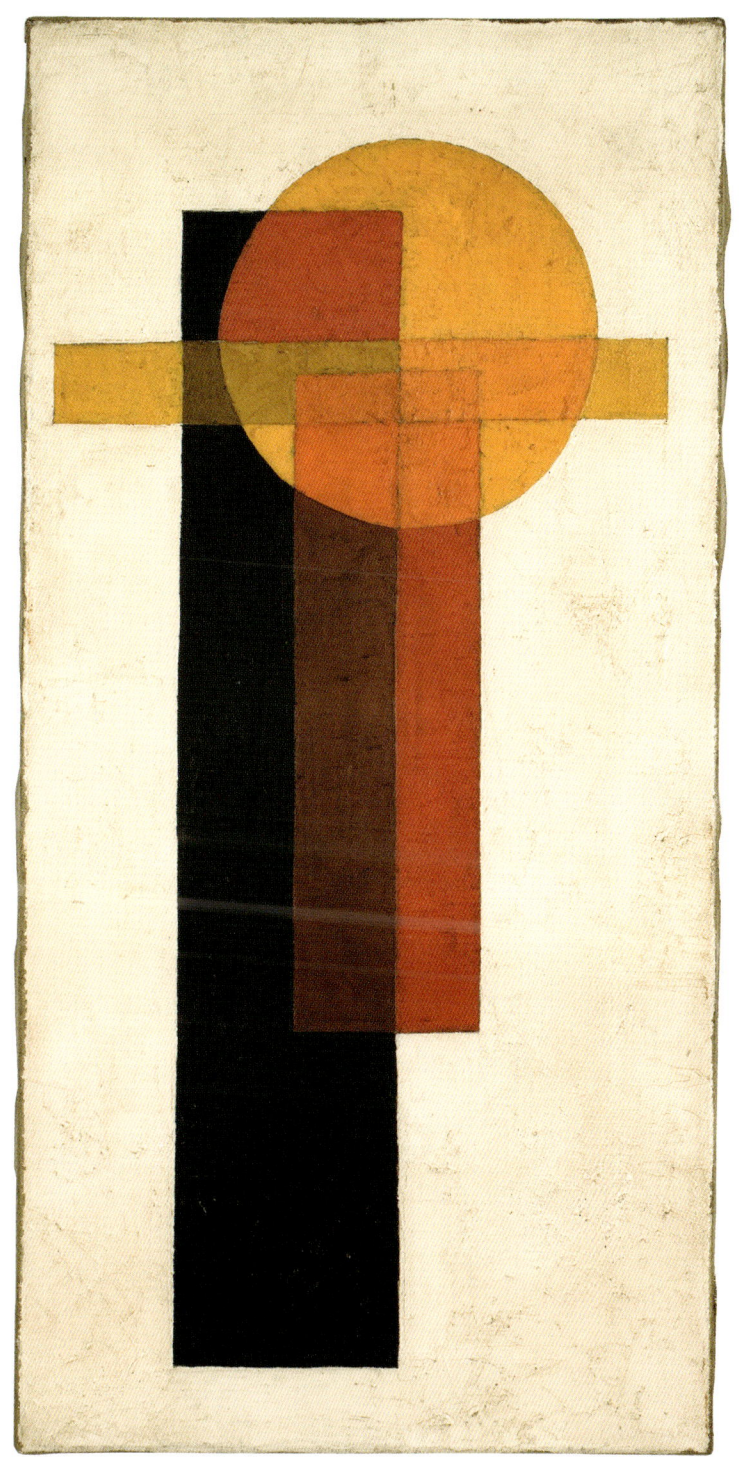

105

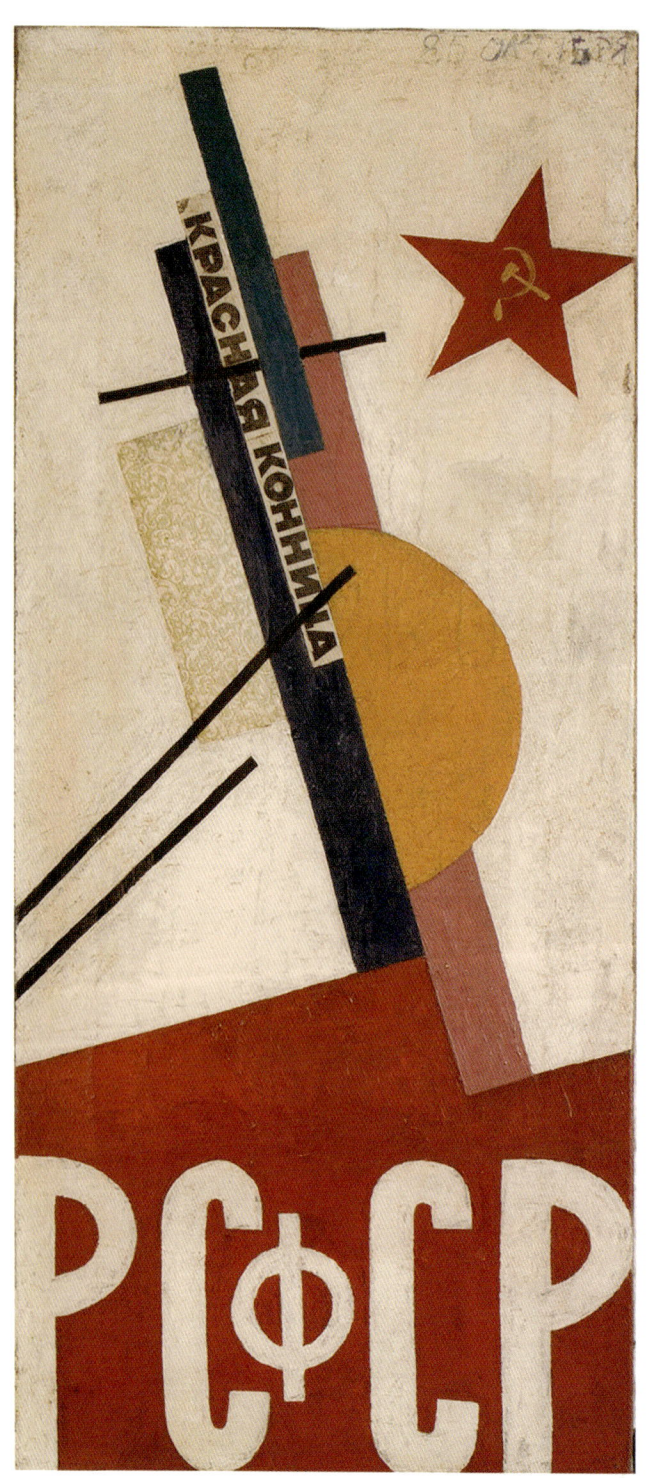

106

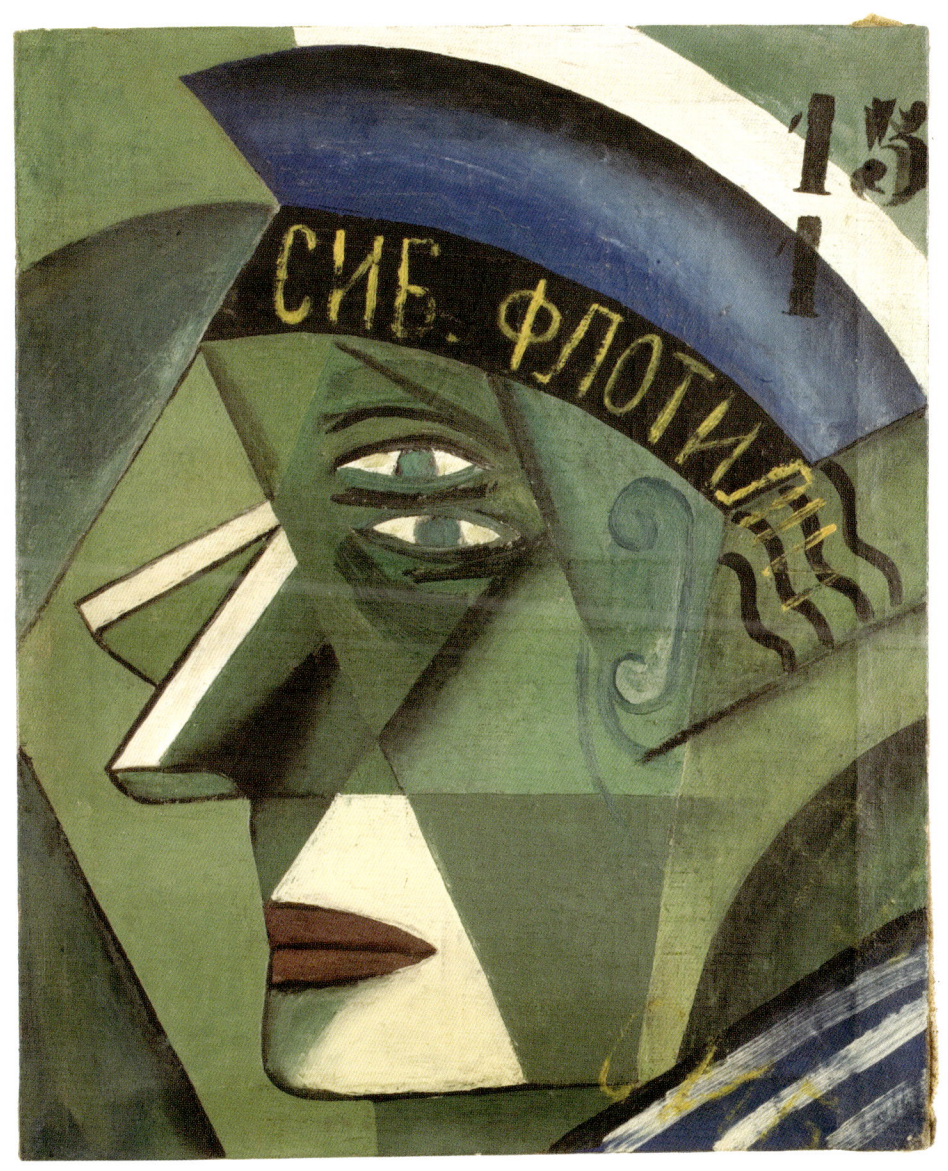

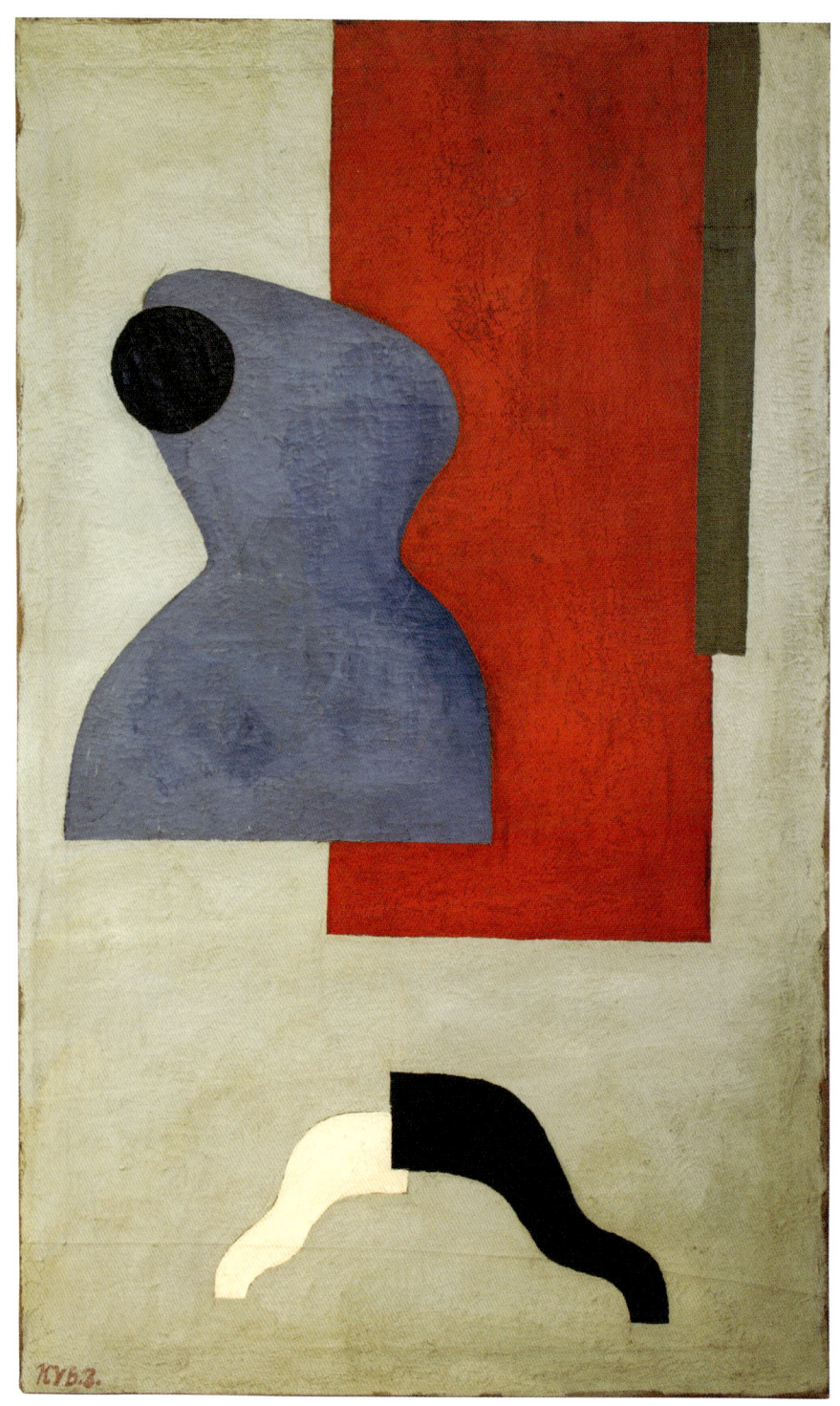

108

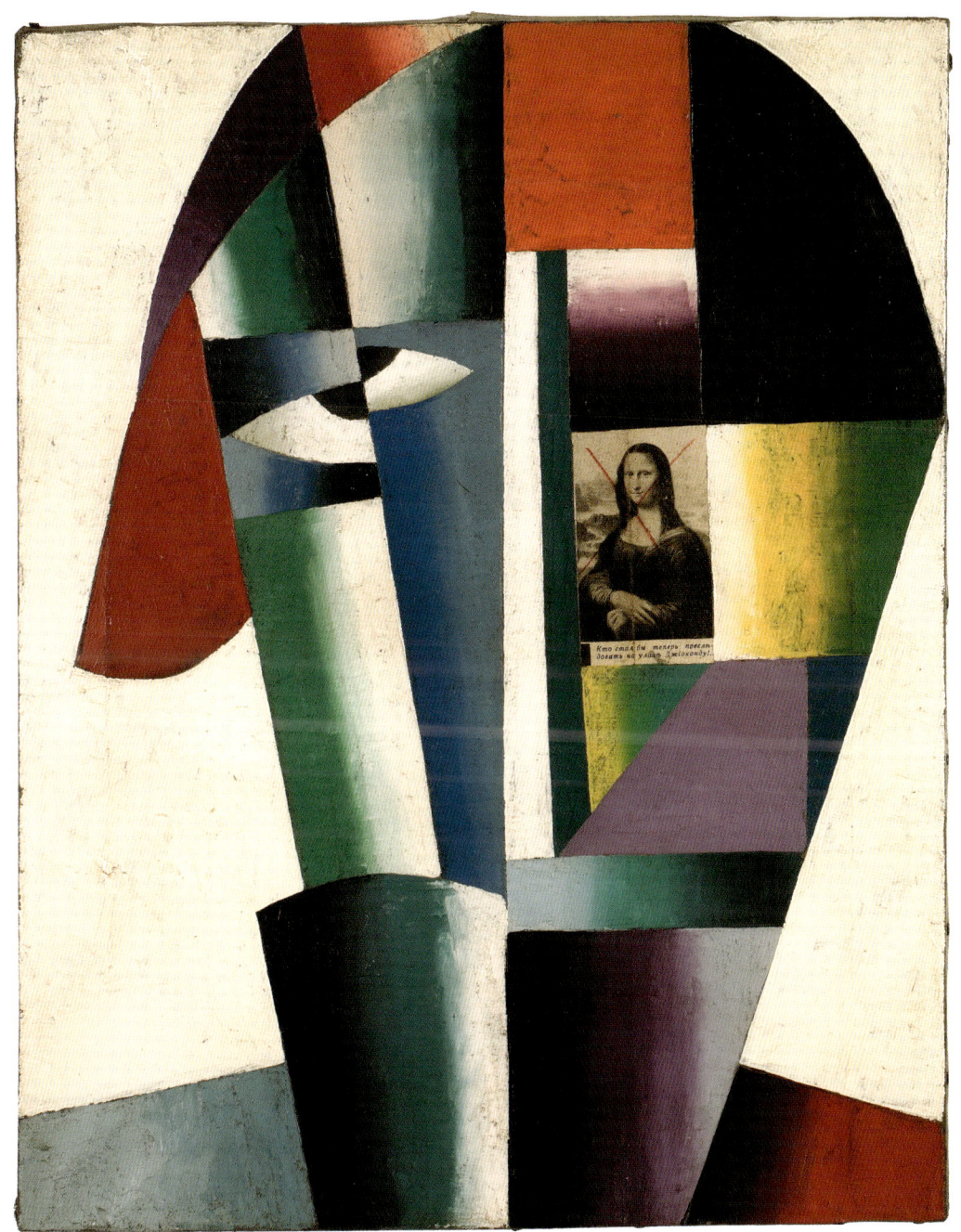

109

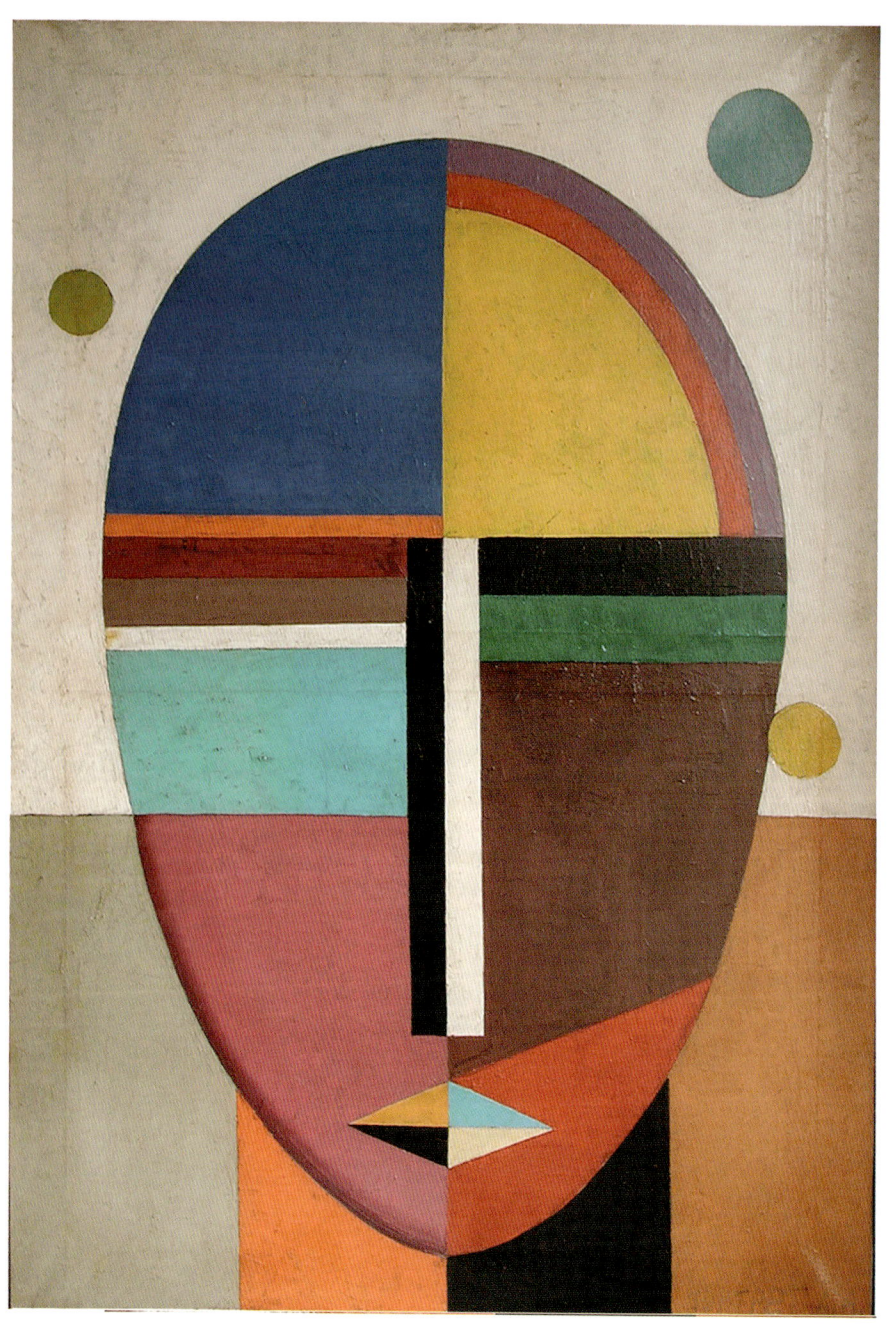

110

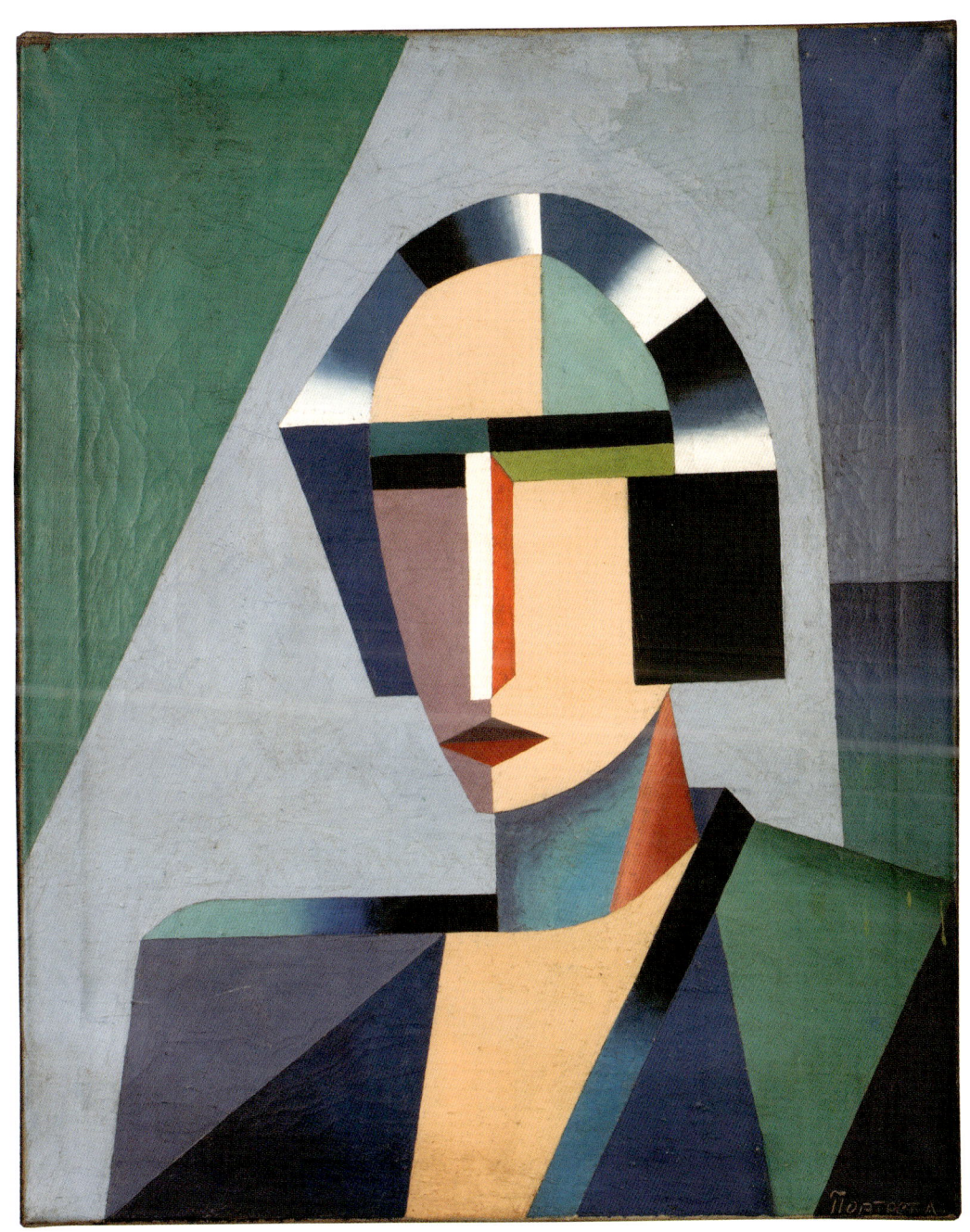

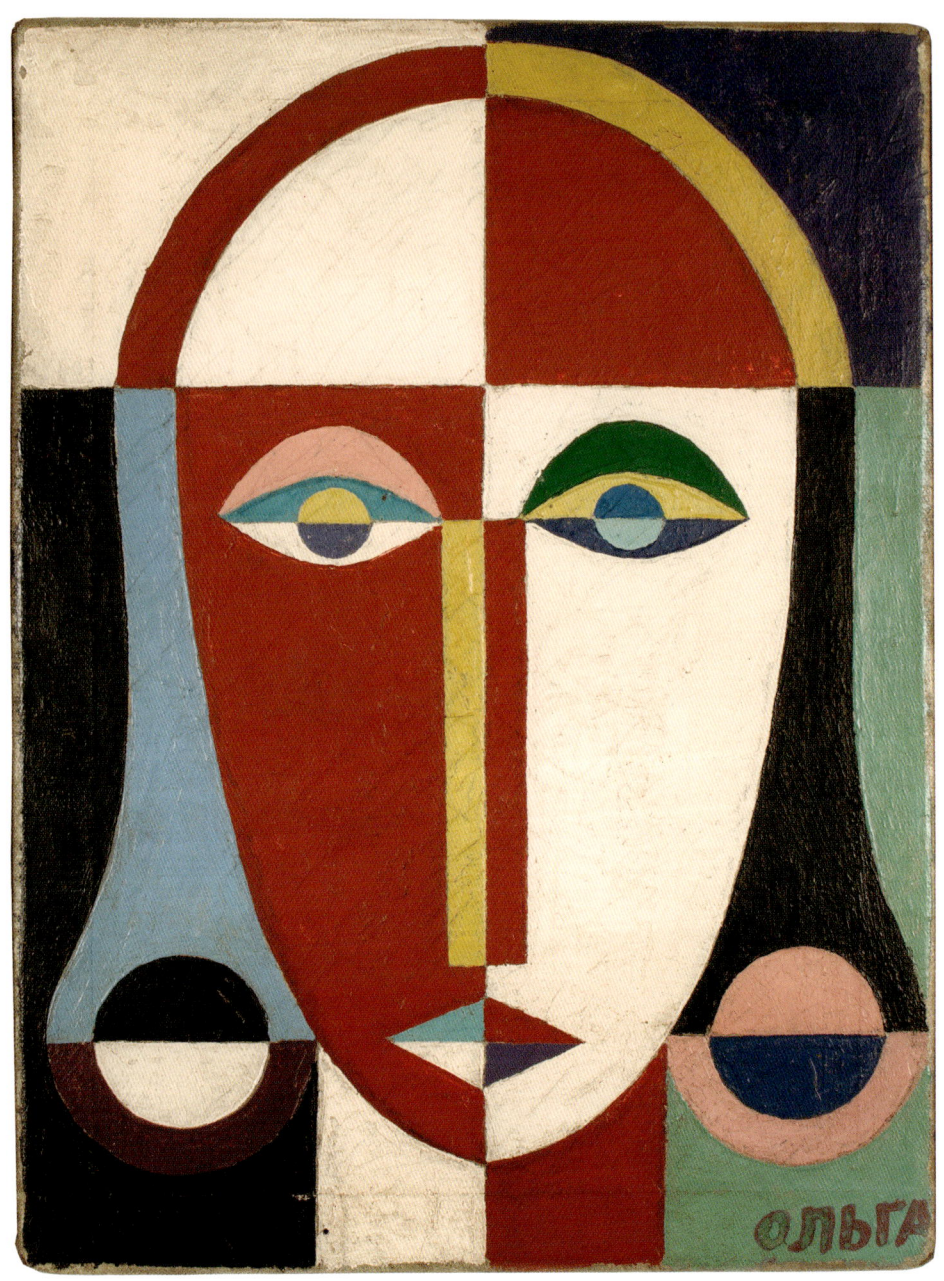

112

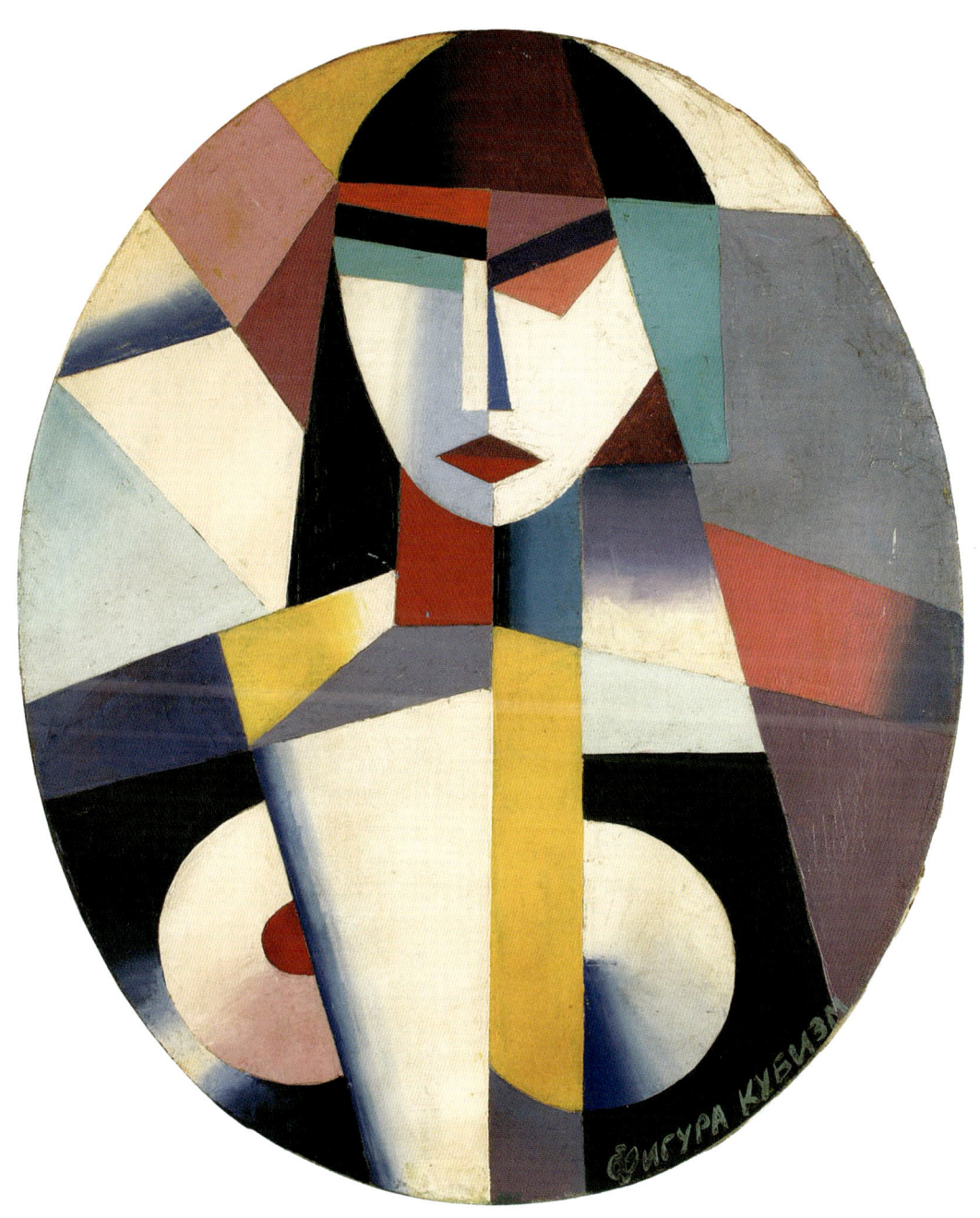

Фигура Кубизм

113

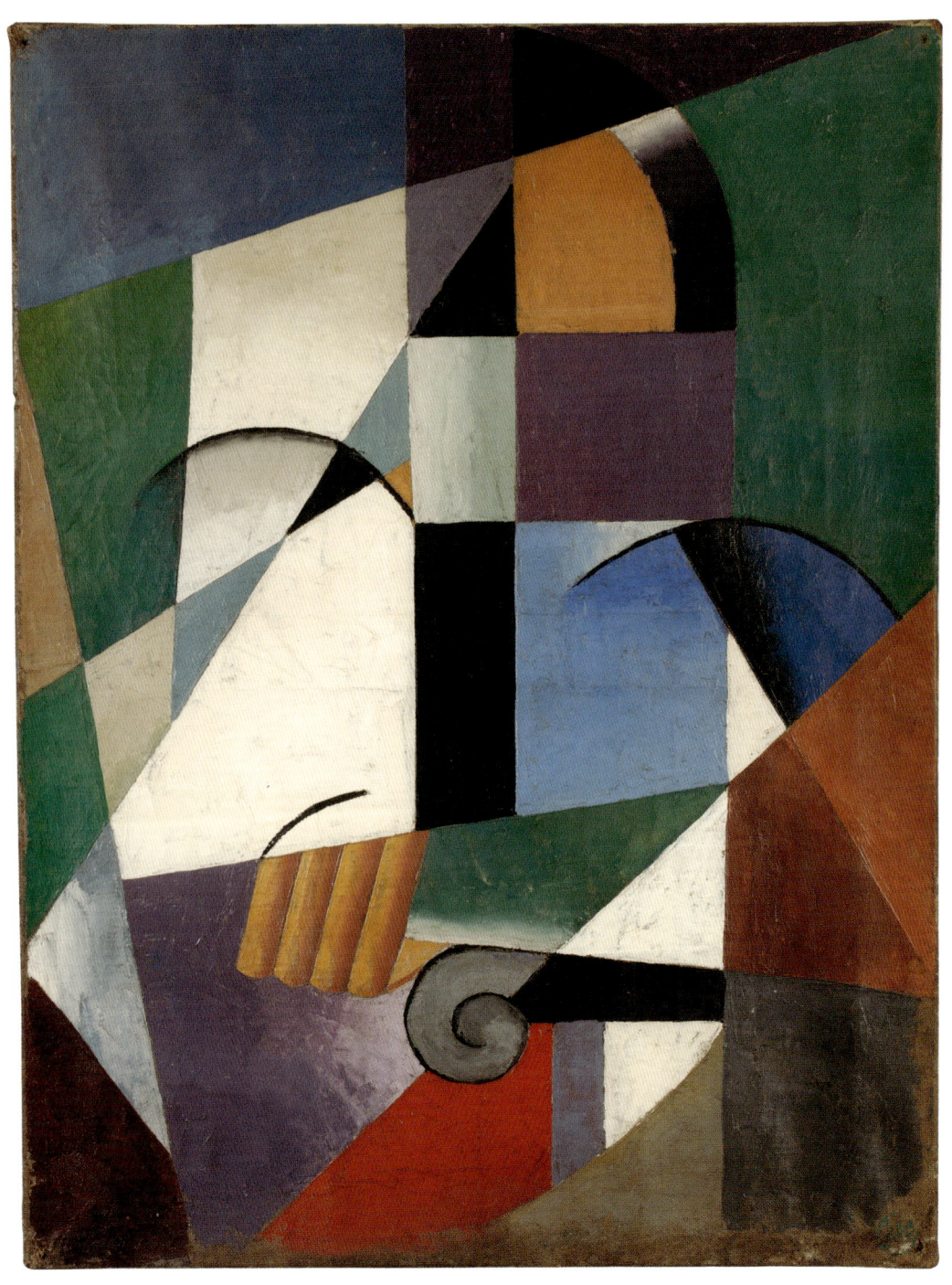

114

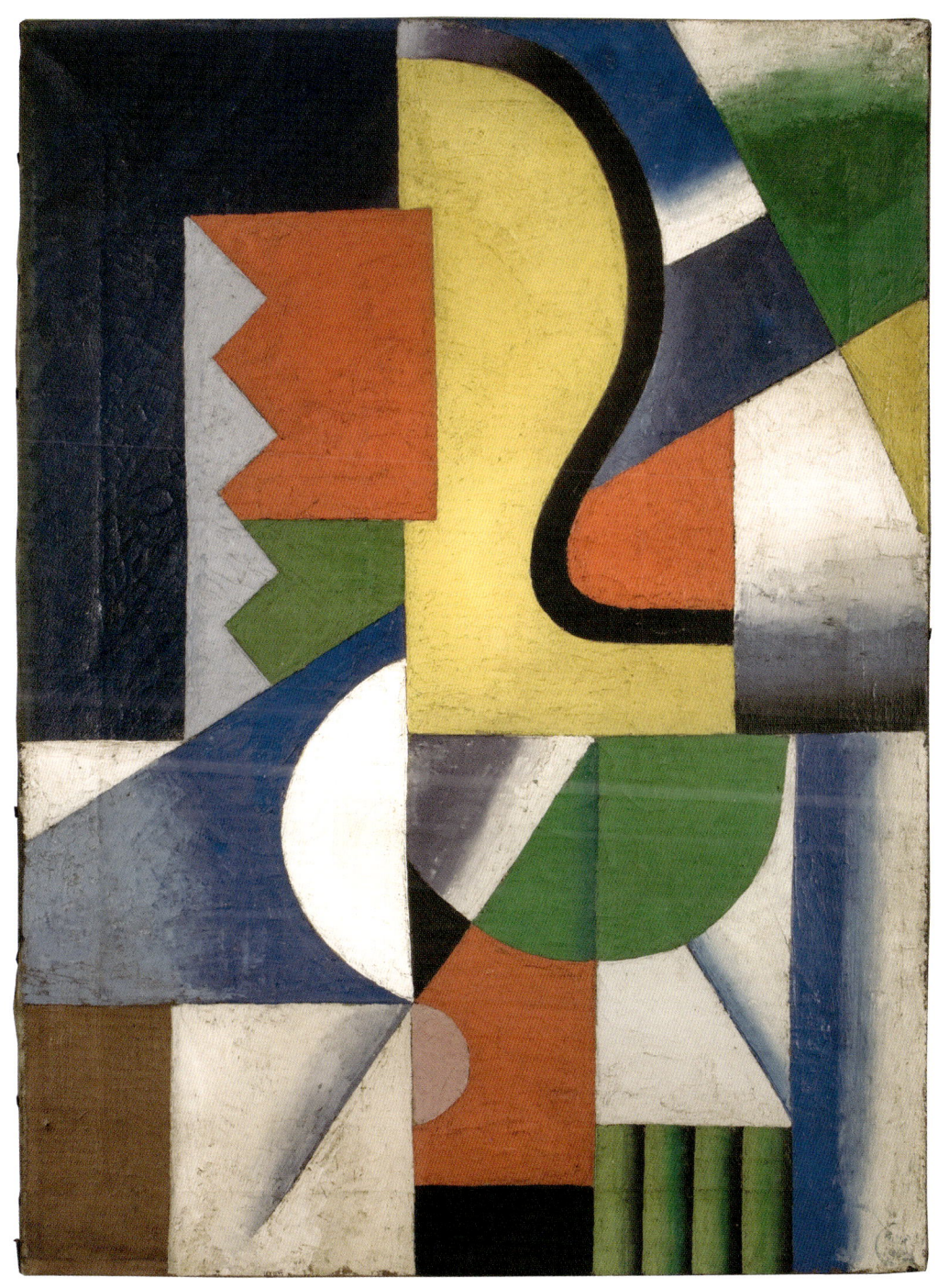

115

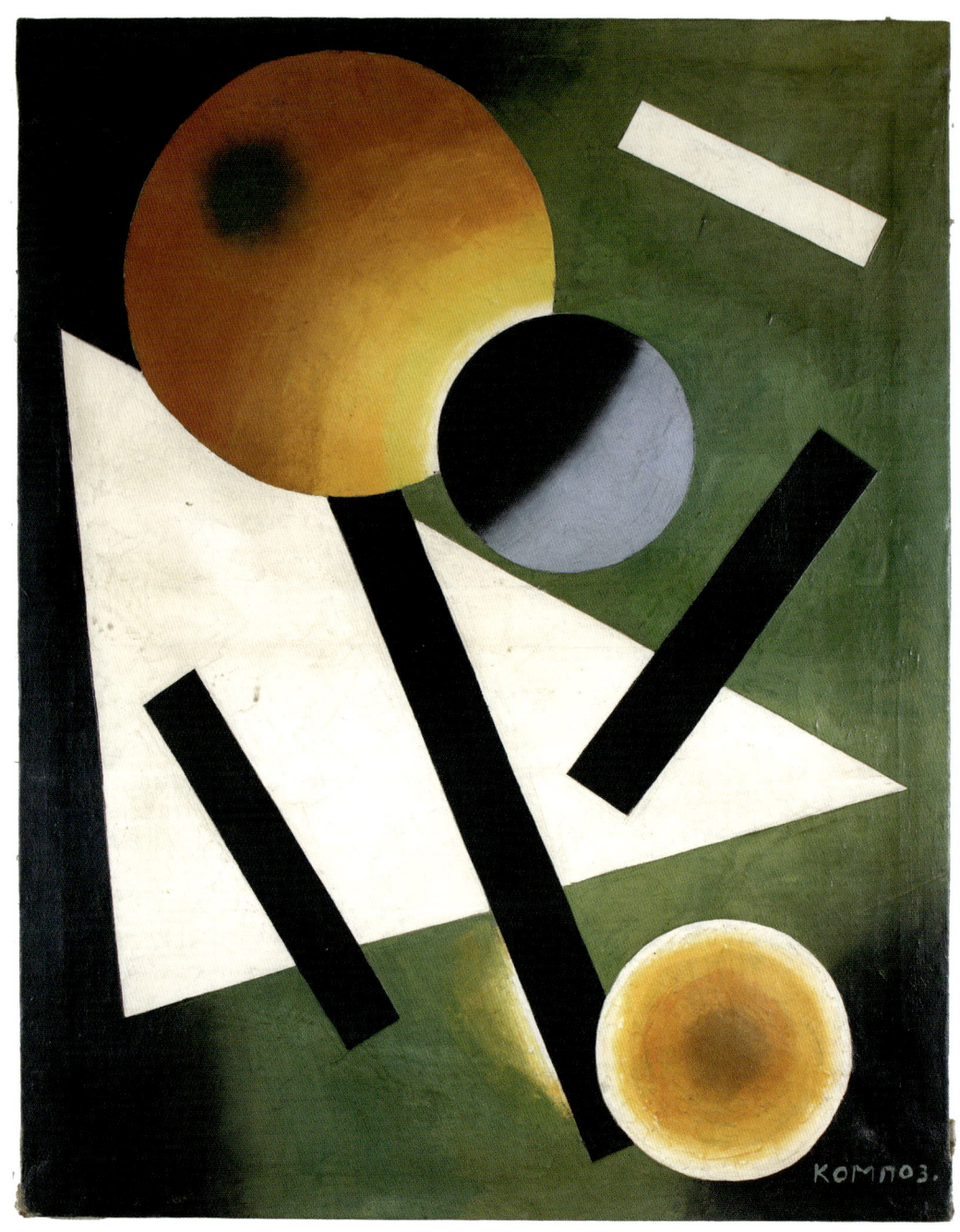

116

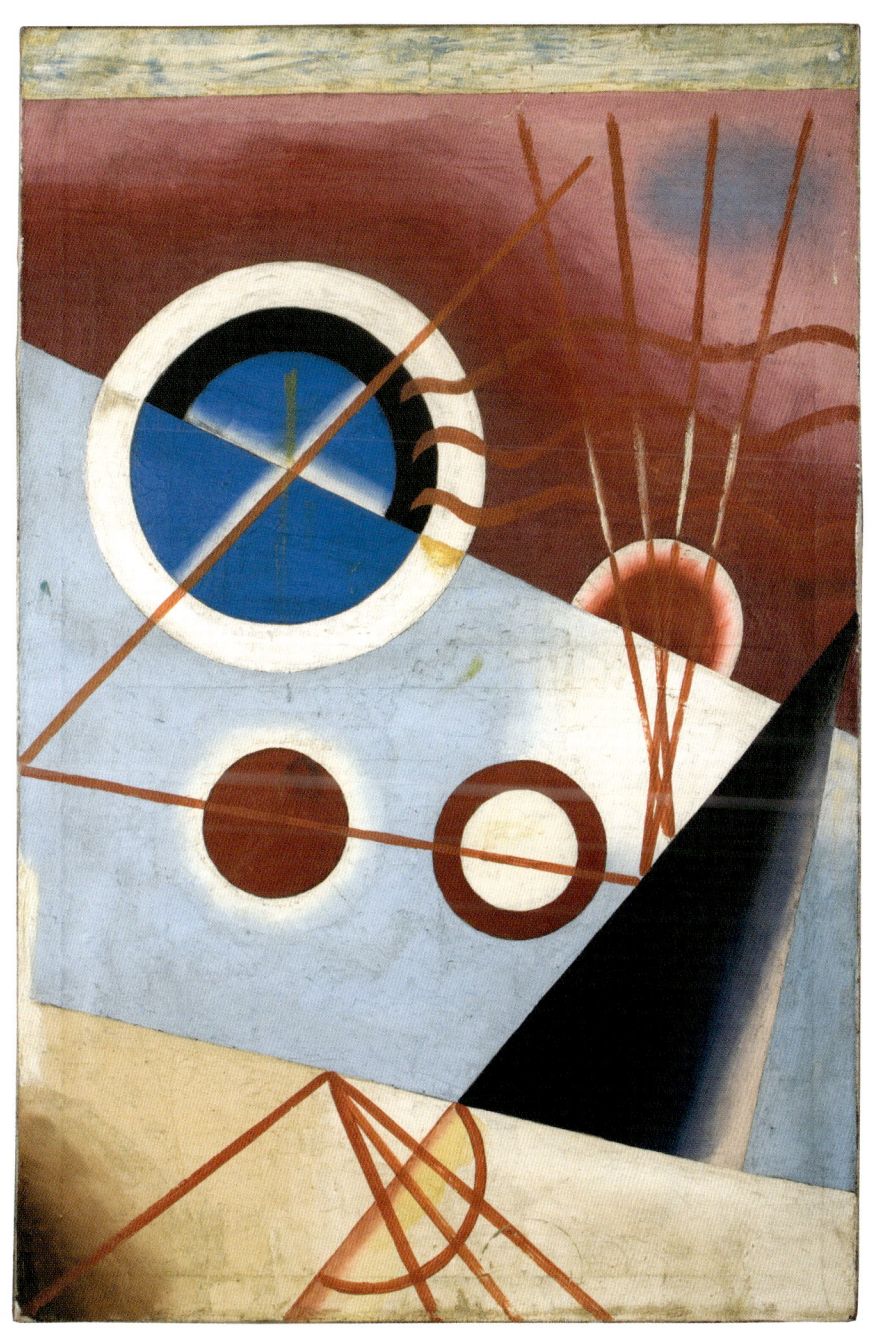

117

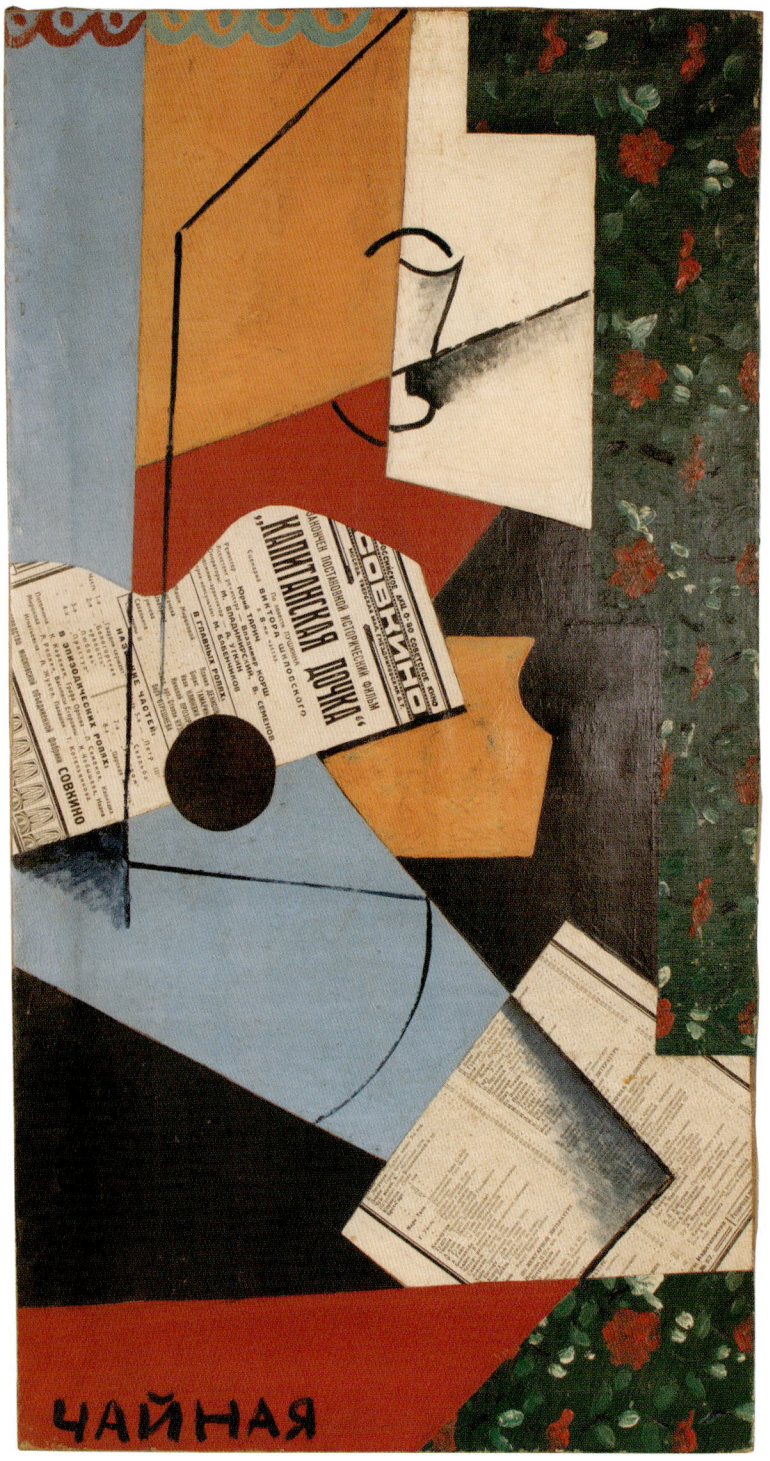

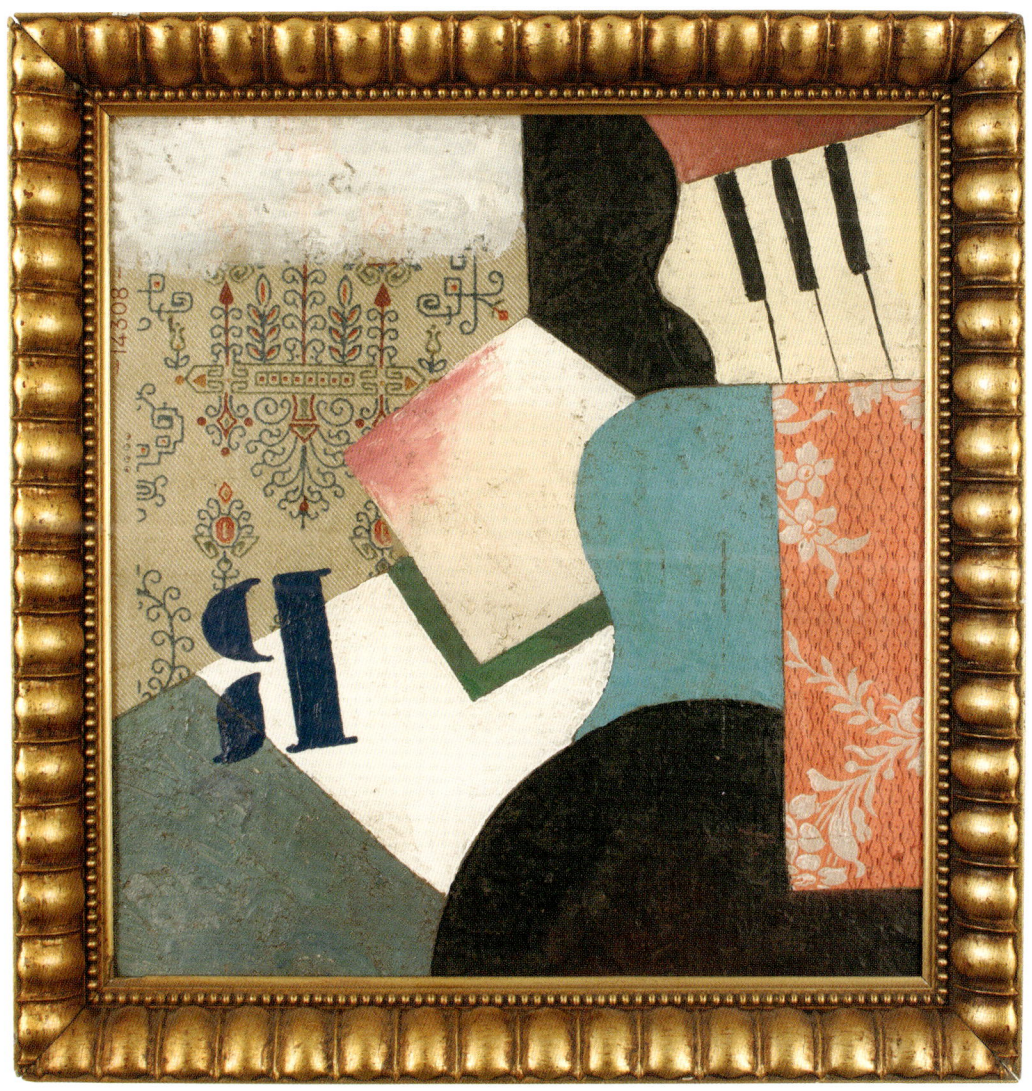

119

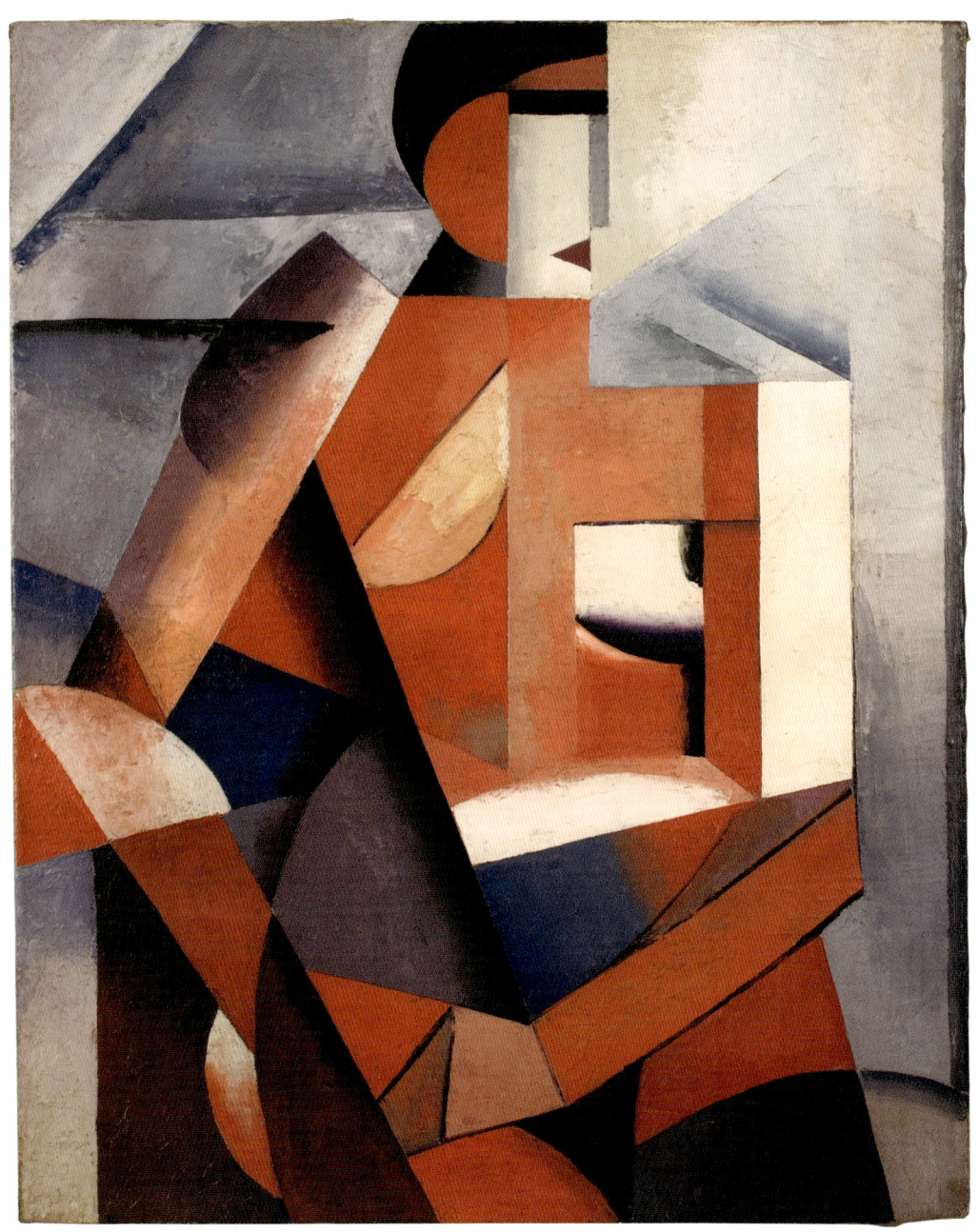

120

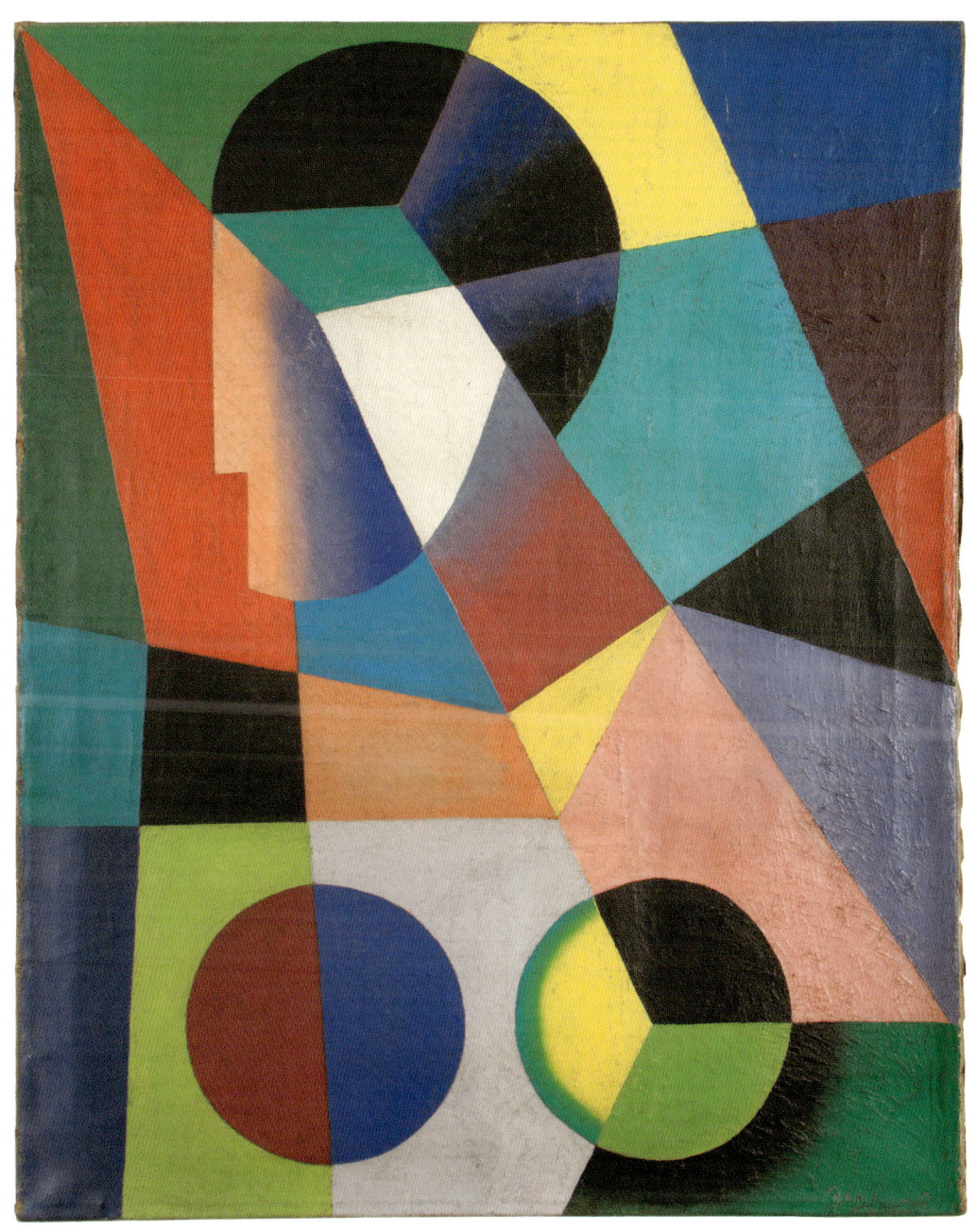

121

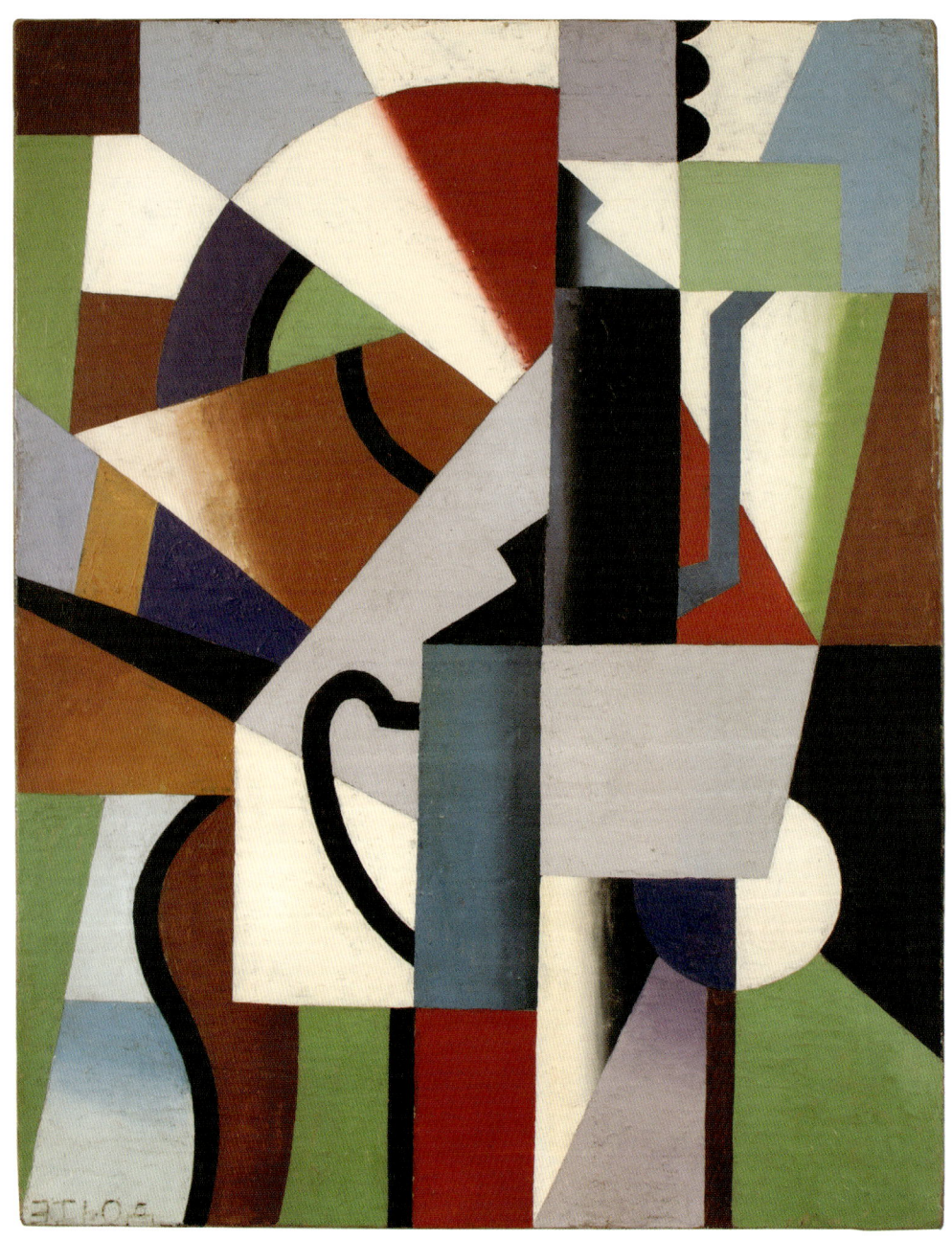

122

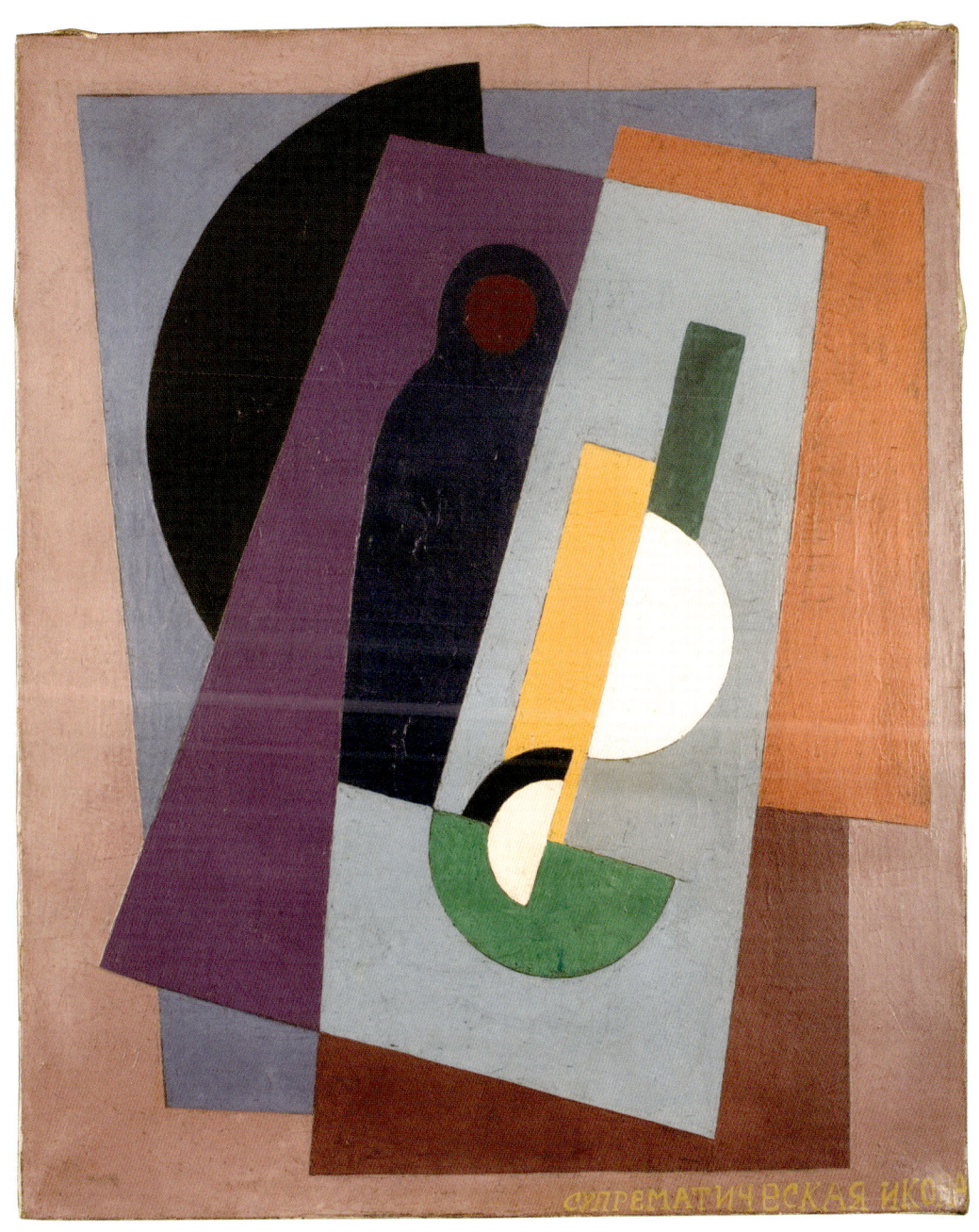

СУПРЕМАТИЧЕСКАЯ ИКОНА

123

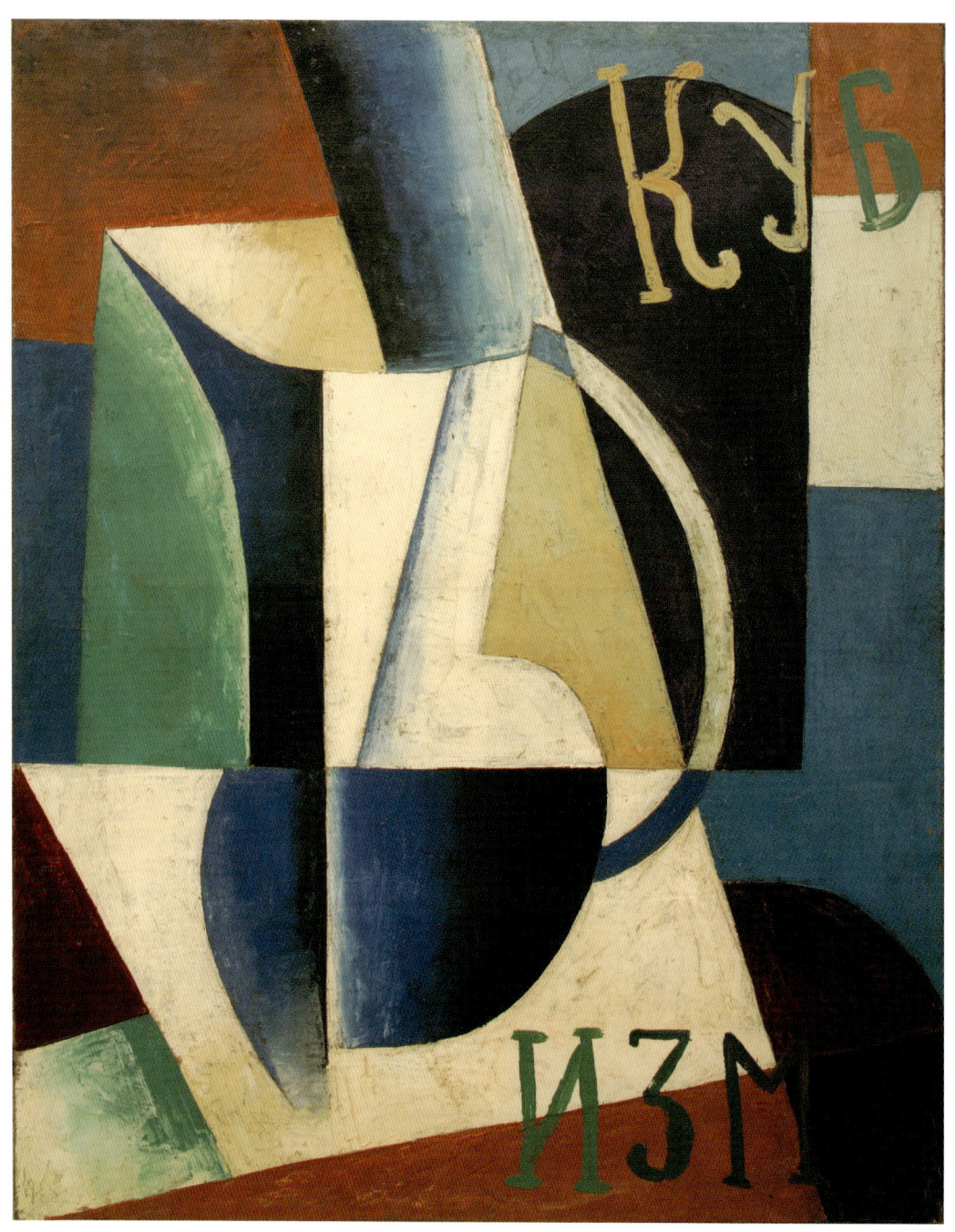

124

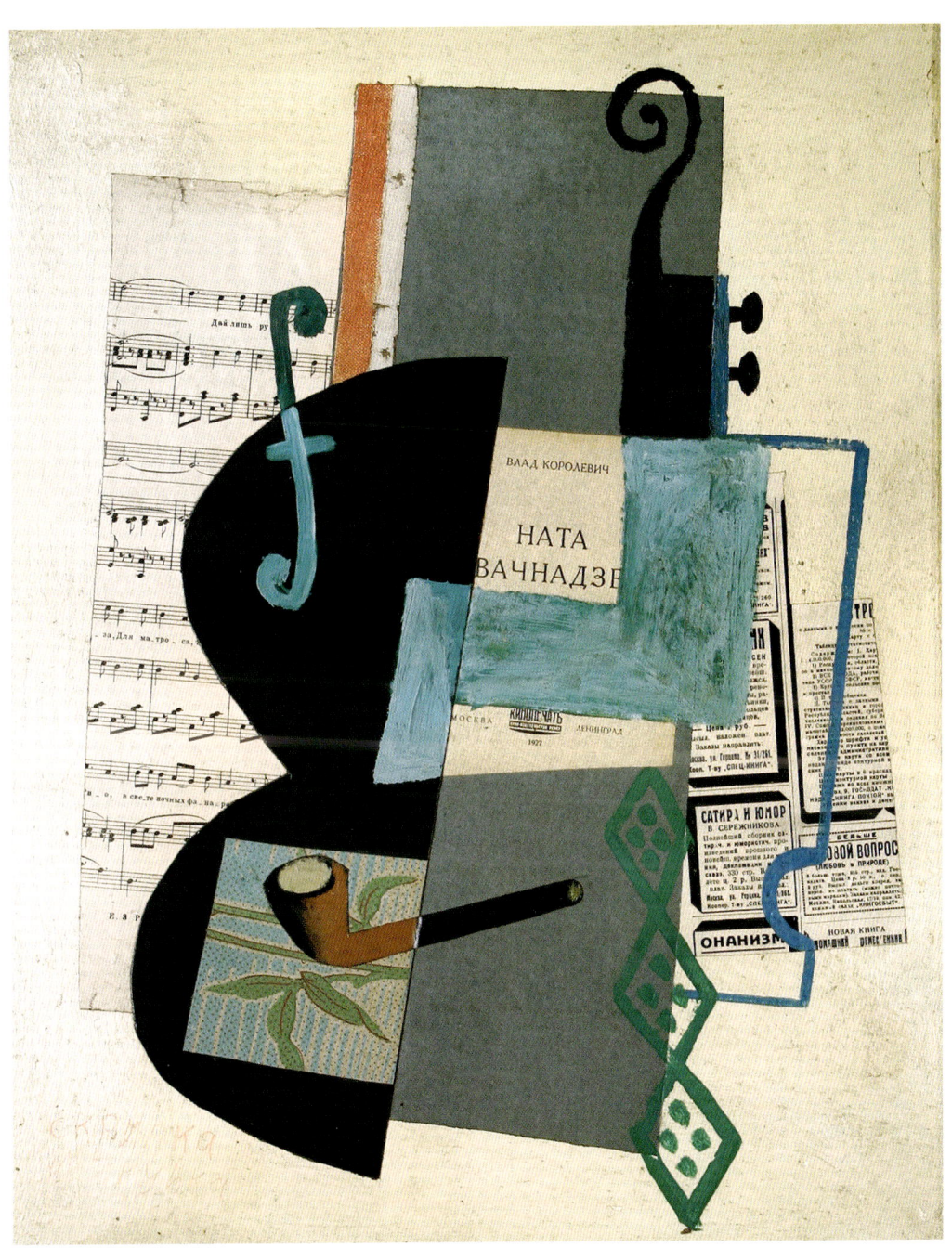

125

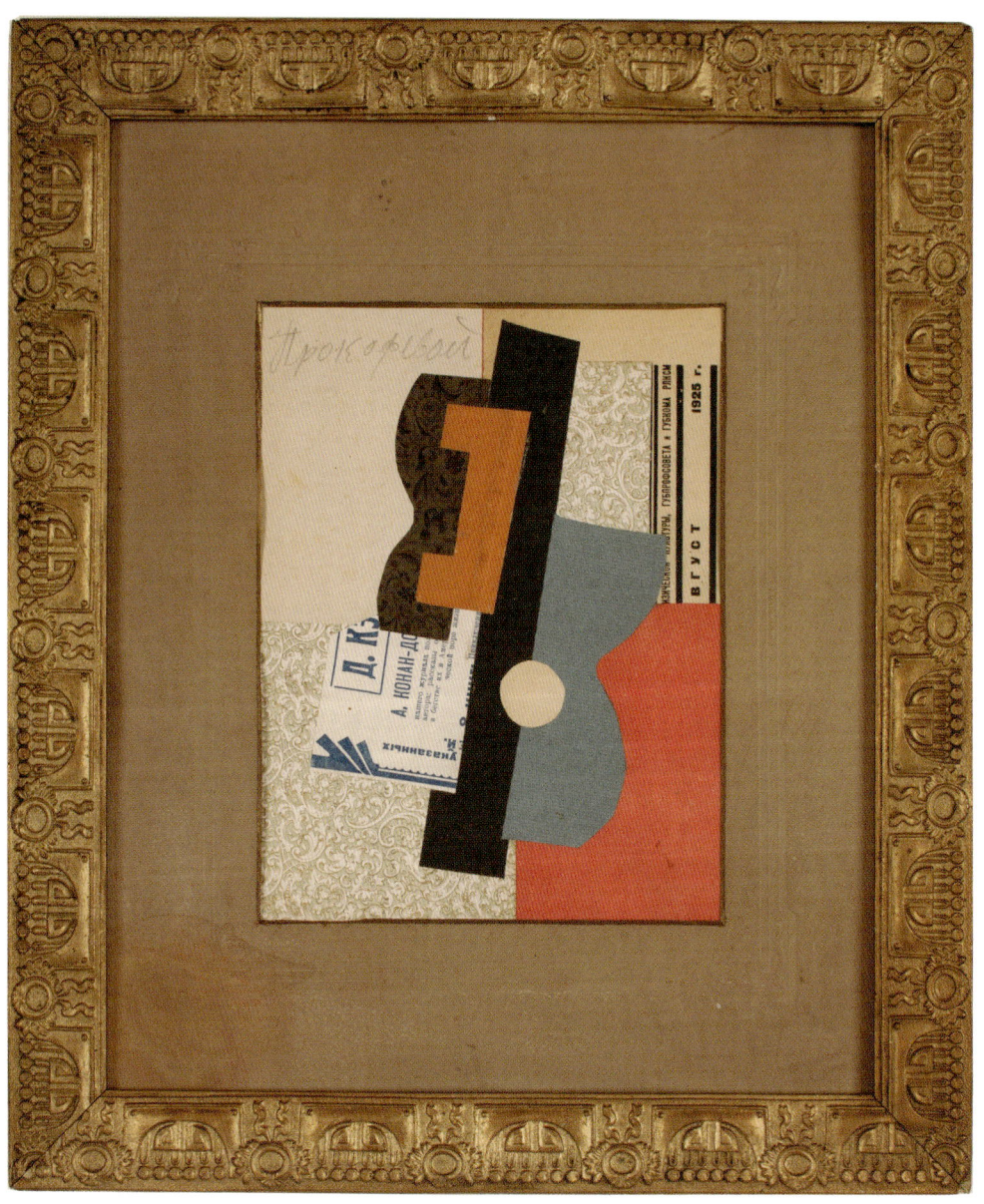

126

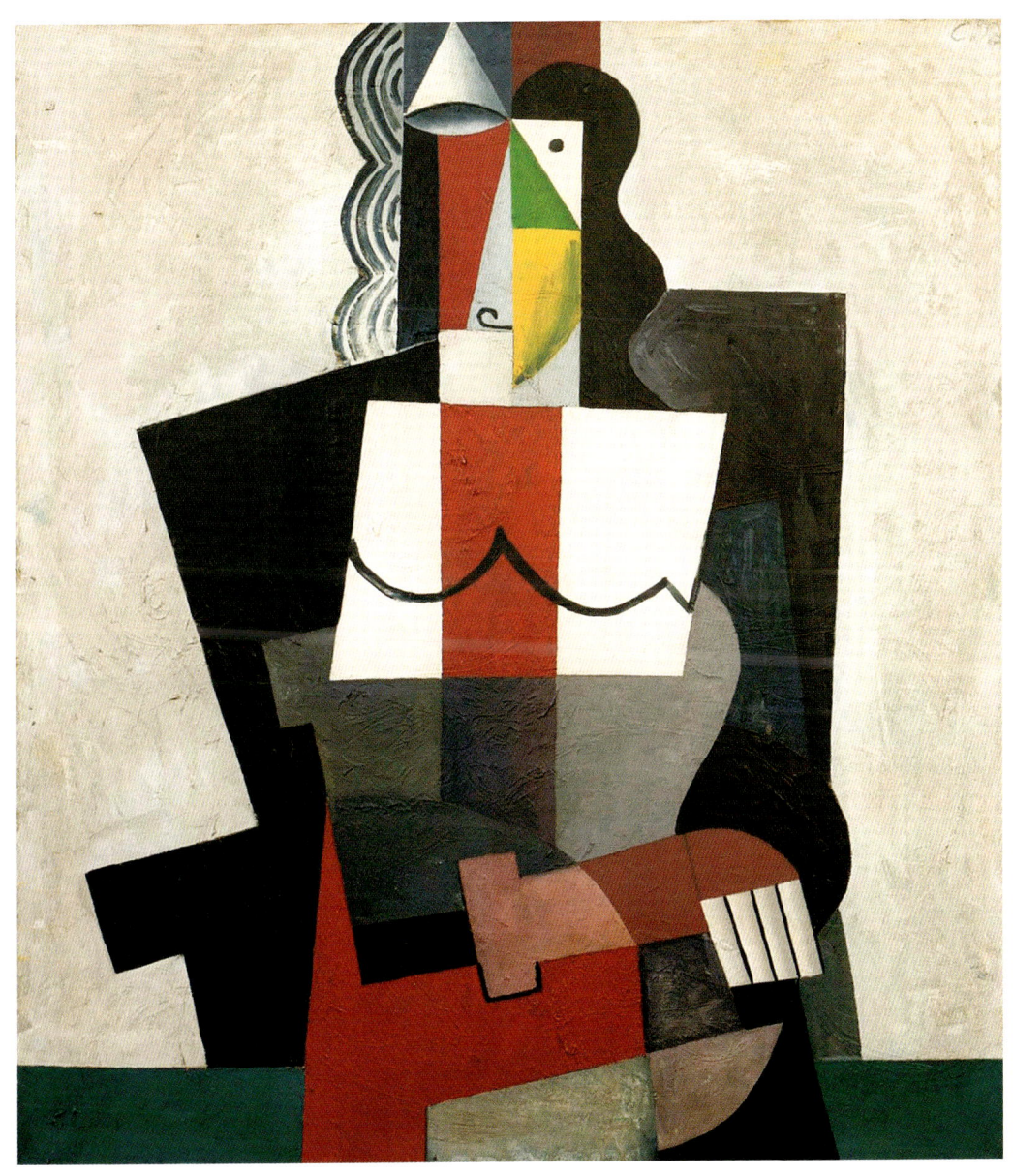

127

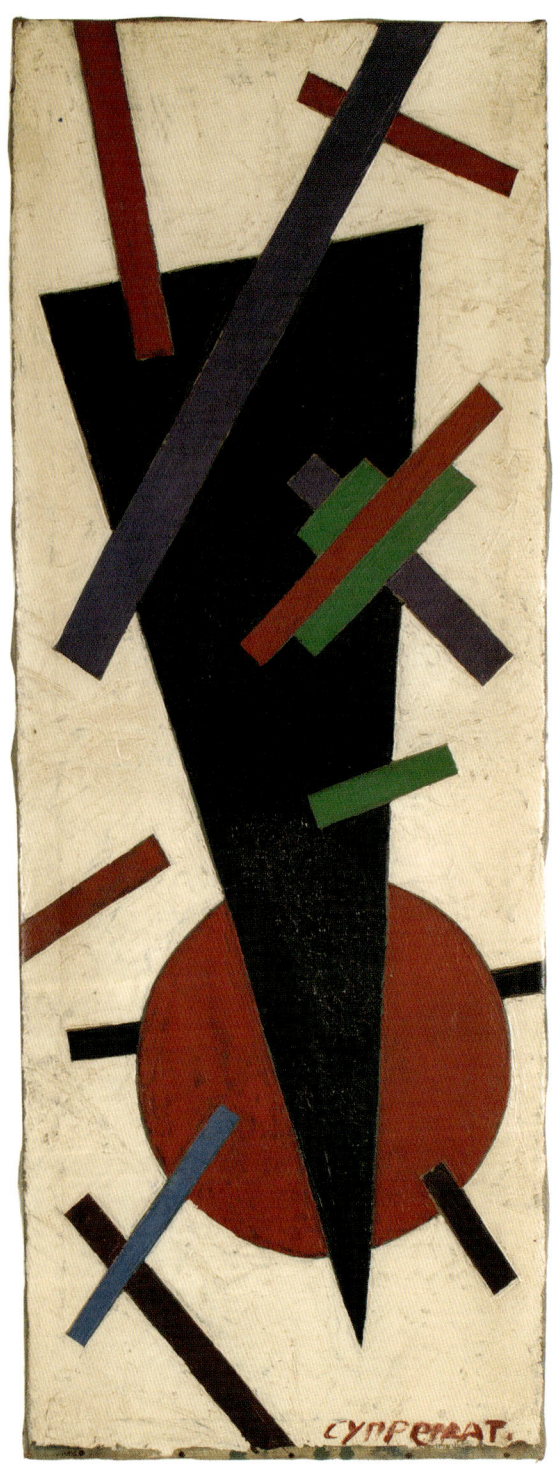

128

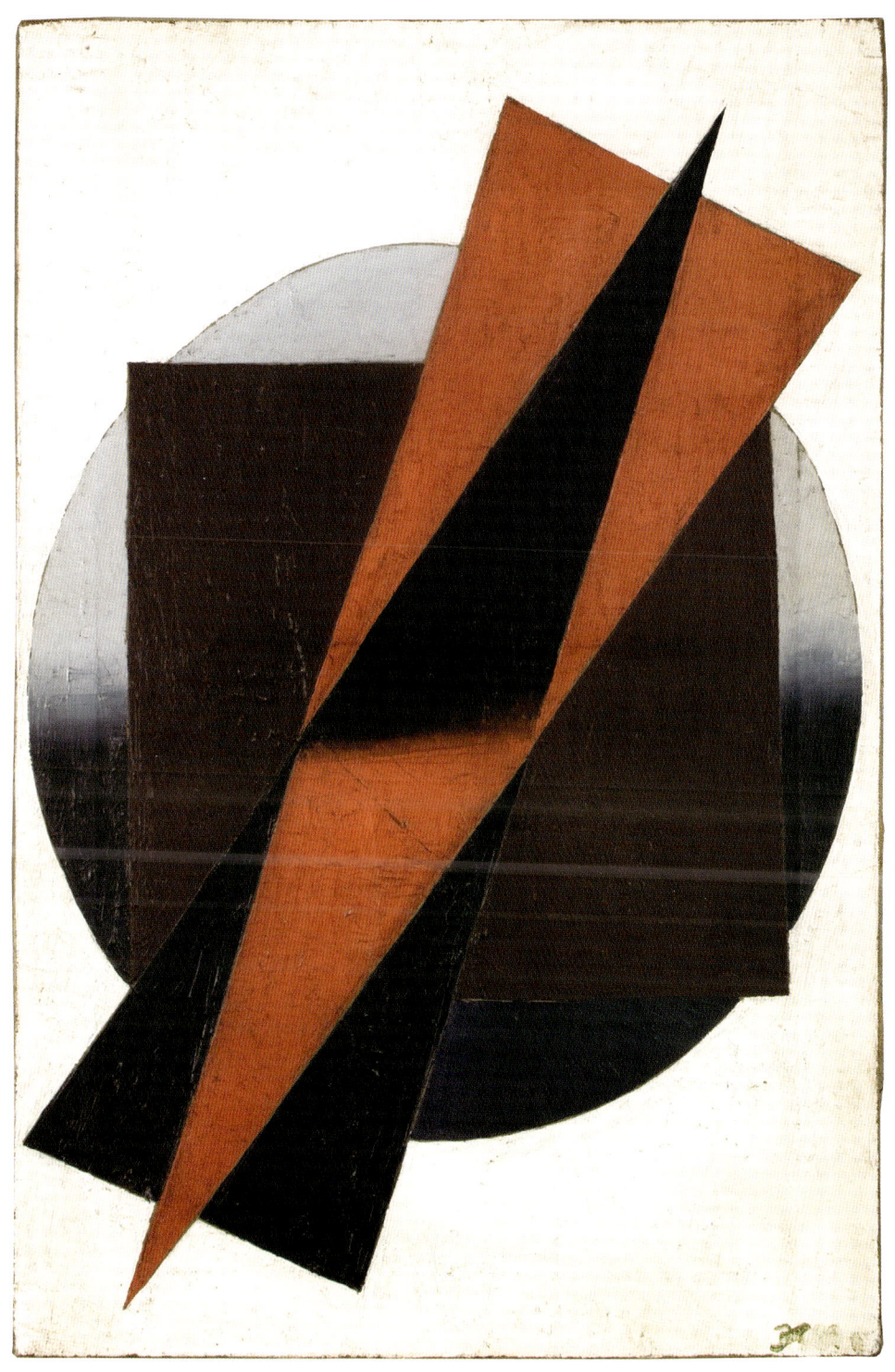

129

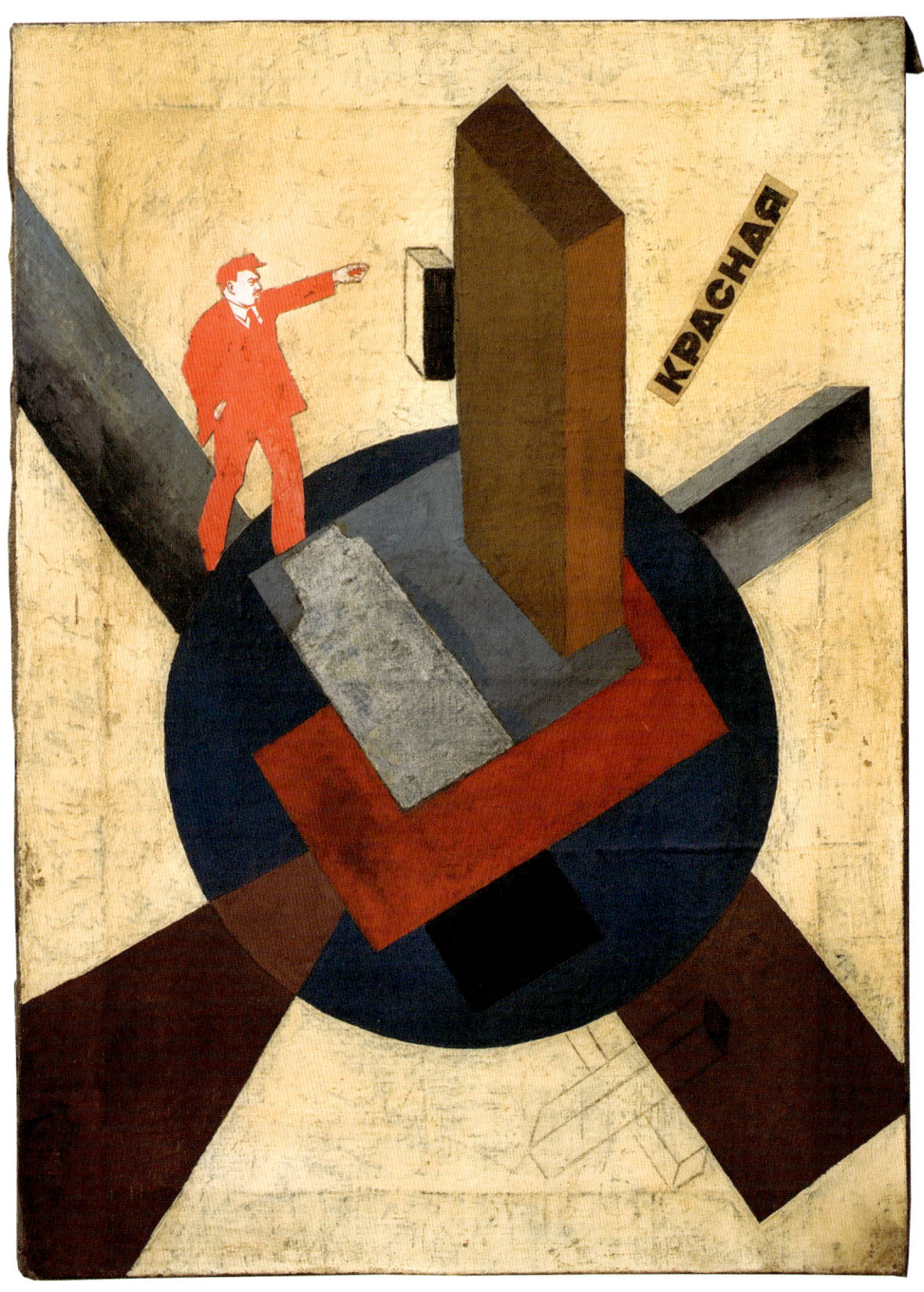

130

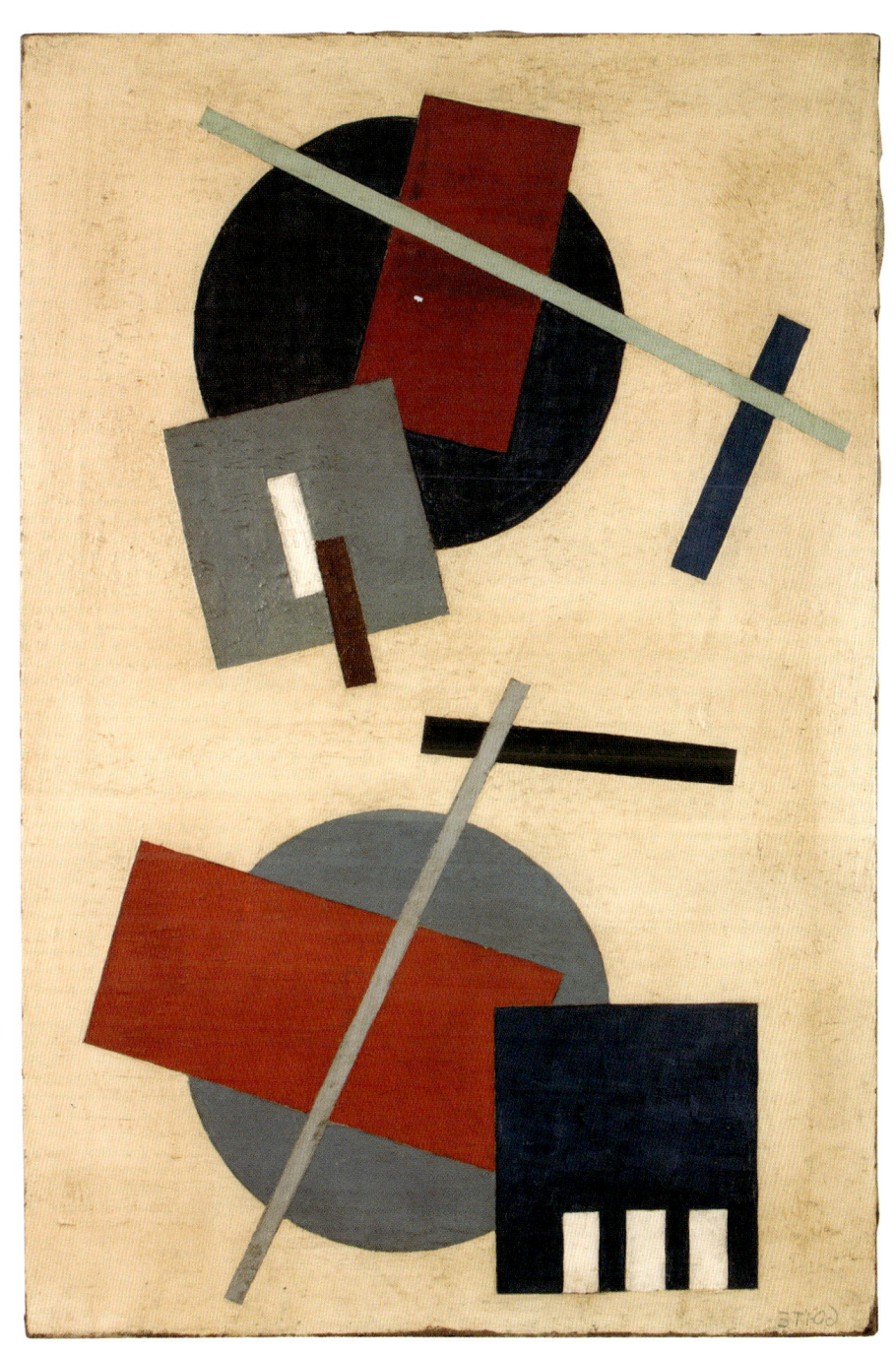

131

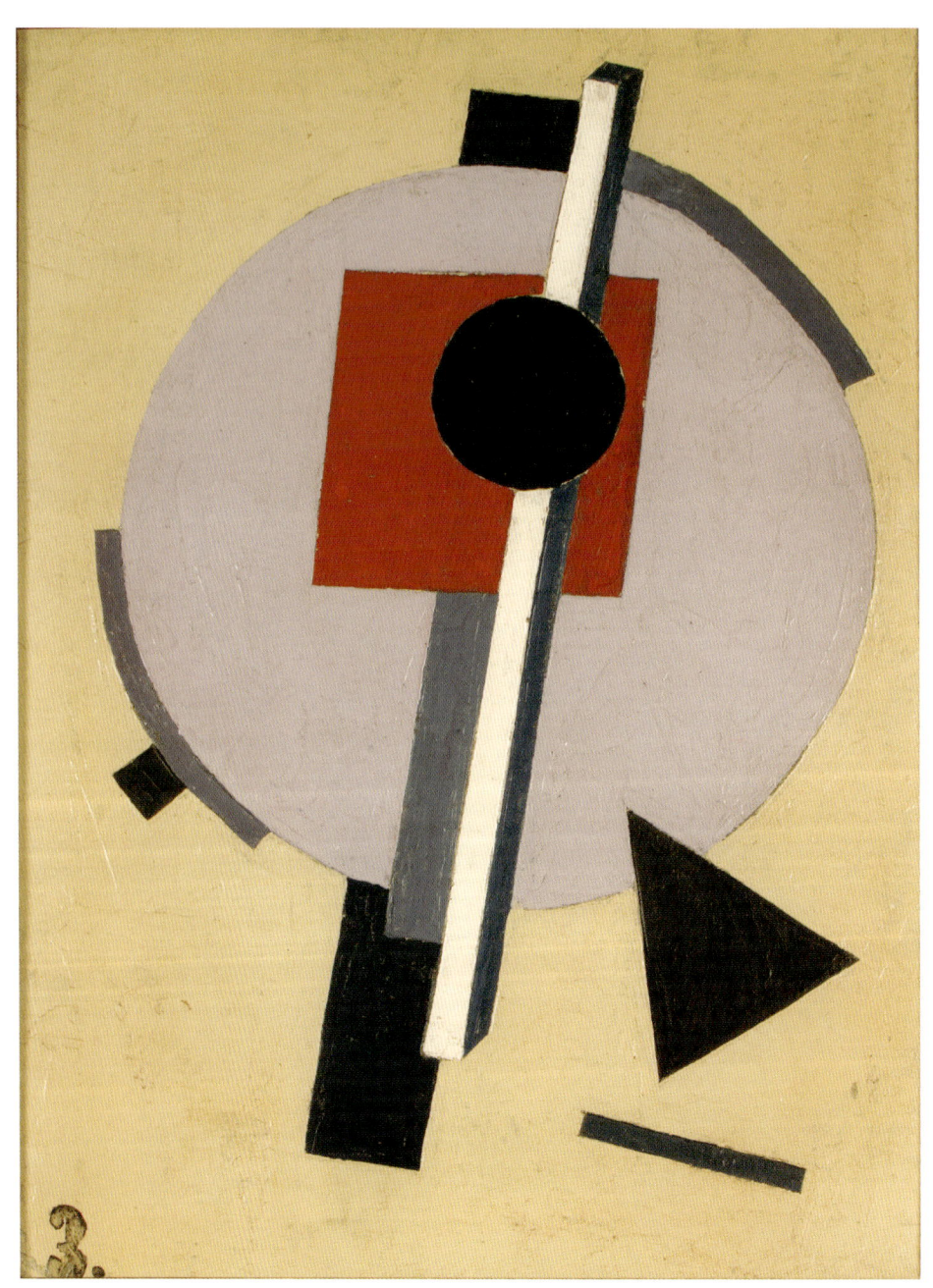

132

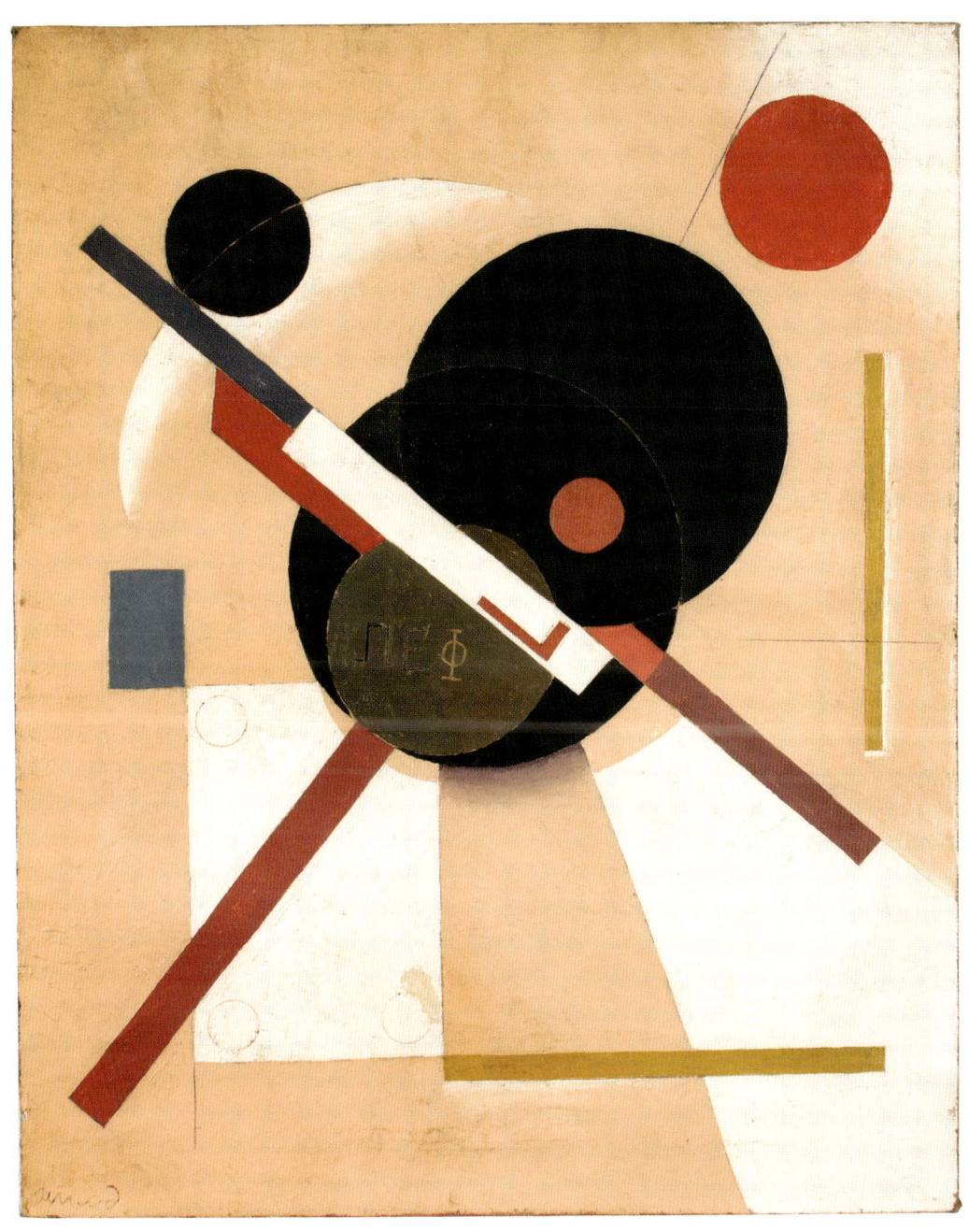

133

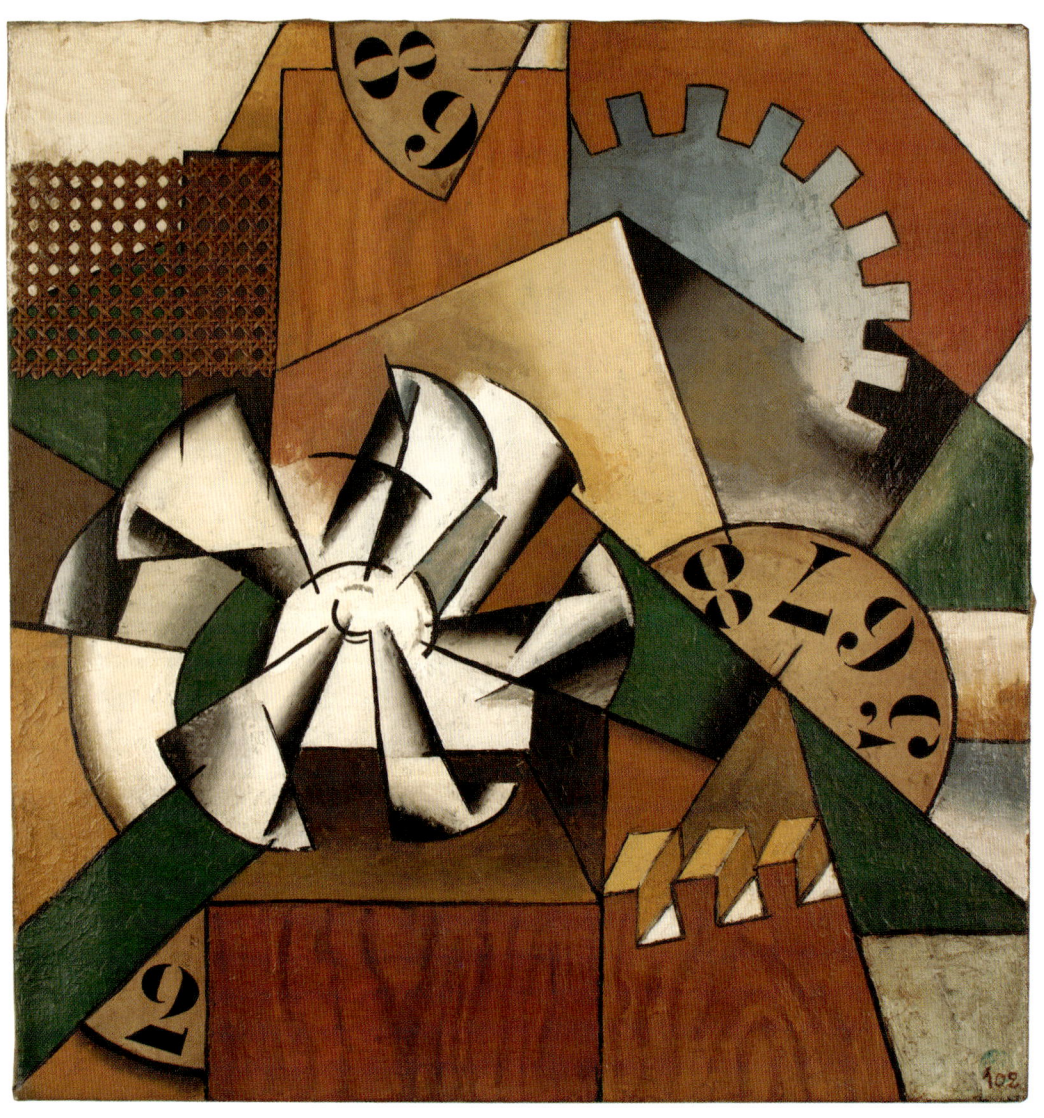

134

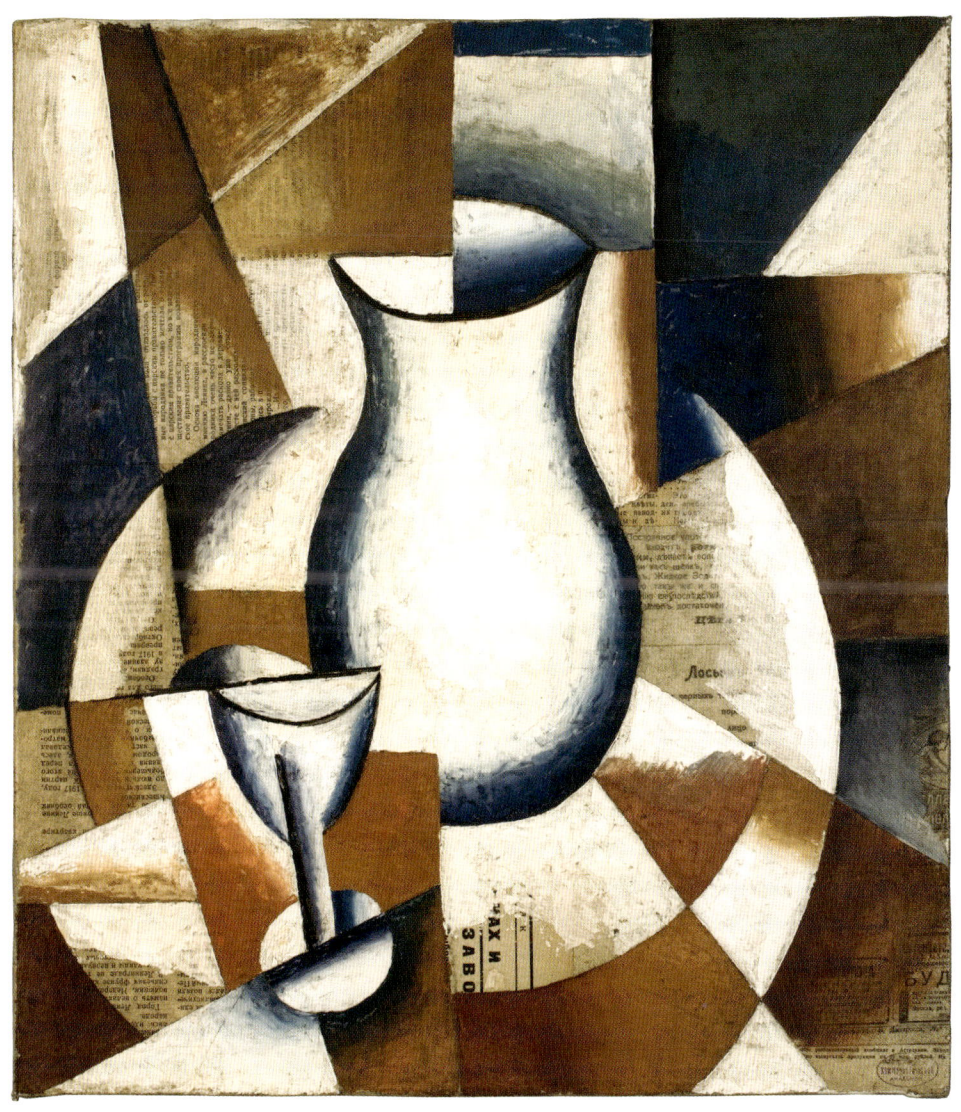

135

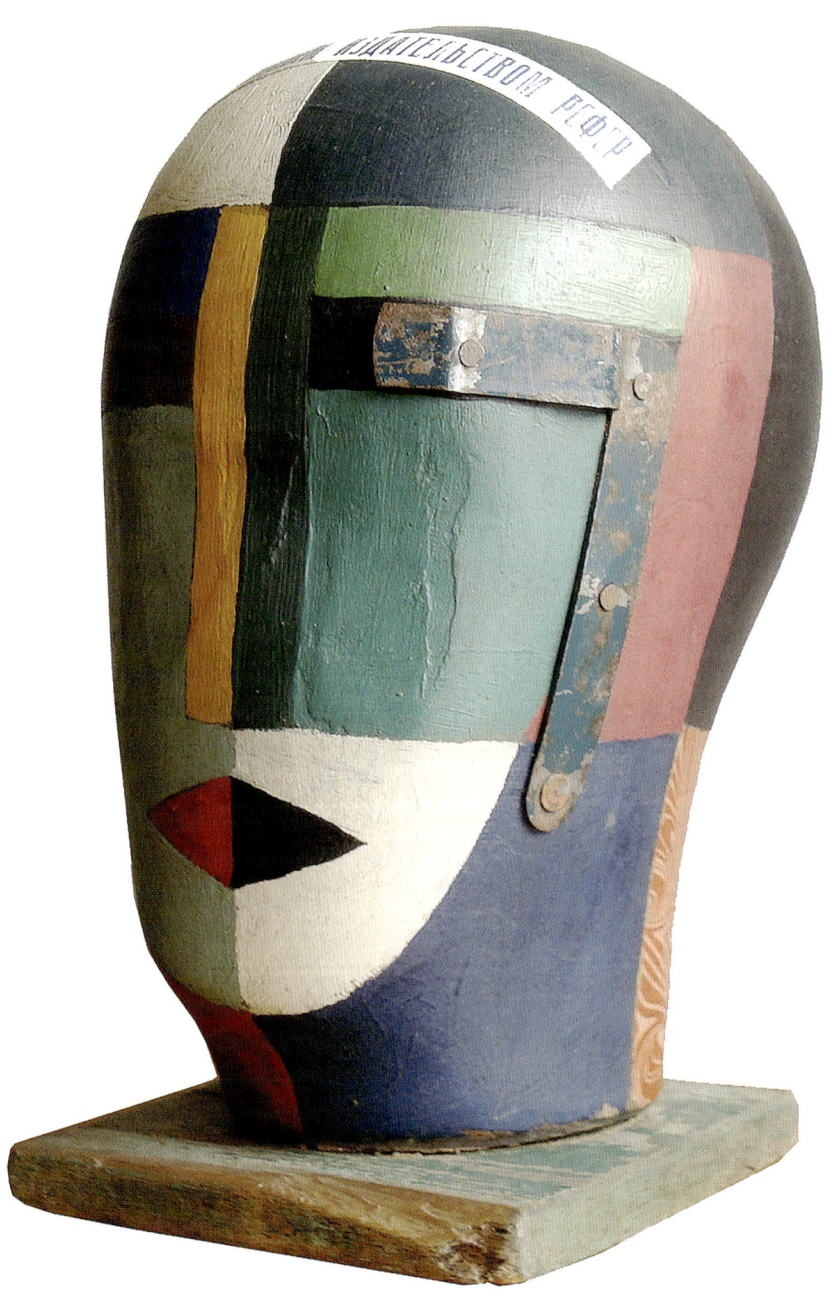

136

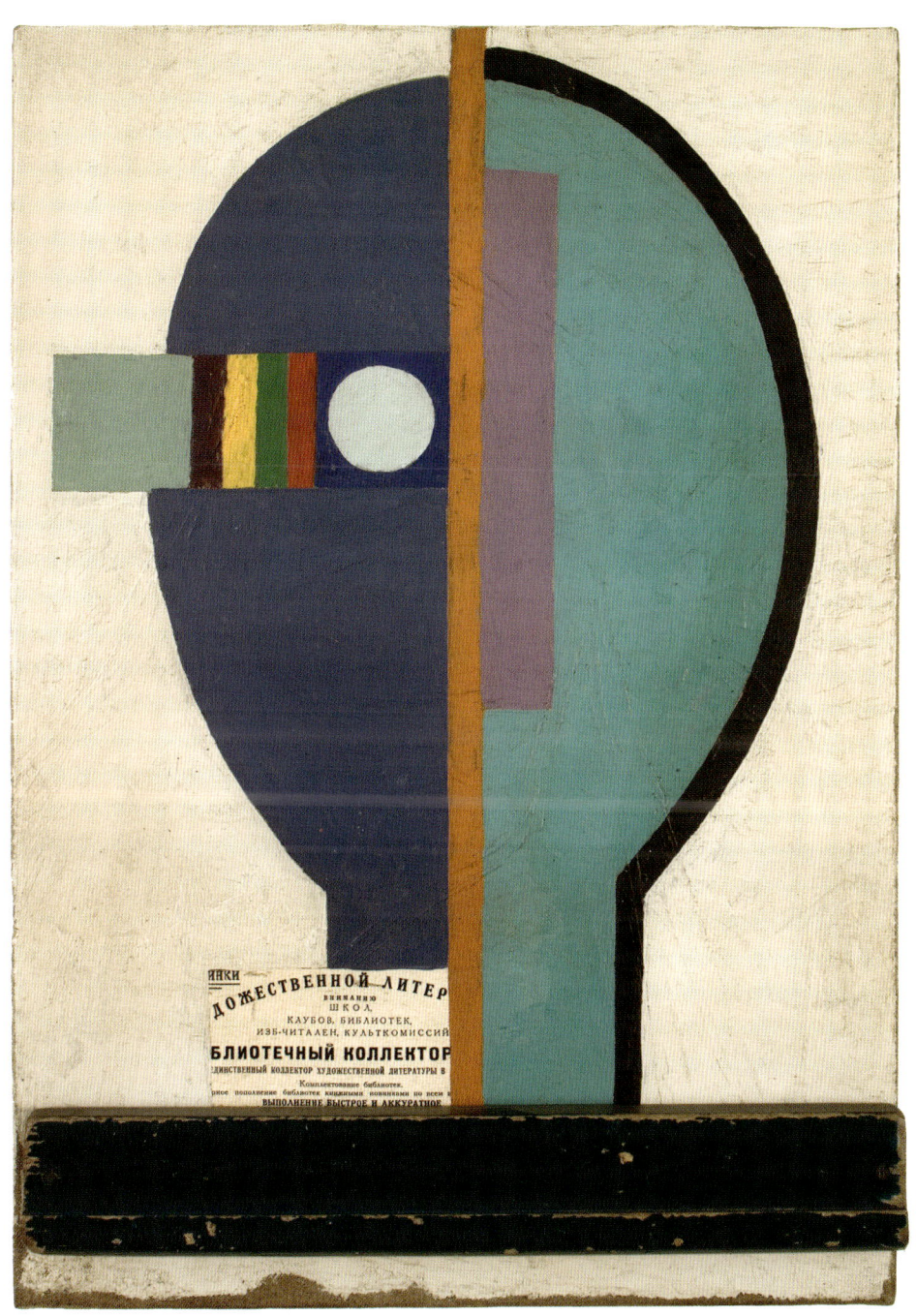

137

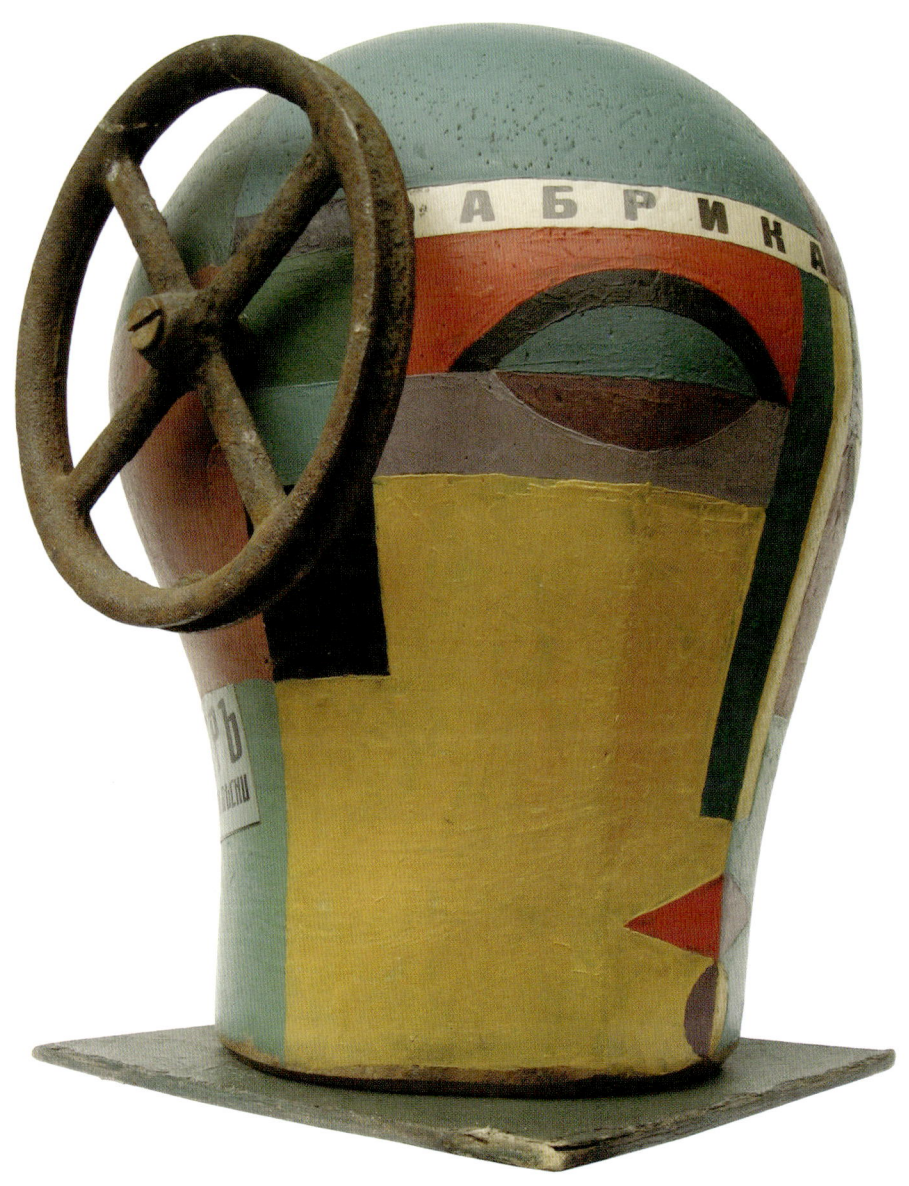

138

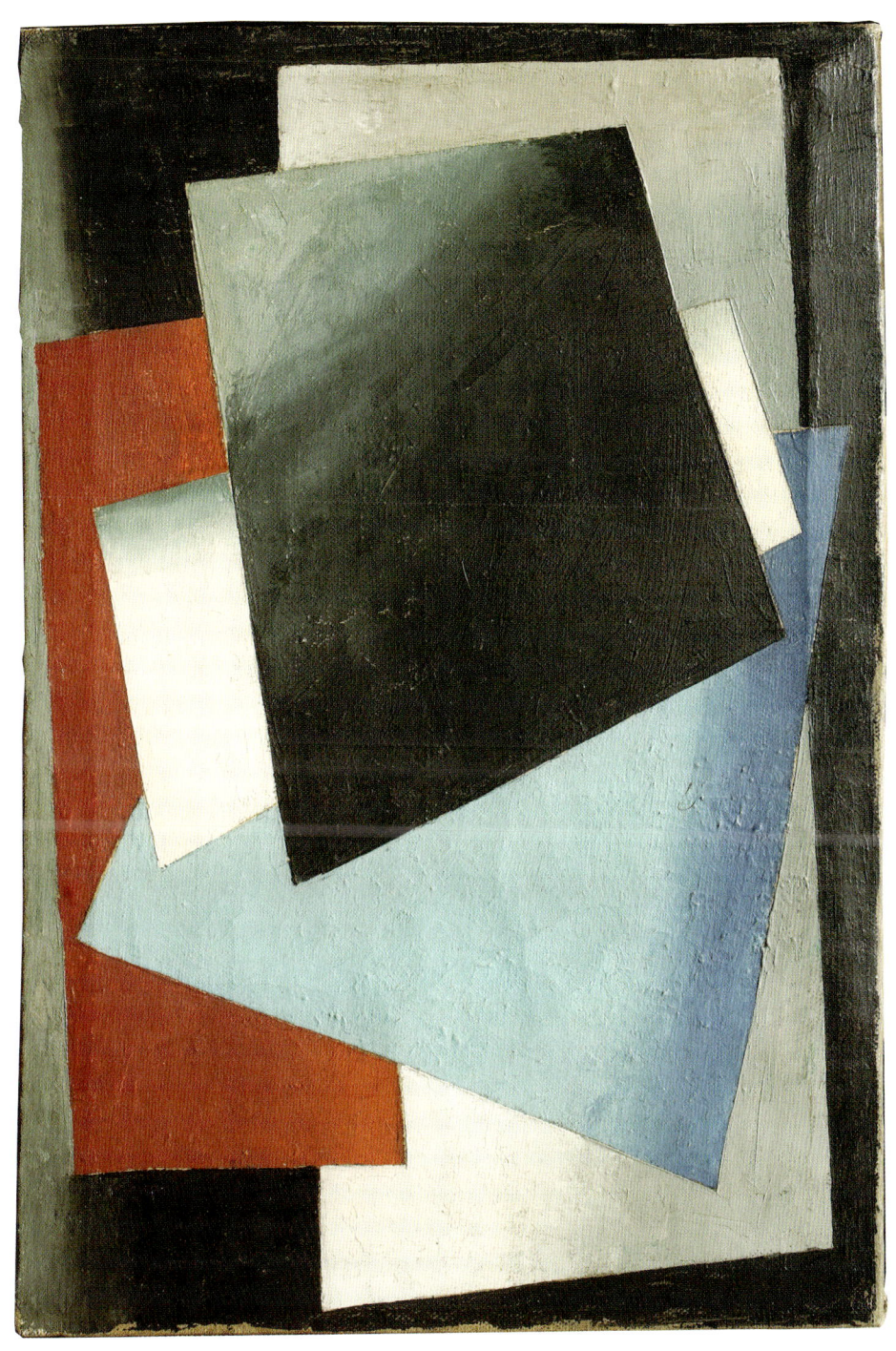

139

APPENDICES

A — **COMPARISON OF THREE UNAUTHENTICATED PAINTINGS WITH AUTHENTICATED WORKS**

B — **EMAIL FROM SELLER ABOUT THE ORIGINS OF THE PAINTINGS**

C — **INVOICE FROM ART RESEARCHER**

D — **TRANSCRIPTION OF MEETING BETWEEN ART RESEARCHER AND MALEVICH SCHOLAR**

E — **TIMELINE OF EVENTS**

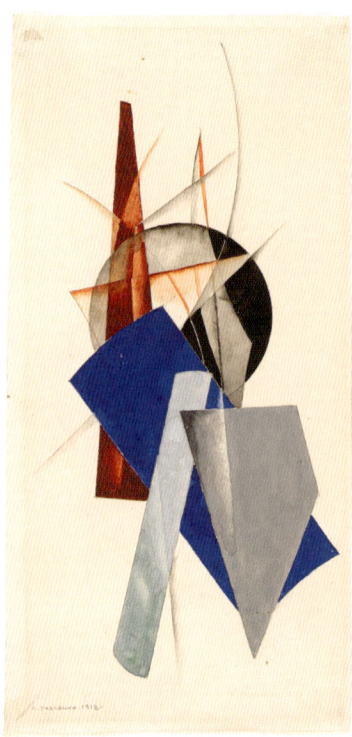

Three comparisons of paintings owned by Ron, Roger, and their friends to works in the collections of major museums suggest that terms such as inauthentic or fake can cover over what may be most interesting about a work of art. The following analyses attempt to delineate the artistic issues at play in works that may otherwise be dismissed.

ALEKSANDR RODCHENKO'S 1918 painting *Composition* [Fig. 63, above] looks so similar to an unidentified painting in Ron's collection [Fig. 64, opposite] that the former seems like it could have been a study for the latter. The authenticated Rodchenko is denser and more vertical, while the unidentified work is loose and centrifugal. The Rodchenko is signed by the artist in its lower-left corner and the unidentified painting is unsigned but has the inscription *Project No. 9* in its lower-right corner. The two paintings are otherwise so much alike that it is difficult to imagine that two artists could have made them independently. ■ The two works share similarities not only in the overall composition of their colors and shapes, but also in their more nuanced elements, especially the relationship between their hard and soft edges. This is particularly visible in the paintings' arced lines, where one side of each line is relatively sharp and the other is feathered. This

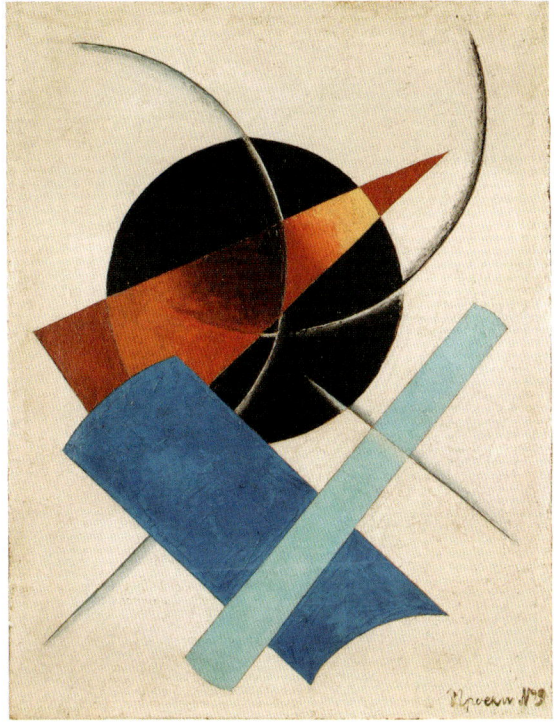

subtle feathering triggers the eye to read the arcs as small gashes or folds in the canvases, but is not obvious enough to give the viewer any confidence that this illusion is intentional. ■ The relationship between the two works becomes more complicated when the way that their lines interact with planes is examined. In the Rodchenko painting, a vertical line passes through the gray field at the bottom of the picture and the paint is gradated in the left corner of the field up to this line. Similarly, a line cuts through the central triangle in the unidentified painting, with the paint gradated on either side of it. Here the triangle is the only shape that is so strongly affected by a line passing through it. ■ The main difference between the two works is in the relationship between each one's major elements. In the Rodchenko work, all the elements are integrated. The long vertical line incorporates the gray shape into the composition. In the unidentified painting, however, the two lower shapes appear disconnected from the center of the composition. It is as if the painter of the unidentified work was able to grasp how Rodchenko connected color and line, but could not see how he used lines to unify the overall composition. ■ By choosing not to fully replicate what Rodchenko achieved in *Composition*, the painter of the unidentified work appears to have been someone who was trying to understand Rodchenko's methods, not just someone trying to copy him. The artist isolated a single effect found in the Rodchenko work and applied it in a different way than the master, while a copyist would be more likely to imitate the appearance of the painting without attempting to integrate its effects in original ways. ■

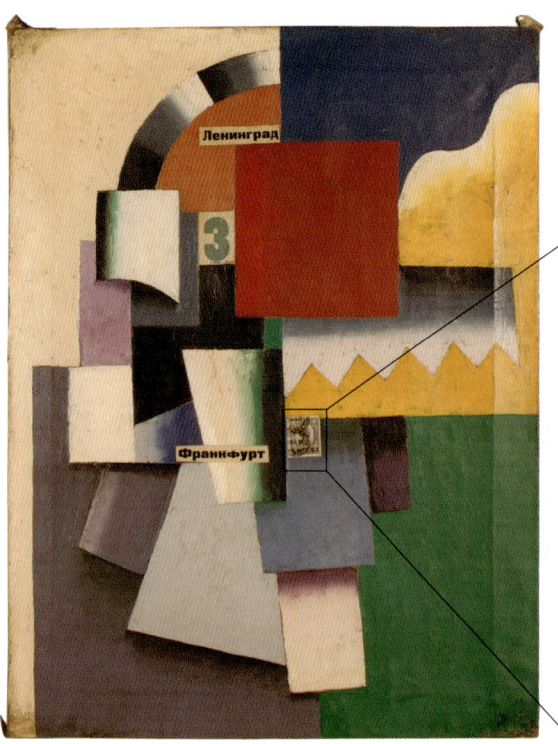

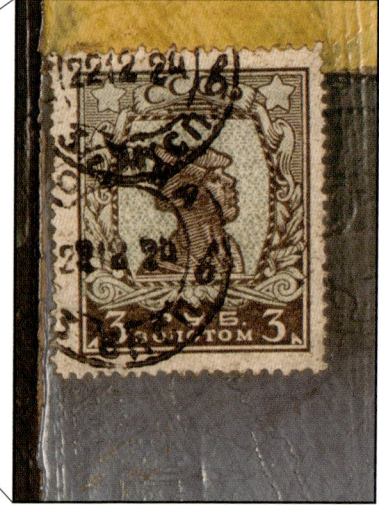

A COMPARISON between another unidentified painting that Ron bought from the Aachen sellers [Fig. 65, above left] and Kazimir Malevich's 1914 work *Reservist of the First Division* [Fig. 67, opposite] brings up many similarities. They are both eccentric interpretations of a standard head-and-shoulder portrait, with a large colored square at or near the place where the face would be. They both have collaged numerals and postage stamps in about the same positions on their canvases. Most importantly, in both, the color squares stand out from the rest of the picture. In Malevich's painting, it looks like someone took a big blue square from another painting and used it to cover up a painstakingly rendered cubist portrait. ■ Malevich was excited about these types of mash-ups when he painted the work in 1914. His paintings from this year are crucial because they show him breaking free from cubism. He realized that a painting did not have to be governed by a single logic—it could

be a portrait *and* a square. In his works of that time, Malevich detached from the entrenched idea that paintings need to reference the natural world and discovered the suspended geometric shapes that became the key elements of his signature style. Within a year, he completely eliminated the fussiness of cubism and abandoned portraiture altogether, instead presenting abstract forms alone on white backgrounds. ■ Given that Malevich's works of 1914 are widely known to anticipate his breakthrough a year later, it is important to note that the postage stamp in the center of Figure 65 has a very obvious cancellation date of 1924. [Fig. 66, above right] Clearly, its creator was not trying to pretend that this painting was by Malevich. If the work was intended to be a forgery, it was either made by a very dumb forger or one who assumed that his customers were very uninformed. ■ The painter of Figure 65 also appears to have been fighting a different battle than Malevich in 1914.

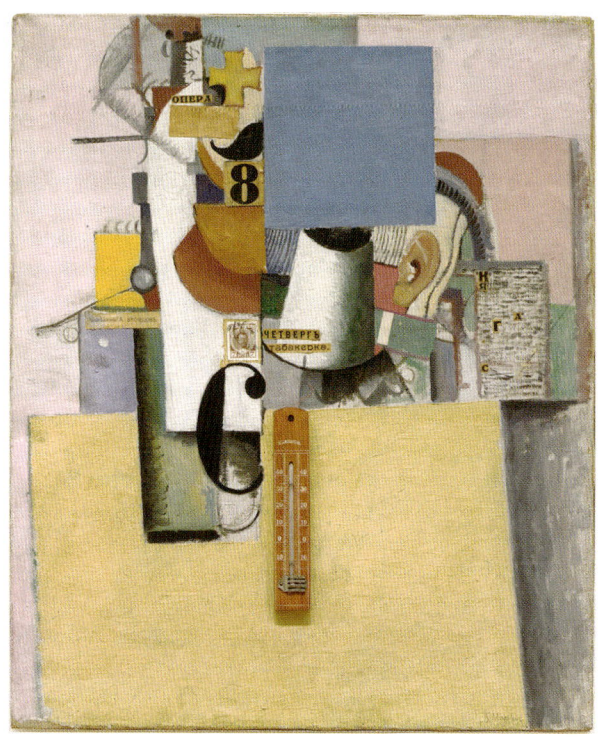

In his painting, Malevich used the blue square to aggressively cancel the cubist minutiae below it. By contrast the unidentified work's red square is at play with other forms of a similar scale in the painting, standing out without seeming to come from another universe. The blue in the upper-right corner of Figure 65 reads as the sky, and the sand-colored form below the sky resembles mountains. The unidentified work does not appear to have been made by an artist at war with cubism. It is less ambitious than Malevich's painting but is also more relaxed and unified. ■ The unauthenticated painting may or may not have been painted in 1924, but since it was definitely not created before then, it most likely is not a work by Malevich, who had moved on to other issues by that time. ■

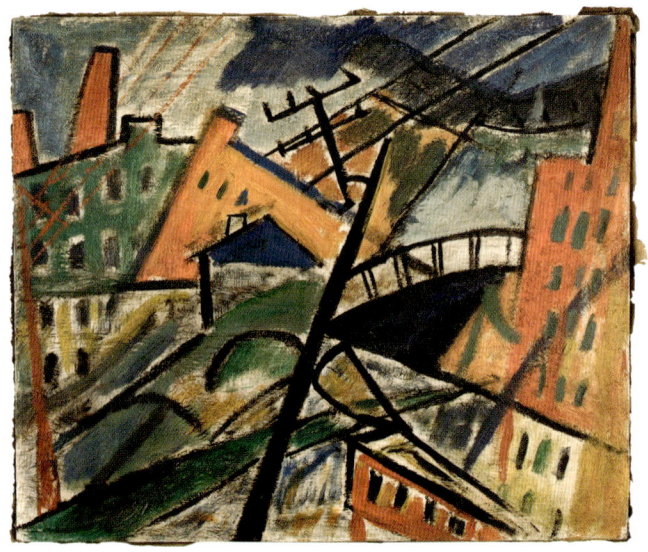

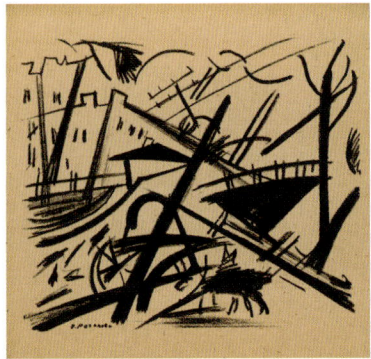

ANOTHER UNAUTHENTICATED paint-
ing from Ron's collection [Fig. 68, left] has an
obvious relationship with Olga Rozanova's
1913 lithograph *Futurist Cityscape* [Fig. 69, right].
Both depict cityscapes that appear to be col-
lapsing in on themselves. The basic structures
of the two works are the same, with the lithograph's crisscrossing lines and strong central line
repeating themselves nearly unchanged in the
unidentified painting. ■ Some differences in subject matter can be found between the two works.
The lithograph has a person on horseback in the
foreground, while the unidentified painting shows
a tram in the same position. The word *tram* is written on the back of this painting in Cyrillic, suggesting that this is its title. [Fig. 70, opposite left]
The major distinction between the two works,
though, is that while their lines are often in the
same places, they define different objects: the tree
in the right of the lithograph is a building in Figure

68, and the pole in the background of the lithograph
is a smokestack in the painting. ■ Lines also have
different levels of predominance in the two works.
In Rozanova's lithograph, the series of thick lines
that tumble from the vertical edge of the building
on the left through the tree on the right dominate
the picture. The unauthenticated painting's corresponding broad lines are more integrated into
the picture, giving the impression that it is a more
mature work than the lithograph by Rozanova.
Only the painting's central pole remains pronounced—like a big, black gash on the surface of
the canvas—while the lithograph's central pole is
less intense in relation to the other strong lines
of the composition. Whoever made the unidentified painting was more in control of its long, bold
lines' power to both provide the basic organization for the picture and also tear the fabric of the
image. The realization that the same lines can both
create and disrupt the structure of a picture is an

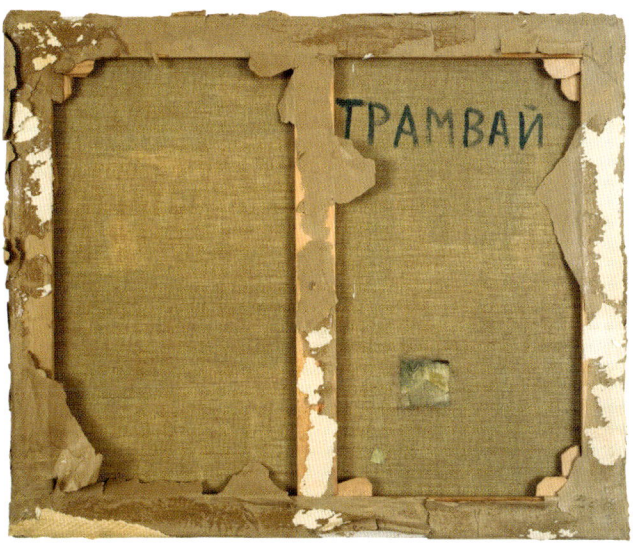
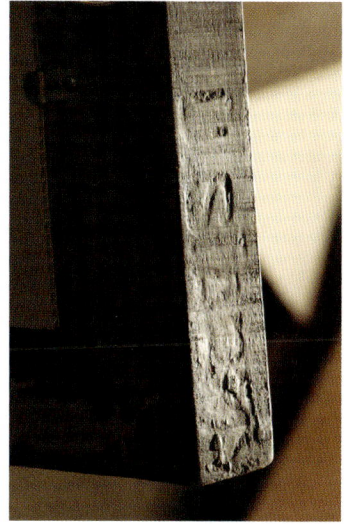

advanced insight for an artist to have about his or her work. A copyist could potentially have this kind of insight, but it is highly unlikely. ■ Other elements may lead someone to believe that the painting was created by the same artist who made the lithograph. When the thick roofline of the building in Rozanova's lithograph crosses over the central vertical line, it thins out into two strands. The same roofline in the painting is blue to the left of the central line and becomes a thin stroke of black after crossing this line. This difference may seem so subtle as to be meaningless. However, it is clear that the artist wanted the roofline to continue past the painting's central vertical line without it being so prominent that it would disrupt the overall balance. Instead of splitting the line into strands, the unidentified work's creator used the opacity of the paint to mitigate the presence of the line. In other words, the artist applied a different technique than that employed in Rozanova's lithograph to achieve the same general effect. It seems improbable that a copyist would make this switch, because copyists tend to imitate techniques and not find alternative ways of obtaining the same effects. ■ A final, enigmatic element of the unauthenticated work may or may not be relevant to its authenticity, but is a significant feature of the object. On the side of the painting, "U.S. ARMY" is stamped into the wood stretcher bar. [Fig. 71, right] Since the word *tram* is written in Cyrillic on the back of the painting, it is much more likely that it was obtained than painted by a member of the U.S. Army. It is unclear when the army would have acquired this painting, though the image's last known place of residence is Germany, so it was probably some time after World War II. Where the painting originated is still a complete mystery. ■

Email from seller about the origins of the paintings

From: ▮▮▮▮▮▮

To: ▮▮▮▮▮▮▮▮▮▮▮, ▮▮▮▮▮▮▮▮▮▮▮

Subject: history

Date: Mon, 25 Apr 2005 22:36:05 +0200 (MEST)

something is not going in the right ways, did you all received
that mail?

hi ▮▮▮▮, das ist gerade raus nach usa!!!

please give a copy to the 3rd person, I can't find the email address

hello @ all, brad, ron & roger
you like to have more information about the history of the paintings:
I collect them since more than 20 years!!! First there were only
a few in Europe, and only a handful of people were interested, mostly
these ugly and dark styles with foxes, deer and castles. I think you
know exactly where I live: Aachen, Aken, Aix la chapelle! That means:
2 minutes to the Netherlands, 3 minutes to Belgium, 45 minutes to
Luxemburg, 1 hour to France and if I like a French-coffee I can get it
in 3 hours in Paris!!! So I live in one of the most international points
of Germany (45 min to cologne, Dusseldorf, 2 hours Frankfurt etc.).
So it was a lucky punch to find the first painting on a market in my
area more than 20 years ago. But the question is, how did the paintings
get from Moscow and St. Petersburg to the markets. I wrote you in the
past that the russians have had a lot schools for paintings, nearly
30 in Moscow, but in the '20s and '30s this art was a non-art for the
government and it was forbidden to paint like that, so you will not find
the signatures on the paintings, sometimes a stamp or only a monogram,
because it was not allowed by the Russian government. A lot of paintings
never left the schools for many years, they were forgotten in the cellar
behind closed doors. Sometimes these doors were broken, or fell down by
the age and people found the paintings, some came via transit by trucks
to Europe. After the "wall" broke down, and the two parts of Germany
east and west were again a union, (I am not making a statement about
good old times because the quotation that things in the past were better
was found on a wall of Spanish castle dated 600 after Christ) the way to
Europe was easier. So the collectors got more. But it is also something
like an elite-circle in Europe and I know some people from Italy,
Sweden, Spain and my area. But I think that a lot of paintings are going
round between the collectors like a "mary goes round." I find a lot of
paintings on the [antiques] markets. I have my special places and

special people who will wait for me. Sometimes I trade paintings with other people. But there was 1 thing, I will never forget, it was told to my by a collector-friend: There was a big container from Russia, all was legal and ok, but the dealers didn't have any money to pay the custom in Germany for the container. This container was in customs for a long time but the owners couldn't pay and so after some time (months or years) the container was broken [open] by German customs and they found Russian icons and paintings...and other arts from Russia. And customs gave the things to an official auction. And I was not invited...*horror!!!!* This is not a fairytale!

It's not measurable how many cellars in Moscow are still closed, but I think there will be more than we 4 ever could pay for. There is still something like a transit from Russia. I think I am the "first-buyer" in Europe for around 40 percent of my paintings; the other 60 percent have been in the possession of 1, 2, or 3 other collectors from Europe. So, that's all for today evening. Now I get an original German weissbier!

I hope that the message is interesting for you. You know that I won't give you the name of my "collector-friends-dealers" :-))) and if you are interested in some new paintings, please let me know.

By the way, I feel like a dealer since I put some paintings on eBay, but I have a normal job in Germany!

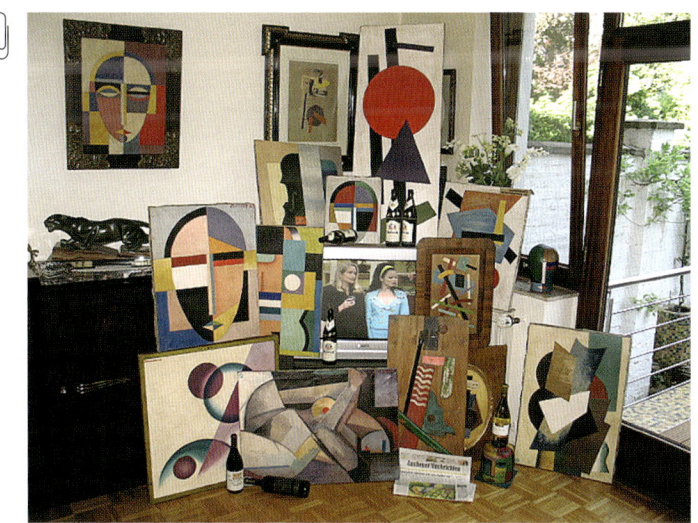

A photograph sent to Ron by one of the Aachen sellers, showing paintings in his home

Invoice from art researcher

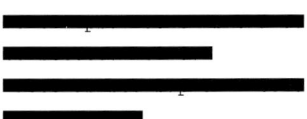

July 23, 2008
Invoice #2

Time detail

Monday, May 5, 2008, Tuesday May 6, 2008
Call from RP, discuss reasons for, goals
of a trip to Denver and begin travel
arrangements (15 min)

Thursday, May 08, 2008
Finalize travel arrangements (10 min)

Sunday, May 11, 2008
Internet research on Museum websites Met,
Guggenheim, MoMA; Read article (May 8,
Bloomberg) on Russian Art fakes business
and check out the author (not at Frick
although there are already 4 volumes) and
Russia's Min of Culture website (only in
Russian, apparently) (15 min)
[Subtotal 40 min]

Friday, May 16, 2008
Go to Guggenheim Museum, only to learn
that no suprematist paintings were on view
(20 min); Go to MoMA (impossible to get in
(free after 4 pm, would have been a 30-min
wait to check umbrellas), no charge
[Subtotal 1 hour]

Monday, May 19, 2008
Go to MoMA study surfaces of 4 Malevich
paintings, and a Lissitzky that was under
glass. (1 hour 10 min)
[Subtotal 2 hrs 10 min]

Travel to Denver (paid separately)

Monday, June 02, 2008
Email from Ron, forwarding summary of plan
and Roger's and Brad's assent, read and
reply (10 min); Receive abbreviated
Malevich book of illustrations
(looseleaf), thank Ron; Communicate re mtg
w/ Larry Kaye [Subtotal 2 hrs 20 min]

Monday, June 09, 2008
Bring it up with ▉▉▉▉ at panel
discussion

Tuesday, June 10, 2008
Arrange meeting with ▉▉▉▉ for Friday,
and let Ron and Michel know (10 min)
[Subtotal 2 hours 30 min]

Friday, June 13, 2008
Meet with ▉▉▉▉ at his office
(40 min) [Subtotal 3 hrs 10 min]

Monday, June 16, 2008
Query from Michel, reply to him and Ron
about Friday meeting and status;
Compose, send email to ▉▉▉▉ (▉▉▉
▉▉ associate), exchange with Michel
and Ron, speak with Frank about how much
info to give to authenticators (25 min)
[Subtotal 3 hrs 35 min]

Tuesday June 17-Thursday, June 19, 2008
Back and forth with Frank Lord re
contacting Charlotte Douglas and Eugena
Ordonez; Send email to Ron and Michel
suggesting times to talk (15 min)
[Subtotal 3 hrs 50 min]

Friday, June 20, 2008
Research ▉▉▉▉▉▉ and ▉▉▉
▉▉▉ on the internet as background for
telephone conference call. (40 min)
Conference call (1 hr) today 1 hr 40 min
[Subtotal 5 hours 30 minutes]

Monday, June 23 – Thursday, June 26, 2008
Efforts to connect with ██████████████,
(Sotheby's) and ██████████████ (U of
Delaware/Winterthur); Let Ron and Michel
know; Speak with ██████████████ and
search the names of the two museum
scholars she provided (the Amsterdam
curator, nothing under his name in the
Frick Library), and the Danish Curator,
just one—a co-author on a loan show
catalogue about a Belgian ceramist. These
do not look promising. EG said she'd also
email Sotheby's Russian specialist, ██████
██████████, and see if we can come up with
any other ideas. (20 min) [Subtotal 5
hours 50 min]

Friday, June 27, 2008
Finally speak with ██████████████████
(10 min) [Subtotal 6 hrs]

Wednesday, July 3, 2008
Try to reach ██████████████, then
Bekkerman's assistant, write to Ron and
Michel to summarize these efforts (15 min)
[Subtotal 6 hrs 15 min]

Monday, July 07, 2008
Call from ██████████'s assistant, says she
will forward expert contact info; she
does, with explanation, and I compose an
email to ██████████████████;
9 pm ██████████ replies and suggests
meeting, unfortunately when I'll be at the
airport on way to Chicago. Reply to her
(20 min) [Subtotal 6 hrs 35 min]

Tuesday, July 08, 2008
Reply from ██████ and reply to her about
meeting next week, speak with Ron to
update and get green light for ██████'s
fee of $300 (15 min)
[Subtotal 6 hrs 50 min]

Wednesday, July 09, 2008
More email w/ ██████ and let Ron and
Michel know mtg set for next Tuesday
(no charge)

Tuesday, July 15, 2008
Meeting with ██████████████████████
(1 hour) [Subtotal 7 hrs 50 min]

Pay expert $300 out of pocket (reimbursed
already)

Wednesday, July 16, 2008
Compose and send email to Ron and Michel
(15 min) [Subtotal 8 hrs 5 min]

Thursday, July 17, 2008
Review notes (10 min), tel con Michel, Ron
(with Roger) (1 hr 10 min)
Today 1 hr 20 min [Subtotal 9 hrs 20 min]

Tuesday, July 22, 2008
Transcribe (verbatim) notes from meeting
(20 min) [Subtotal 9 hrs 40 min]

Wednesday, July 23, 2008
Write more narrative report of that
meeting, filling in between the notes.
Send to Ron and Michel (50 min)
[Subtotal 10 hrs 30 min]

Total 10.5 hours @ $300 = $3,150.00
Please make check payable to "██████████████
██████."

Transcription of meeting between art researcher
and Malevich scholar

11:27
I met ▆▆▆▆▆▆▆▆▆▆ in the entrance lobby of the New York
Public Library at 42nd Street, where there are some marble
benches halfway up the side staircases that afford a quiet and
private spot for conversation.

I thanked her, explained a little bit more who I was and how the
four gentlemen who are my clients purchased these paintings in
the last six years or so from Germany. I said that you really
wanted to know what you have. She had asked for provenance so I
wrote down a list of the names you had sent me with the cities
but nothing else. She did not seem to recognize these names.

I brought photos of four of our most like Malevich pictures as
this artist is her specialty.
. . .

The first photo I showed was
Geometric multi [Fig. 54]
because I personally have the hardest time determining what was
in the artist's mind as he chose his shapes and colors and their
relationships in space. In my pre-Denver visit to MoMA, I had
determined that this was not physically painted the same way (in
terms of the brushtrokes [sic], the amount of paint, and how the
edges of the colored shapes met the white background. This struck
me as a typically recognizable type of Malevich composition.

Late 1970s (1915)
Many fakes
No understanding
Malevich white background abyss
This is white
This is flat
Decorative color

She seemed unhappy during her first few moments looking at it,
and then she gave a big sigh and began to speak. Her comments
went to the question of Malevich's concept in creating
suprematism (she has studied and published his extensive

writings) and how slowly and painstakingly he designed his compositions (in drawings first, sometimes altering one shape in a tiny amount, moving it, or making it larger or smaller relative to the canvas). His execution was very slow and deliberate. The application of the paint took days and days. She did not recognize the mind or the process of Malevich here.

Later she came back to it, observing the dark red cross shape in the upper half, that sits on an angle that descends from left to right. She told me that the cross shape as a motif did not enter Malevich's vocabulary until fifteen years after the style that this painting is imitating and could not appear in a Malevich of this period of his work.

. . .

Some fakers or owners of fakes are in cahoots with dishonest scholars who, for a consideration, include the fakes in publications to give them credibility. Only as credible as the scholars, of course, but many buyers do not distinguish between publications.

Boris Nakov includes fake drawings more than fake oils in his catalogue raisonné. We discussed his role in the Larionov scandal in Switzerland some years ago, where a Geneva court shut down and seized an entire exhibition of Larionov—organized, owned, and with a catalogue written by Boris Nakov.

In her view, there are about 350 genuine paintings by Malevich.

. . .

Then I showed her a much simpler image:
Black and White Cross [Fig. 37]

She observed that this probably was painted after a similar Malevich in a provincial Russian museum was first published.

Made in late 1980s after a provincial museum published its Malevich in the 80s
Artificial craquelure
No understanding of the placement of the square-ish shapes in the corners

Malevich had an energy, intensity in his work that she does not see in this composition. She did not use the word liveliness, but I thought I understood that, for her, the most apparently simple

Malevich practically throbs within the limits of its geometric shapes—because he did not see it as an arrangement of flat colors or shapes on a flat surface, but something suspended in the cosmos on a plane in an unearthly continuum.

Woman with Saw [Fig. 47]
Paintings from the 1930s have no craquelure and this one does
Post sup(rematist) fakes appear in 1990s
Saw (motif) from Suetin a follower/student of Malevich's
The points are exactly at the bottom (line) and this is too schematic to be genuine
Handwriting (never title on it) I didn't ask about the handwriting itself; I did not take the hours required to review all our material prior to this meeting, because I wasn't going to discuss, only to learn her reactions to our photos. It was clear that she had never seen the title of a work written on the front of the canvas, so this struck her as wrong.

We returned to the circumstances of when and how these could have been produced. She said that the people who made them took old canvases, stripped or scraped the paintings down to the preparatory layer which already had carckle [sic] or not.

Old canvas
Nothing on back
Later fakes have more on the back and those she believes were made in Germany in the 1980s
Ger. Early 80s
Leningrad fakes for Jewish émigrés esp to Germany. Jews who managed to get permission to leave the Soviet Union were not allowed to take money out, only possessions. A little industry arose in Leningrad, making Russian Avant Garde pictures that they could sell in the West—purportedly a currency equivalent— to finance the émigrés in their new country.

Often that was Germany, and there a second type of production occurred, she thinks after the Leningrad made-for-export works started showing up in Germany. Those have more info and writing on the back.
Next came

Last painting [index, plate 92]
Imitates M "Matyushi Portrait" 1930–1940
Scallops OK but NO DOTS

Too many straight (areas)

Simplicities in the composition not thought-through for balance and vigor (not her words). Should be more muscular (my interpretation).

Ukrainian inspiration

Folk song (the paper with the writing in a curve)

Fakers know he was born in Kiev

The letter b at the end of one of the words disappeared in 1918

Malevich used only contemporary newspapers NEVER BOOK PAGES

Magazines or newspapers

Done in Germany if a book page

If old newspaper could be made in Leningrad

She also said, though I did not jot it down, that the black arc with highlights in the upper let [*sic*] quadrant is supposed to be a cubist version of hair (as in Léger), but looks like a fragment of a phonograph record.

I did not ask her to document what she said about how and why the fakes were made and came on the market.

I promised her she would not be mentioned by name, and she asked for photos for her files. I said I would try for that.

*Timeline of events, as recorded by Roger, October 2004
to July 2006 (with author's notes in red)*

October 04

Ron shows paintings to a neighborhood friend, an art conservator, who specializes in Russian icons. Though non-committal, <u>felt the paintings were "right"</u> based on a cursory look at their physical qualities. Advises that painting be "secured."

*Not a term
conservators use.*

Ron lends an art collector friend two paintings to "live with." He examines them and feels they are of the period and is impressed by their naïveté. He mentions he is vacationing in London and is willing to show detailed photos to his friends who own a gallery. They also feel they are real but convey the difficulties of bringing them to market, suggesting the European market may be a better place to work.

Ron's collector friend recommends he speak to a second Denver-based art conservator he knows. This conservator views two of the paintings and is impressed with them. Thinks they look right but mentions that the Russians are crafty. Says the paintings have a great painterly quality. Recommends contacting an appraiser who is a friend.

<u>Ron contacts appraiser</u>. It is assumed that the paintings need to be appraised before moving on. Appraiser mentions she has friend in Canada who might be able to sell a painting. Ron is not comfortable with this given new understanding of due diligence and ownership issues.

*Appraisal before works
authenticated?
Assumed authentic?*

05/19/05

Connect with ALR, UK-based organization with offices in NYC, Germany, Netherlands, and France. Manages database of registered art currently owned by collectors and institutions. Additionally, houses data on stolen art, which is cross-checked with registered art. Used extensively by museums to confirm art in collections are not stolen. Considered a key component in establishing due diligence. Entire collection is eventually registered.

07/01/05

Random images of paintings are slightly altered. A technique known as "trap streets" used by mapmakers for copyright. Fear that someone acquiring the image could forge documents and claim ownership.

*Roger is a mapmaker.
Ev. of paranoia or
Roger's interest in being
involved?*

Conference call with both attorneys. Second attorney recommends contacting the FBI Art Crime division. He mentions that it is better that you go to them than have them come to you. He sets up conference call with a special agent.

07/29/05

Conference call takes place with an FBI Special Agent from the Salt Lake <u>Art Crime Division</u>, including Ron, Roger, both attorneys, and Michel, an architect friend of Ron's in Connecticut. Story is conveyed to agent. Agent says he will pass on to the FBI <u>art theft division</u> and check possibilities of looted art. Later mentions nothing was found. The information is filed with the office for future reference. The conversation is recorded.

*INCONSISTENT
Is agent with art crime
division or not?*

10/27/05

Ron relays researcher's negative comments to conservator friend who first looked at the paintings and she still feels the paintings are real and that something's fishy.

*Trust network of
friends more than
experts — consistent.*

Ron further involves his friend Michel Pariseau, a Connecticut-based architect with many connections on the east coast art/business world. He is an articulate spokesman with keen insight of many issues. Michel is instrumental in bringing together important figures in the process.

12/11/05

Ron emails photos of three paintings to curator and scholar, formerly at the Guggenheim Museum, who is a specialist on Malevich. No reply. First Russian avant-garde expert approached. Later expert gives talk in Anchorage. Roger talks with him and shows photos of the paintings. Expert acts as if the paintings are radioactive. Replies that unless there is solid provenance he doesn't want to see them.

*Why no mention of
handwriting analysis
in timeline? Best ev.
of authenticity.
Why did Roger make
this timeline?*

IFAR authenticates art.
Why not use them?

Appraiser contacts conservator who specializes in Russian avant-garde art. Conservator offers to look at the paintings if she comes to Denver. Her sister lives in Boulder.

Ron finds International Foundation for Art Research (IFAR) article on provenance and due diligence. Enlightening article which shifts the thought of simply selling the paintings to establishing ownership. The article addresses the concept of repatriation. Paintings are then sent to the Art Loss Register (ALR) as advised by the article and other references.

Ron travels to NYC to look at paintings at MoMA. Considers paintings "dead-on."

Ev. of Ron's confidence
in his own taste—
mistrust of experts.

Contact attorney, who recommends involving a second attorney, knowledgable in asset management, who may lend some insight from an international perspective. Sets up conference call with second asset management attorney to discuss due diligence and ownership issues.

$ $ $

Four paintings are sent to lab in Chicago, notable for analyzing highly publicized discoveries of art and artifacts. Director of Scientific Imaging and Research Microscopist analyzed four paintings, including the White Cross. After the analysis, researcher provided a report that was questioned by Denver-based analysts as nonconclusive. Researcher states that the white cross painting is a "very, very good simulation of an authentic painting," then recommends that it be shipped back to Denver using a professional art shipping company instead of FedEx.

What about the other
100 + paintings?

BUT did not perform
2nd analysis

Ron tells researcher about art conservator in the field of Russian avant-garde art, who had earlier been referred to Ron by the art appraiser. Researcher is very upbeat on the analysis to this point. Contacts conservator. The following Monday he has taken a 180-degree mood swing and is questioning the White Cross. Conservator had been sued in the past after being hired to authenticate Russian avant-garde art. Speculation that researcher's conclusions were influenced by fear of liability.

Believe the deck
is stacked
against them.
May be correct.

Contact the brother of Roger's friend, a Manhattan investment banker tied to the art scene and New York Alliance for the Arts. He is friends with head of a major New York auction house.

Contact friend and mentor of Michel, who is president of a foundary that produces large scale art sculptures. He is a member of Yale Skull and Bones Society. He is impressed with the paintings and connects us with his friend, an art dealer who is also friends with the head of the New York auction house.

Contact art dealer, who connects with an art gallery that sells Russian avant-garde art. Dealer is told that "if they're not fake, they're stolen." Head of gallery does not want to speak to the dealer.

Contact friend of Michel, who is a writer at a major international law firm and formerly on the editorial board of the New York Times. She recommends we contact her law firm's art specialist.

Compare w/ emails from this time—
Michel is promised % of income from sale.

INDEX OF WORKS

Ron, Roger, and their friends purchased their last painting from the sellers in Aachen on December 11, 2008, the 166th work they had acquired. Though their German counterparts did not offer them any more works or, to their knowledge, place any on eBay, the American collectors continued to buy online and through auction houses paintings they believed to have the same origins as the ones they purchased earlier. The following section includes the entire collection of 181 paintings—119 owned by Ron and Roger, 51 by Brad, and 11 by other friends—purchased from 2004 until this book went to press in 2013. Most of the works are in storage, many of them in the bank vault.

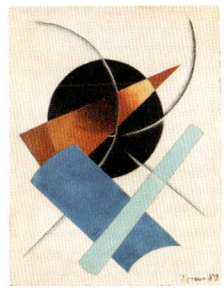

01 Figs. 10 + 64
(pages 21 + 143)
Artist unknown. In the style of
Aleksandr Rodchenko, n.d. Oil
on canvas, 23.5 × 19.5 inches.

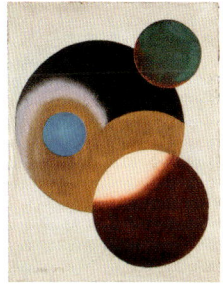

02 Fig. 11 (page 21)
Artist unknown. In the style of
Aleksandr Rodchenko, n.d.
Oil on canvas, 23.5 × 19.5
inches.

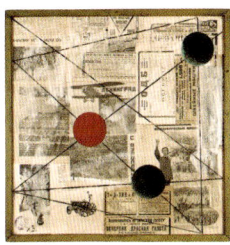

03 Fig. 12 (page 22)
Artist unknown, n.d.
Oil and collage on plywood,
25.5 × 25.5 inches.

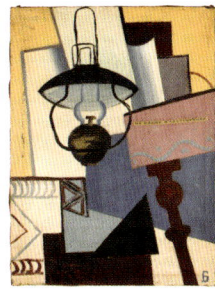

04 Fig. 14 (page 23)
Artist unknown. In the style of
Ivan Puni, n.d. Mixed media on
canvas, 25.5 × 19.5 inches.

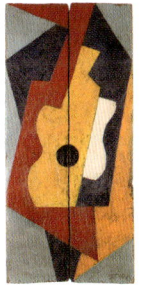

05 Fig. 15 (page 23)
Artist unknown. In the style of
Ivan Kliun, n.d. Oil on wood,
22 × 10 inches.

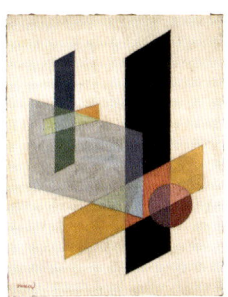

06 Fig. 16 (page 24)
Artist unknown. In the style of
László Moholy-Nagy, n.d. Oil on
canvas, 27.5 × 20.75 inches.

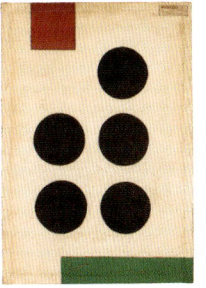

07 Fig. 20 (page 25)
Artist unknown. In the style of
Kazimir Malevich, n.d. Oil on
canvas, 20 × 14 inches.

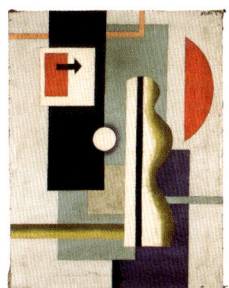

08 Fig. 21 (page 26)
Artist unknown. In the style of
Ivan Kliun, n.d. Oil on canvas,
35.75 × 28.75 inches.

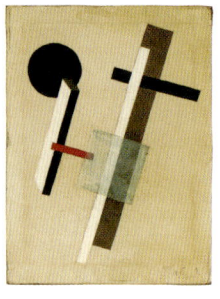

09 Fig. 23 (page 27)
Artist unknown. In the style of
El Lissitzky, n.d. Oil and collage
on canvas, 15.75 × 11.75 inches.

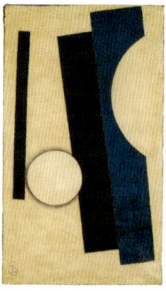

10 Fig. 25 (page 28)
Artist unknown. In the style of
Liubov Popova, n.d. Oil on
canvas, 32.5 × 19.75 inches.

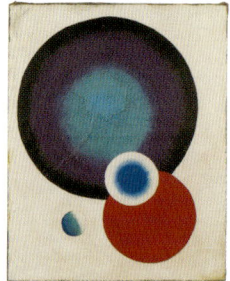

11 Fig. 29 (page 33)
Artist unknown. In the style of
Aleksandr Rodchenko, n.d. Oil
on canvas, 31.75 × 24 inches.

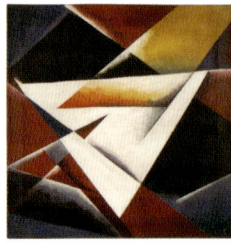

12 Fig. 30 (page 34)
Artist unknown. In the style of
Liubov Popova, n.d. Oil on
canvas, 23.5 × 23.5 inches.

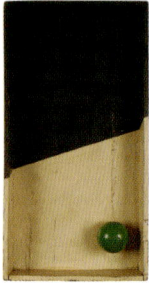

13 Fig. 31 (page 35)
Artist unknown. In the style
of Ivan Puni, n.d. Mixed
media construction,
21.25 × 11.75 × 1 inches.

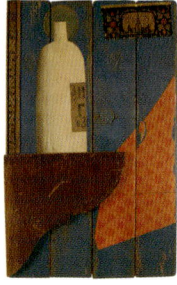

14 Fig. 32 (page 36)
Artist unknown, n.d. Mixed
media wood construction,
20 × 13.5 inches.

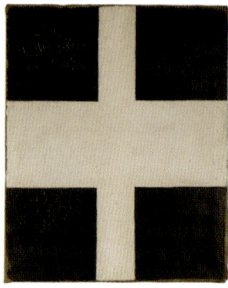

15 Fig. 37 (page 39)
Artist unknown. In the style of
Kazimir Malevich, n.d. Oil on
canvas, 23.5 × 20 inches.

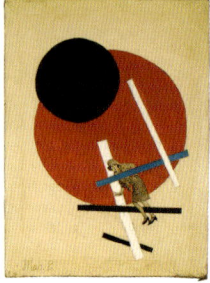

16 Fig. 38 (page 40)
Artist unknown. In the style of
El Lissitzky, n.d. Mixed media on
canvas, 15.75 × 11.75 inches.

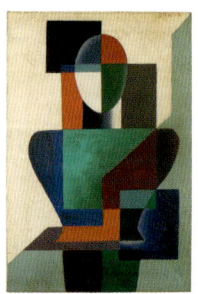

17 Fig. 40 (page 46)
Artist unknown, n.d. Oil on
canvas, 23.5 × 15.75 inches.

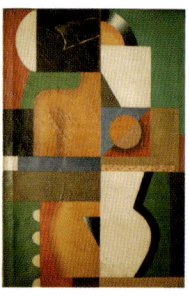

18 Fig. 41 (page 47)
Artist unknown, n.d. Oil on
canvas, 26.25 × 17.75 inches.

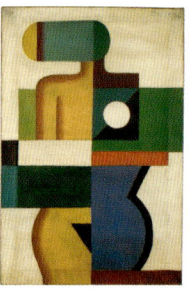

19 Fig. 42 (page 47)
Artist unknown, n.d. Oil on
canvas, 22 × 15 inches.

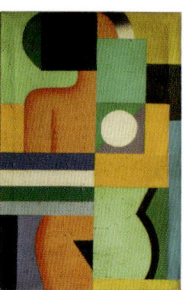

20 Fig. 43 (page 48)
Artist unknown, n.d. Oil on
canvas, 21.25 × 14 inches.

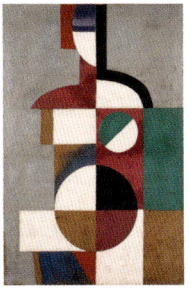

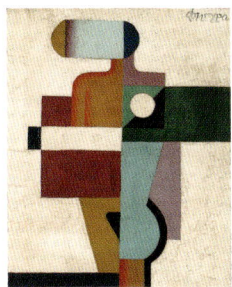

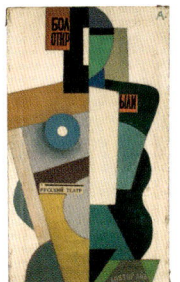

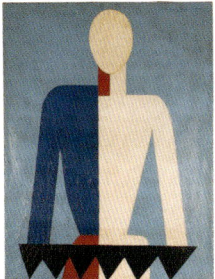

21 Fig. 44 (page 48)
Artist unknown, n.d. Oil on canvas, 28 × 19 inches.

22 Fig. 45 (page 48)
Artist unknown, n.d. Oil on canvas, 18 × 15 inches.

23 Fig. 46 (page 49)
Artist unknown, n.d. Oil on canvas, 23.5 × 13.75 inches.

24 Fig. 47 (page 50)
Artist unknown. In the style of Kazimir Malevich, n.d. Oil on canvas, 35.5 × 27.5 inches.

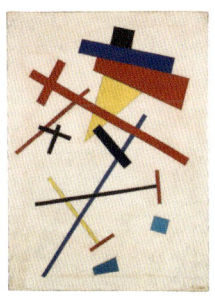

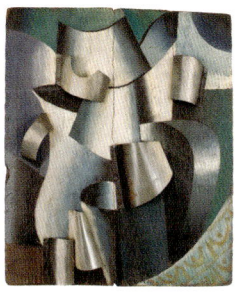

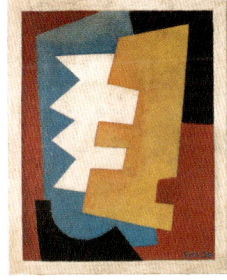

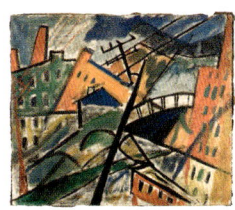

25 Fig. 54 (page 57)
Artist unknown. In the style of Kazimir Malevich, n.d. Oil on canvas, 28.75 × 21.25 inches.

26 Fig. 57 (page 62)
Artist unknown. In the style of Liubov Popova, n.d. Mixed media on wood, 15.25 × 13 inches.

27 Fig. 59 (page 63)
Artist unknown. In the style of Alexandra Exter, n.d. Oil on canvas, 15.75 × 11.75 inches.

28 Fig. 68 (pages 77 + 146)
Artist unknown. In the style of Olga Rozanova, n.d. Oil on canvas, 19.75 × 23.75 inches.

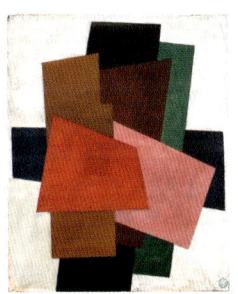

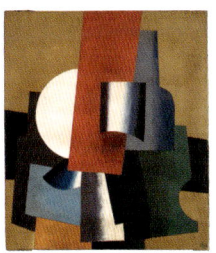

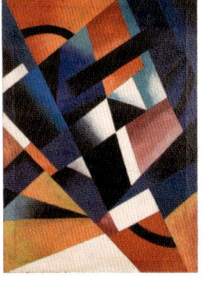

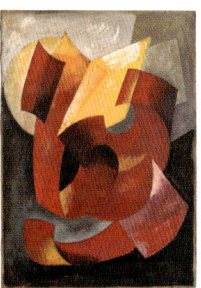

29 (page 78)
Artist unknown. In the style of Liubov Popova, n.d. Oil on canvas, 23.5 × 19.5 inches.

30 (page 79)
Artist unknown. In the style of Liubov Popova, n.d. Oil on canvas, 27.75 × 23.5 inches.

31 (page 80)
Artist unknown. In the style of Alexandra Exter, n.d. Oil and gouache on canvas, 30.25 × 22.5 inches.

32 (page 81)
Artist unknown. In the style of Alexandra Exter, n.d. Oil on canvas, 23.5 × 21.25 inches.

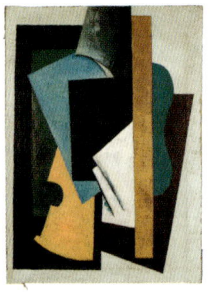

33 (page 82)
Artist unknown. In the style
of Nadezhda Udaltsova, n.d.
Oil on canvas, 28.75 × 23.5
inches.

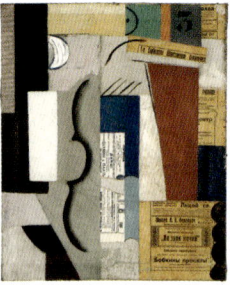

34 (page 83)
Artist unknown. In the style
of Kazimir Malevich, n.d.
Mixed media on canvas,
22 × 18 inches.

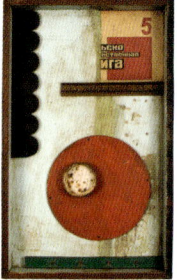

35 (page 84)
Artist unknown, n.d.
Mixed media construction,
21.5 × 13.25 inches.

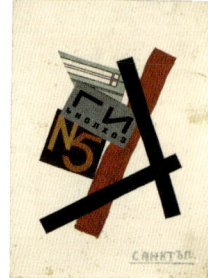

36 (page 85)
Artist unknown. In the
style of Varvara Stepanova,
n.d. Collage on paper,
9 × 6.75 inches.

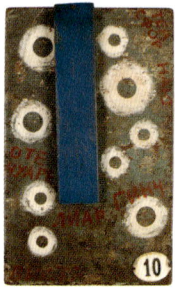

37 (page 86)
Artist unknown, n.d.
Mixed media construction,
23.25 × 14.5 inches.

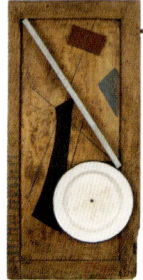

38 (page 87)
Artist unknown, n.d.
Mixed media construction,
33 × 15.75 inches.

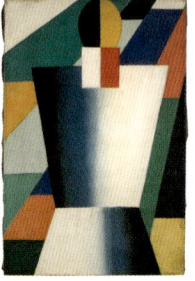

39 (page 88)
Artist unknown. In the style of
Kazimir Malevich, n.d. Oil on
canvas, 23.5 × 15.75 inches.

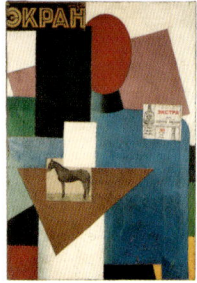

40 (page 89)
Artist unknown. In the style
of Kazimir Malevich, n.d.
Mixed media on canvas,
26.25 × 17.75 inches.

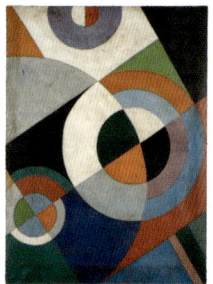

41 (page 90)
Artist unknown. In the style of
Aleksandr Rodchenko, n.d. Oil
on canvas, 40 × 33.5 inches.

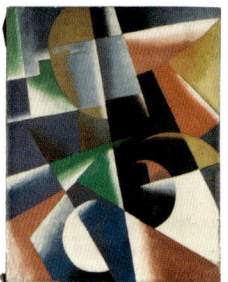

42 (page 91)
Artist unknown. In the style of
Liubov Popova, n.d. Oil on
canvas, 21.5 × 17 inches.

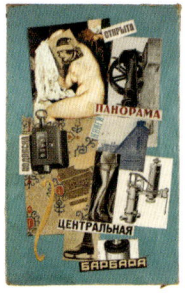

43 (page 92)
Artist unknown. In the style of
Aleksandr Rodchenko, n.d.
Mixed media on canvas,
14.25 × 10.25 inches.

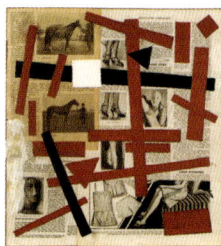

44 (page 93)
Artist unknown, n.d.
Oil and collage on board,
16.25 × 15 inches.

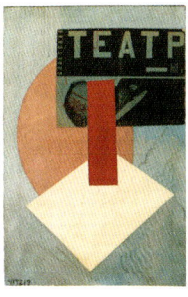

45 (page 94)
Artist unknown, n.d.
Mixed media on canvas,
23.5 × 15.75 inches.

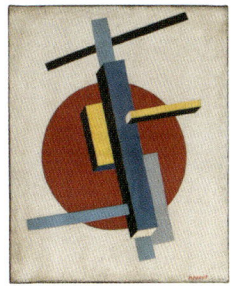

46 (page 95)
Artist unknown, n.d. Oil on
canvas, 29 × 23.5 inches.

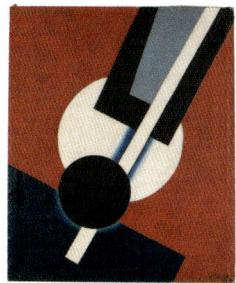

47 (page 96)
Artist unknown. In the style of
Aleksandr Rodchenko, n.d. Oil
on canvas, 23.5 × 19.5 inches.

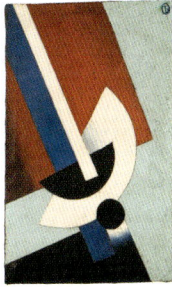

48 (page 97)
Artist unknown. In the style of
Aleksandr Rodchenko, n.d. Oil
on canvas, 32.5 × 21 inches.

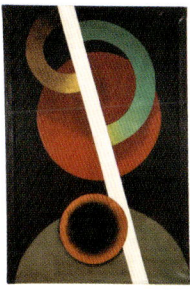

49 (page 98)
Artist unknown. In the style of
Aleksandr Rodchenko, n.d. Oil
on canvas, 35.5 × 23.5 inches.

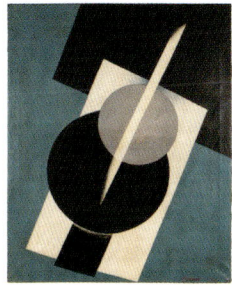

50 (page 99)
Artist unknown. In the style of
Aleksandr Rodchenko, n.d. Oil
on canvas, 39 × 31.5 inches.

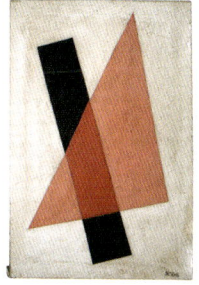

51 (page 100)
Artist unknown. In the style of
Liubov Popova, n.d. Oil on
canvas, 25.75 × 15.75 inches.

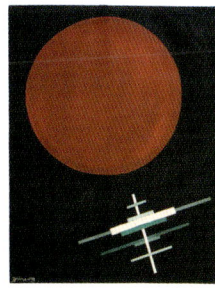

52 (page 101)
Artist unknown. In the style of
Il'ia Chashnik, n.d. Oil on
canvas, 39 × 30 inches.

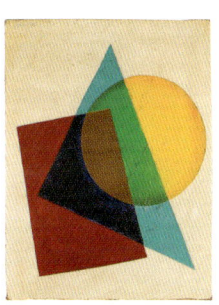

53 (page 102)
Artist unknown. In the style of
Ivan Kliun, n.d. Oil on canvas,
23.5 × 17.75 inches.

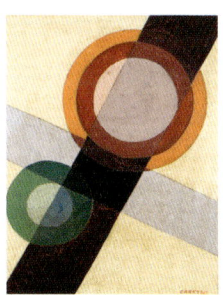

54 (page 103)
Artist unknown. In the style of
Ivan Kliun, n.d. Oil on canvas,
25.5 × 16.25 inches.

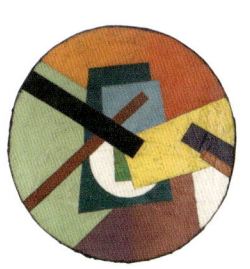

55 (page 104)
Artist unknown. In the style of
Ivan Kliun, n.d. Oil on canvas,
19.5-inch diameter.

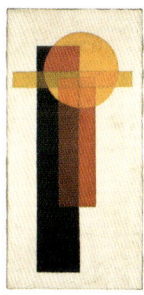

56 (page 105)
Artist unknown. In the style of
Ivan Kliun, n.d. Oil on canvas,
23.5 × 11 inches.

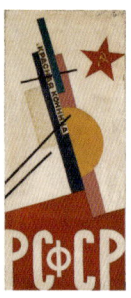

57 (page 106)
Artist unknown. In the style of Nathan Altman, n.d. Mixed media on canvas, 24.5 × 11 inches.

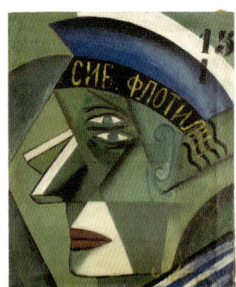

58 (page 107)
Artist unknown, n.d. Oil on canvas, 18 × 15 inches.

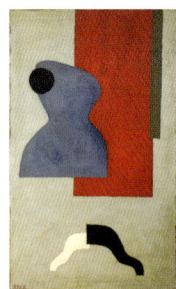

59 (page 108)
Artist unknown. In the style of Vladimir Lebedev, n.d. Oil on canvas, 39 × 23.5 inches.

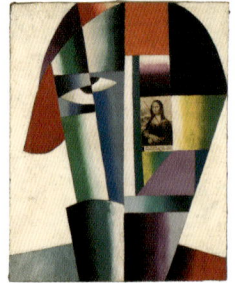

60 (page 109)
Artist unknown. In the style of Kazimir Malevich, n.d. Mixed media on canvas, 19.5 × 15.5 inches.

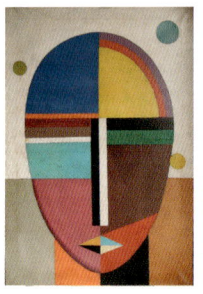

61 (page 110)
Artist unknown, n.d. Oil on canvas, 39 × 27.5 inches.

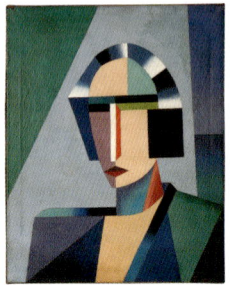

62 (page 111)
Artist unknown, n.d. Oil on canvas, 31.5 × 25.5 inches.

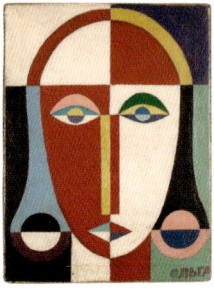

63 (page 112)
Artist unknown, n.d. Oil on canvas, 15.75 × 11.75 inches.

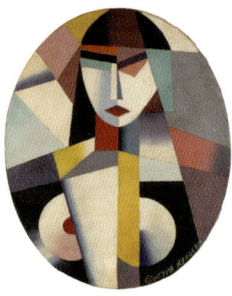

64 (page 113)
Artist unknown, n.d. Oil on canvas, 25.5 × 21.25 inches.

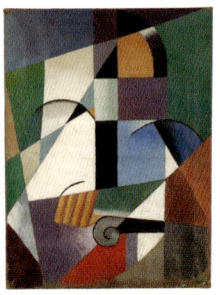

65 (page 114)
Artist unknown, n.d. Oil on canvas, 23.5 × 18 inches.

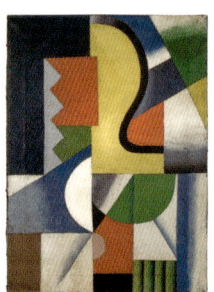

66 (page 115)
Artist unknown, n.d. Oil on canvas, 25.5 × 19.5 inches.

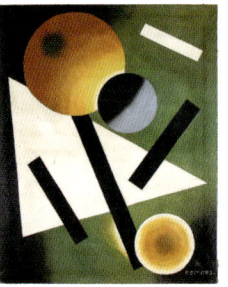

67 (page 116)
Artist unknown. In the style of Aleksandr Rodchenko, n.d. Oil on canvas, 29 × 23.5 inches.

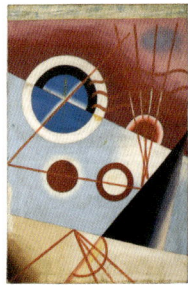

68 (page 117)
Artist unknown. In the style of Bela Uitz, n.d. Oil on canvas, 35.5 × 21.5 inches.

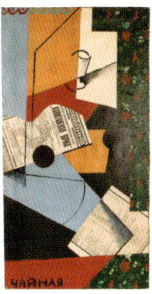

69 (page 118)
Artist unknown, n.d.
Mixed Media on canvas,
33 × 17.5 inches.

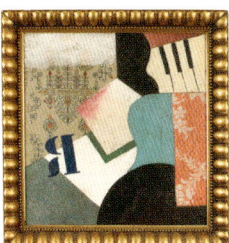

70 (page 119)
Artist unknown. In the
style of Vera Pestel, n.d.
Mixed media on plywood,
15.25 × 15.75 inches.

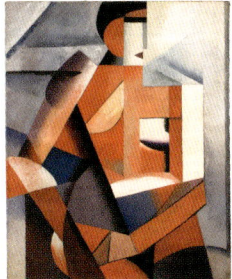

71 (page 120)
Artist unknown. In the style of
Nadezhda Udaltsova, n.d. Oil on
canvas, 38 × 31.5 inches.

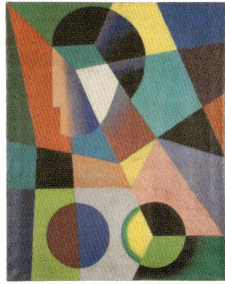

72 (page 121)
Artist unknown, n.d. Oil on
canvas, 26.75 × 21.5 inches.

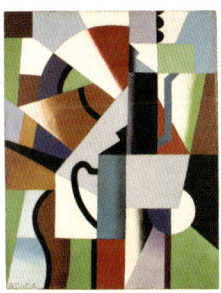

73 (page 122)
Artist unknown. In the style of
Lev Lapin, n.d. Oil on canvas,
28.75 × 22.5 inches.

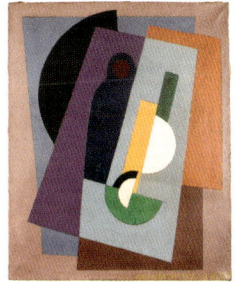

74 (page 123)
Artist unknown, n.d. Oil on
canvas, 28.25 × 23.5 inches.

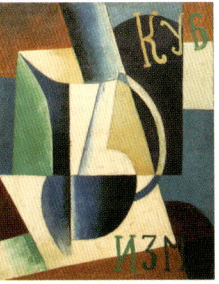

75 (page 124)
Artist unknown, n.d. Oil on
canvas, 19.5 × 15.75 inches.

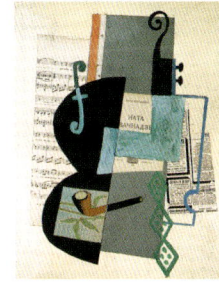

76 (page 125)
Artist unknown, n.d.
Mixed media on cardboard,
24 × 16 inches.

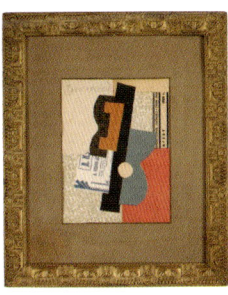

77 (page 126)
Artist unknown. In the style of
Nadezhda Udaltsova, n.d.
Paper collage, 8.5 × 6.25 inches.

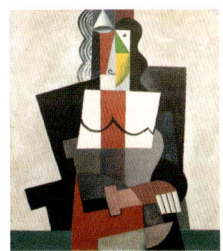

78 (page 127)
Artist unknown, n.d. Oil on
canvas, 39 × 35.5 inches.

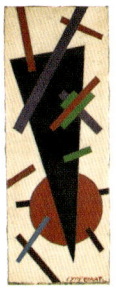

79 (page 128)
Artist unknown, n.d. Oil on
canvas, 23.5 × 9 inches.

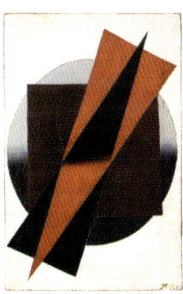

80 (page 129)
Artist unknown. In the style of
Kliment Redko, n.d. Oil on
canvas, 23.5 × 15.25 inches.

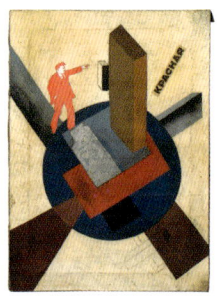

81 (page 130)
Artist unknown. In the style of Gustav Klutsis, n.d. Mixed media on canvas, 21.5 × 15.75 inches.

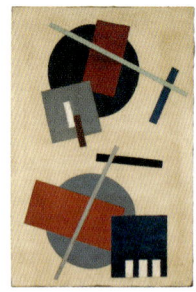

82 (page 131)
Artist unknown. In the style of Ivan Kliun, n.d. Oil on canvas, 32 × 21.5 inches.

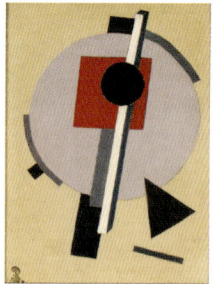

83 (page 132)
Artist unknown. In the style of El Lissitzky, n.d. Oil on canvas, 15 × 11.5 inches.

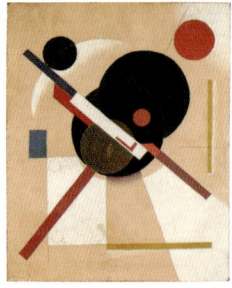

84 (page 133)
Artist unknown. In the style of David Zagoskin, n.d. Oil on canvas, 32.5 × 26.75 inches.

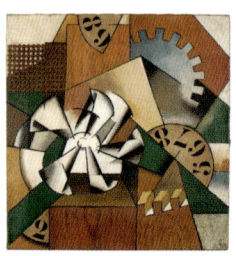

85 (page 134)
Artist unknown. In the style of Ivan Kliun, n.d. Mixed media on canvas, 23.5 × 25.5 inches.

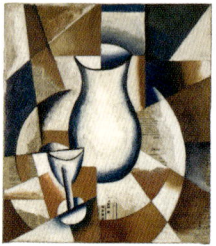

86 (page 135)
Artist unknown, n.d. Mixed media on canvas, 19.5 × 17.75 inches.

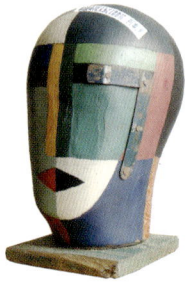

87 (page 136)
Artist unknown, n.d. In the style of Sophie Taeuber-Arp. Mixed media on wooden hat block, 9.5 × 5.5 × 4.75 inches.

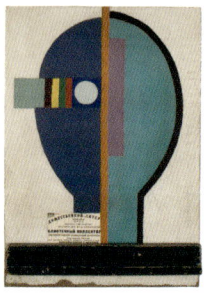

88 (page 137)
Artist unknown, n.d. Mixed media on canvas, 11 × 13 inches.

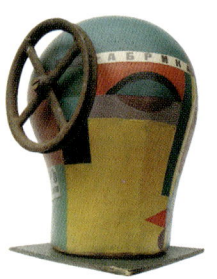

89 (page 138)
Artist unknown, n.d. In the style of Sophie Taeuber-Arp. Oil, metal, and paper on wood, 10.5 × 7 × 8 inches.

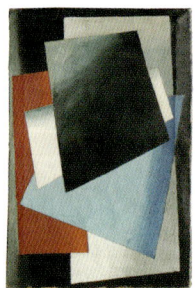

90 (page 139)
Artist unknown. In the style of Alexander Vesnin, n.d. Oil on canvas, 22 × 15 inches.

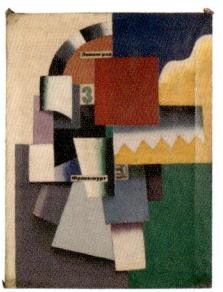

91 Fig. 65 (page 144)
Artist unknown. In the style of Kazimir Malevich, n.d. Mixed media on canvas, 22.5 × 17.25 inches.

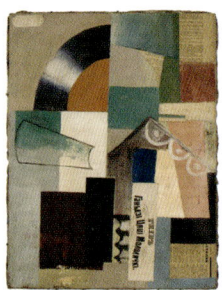

92
Artist unknown. In the style of Kazimir Malevich, n.d. Mixed media on canvas, 26.25 × 19.75 inches.

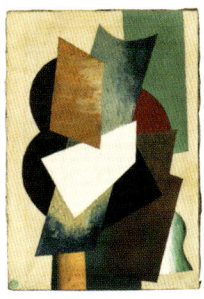

93
Artist unknown. In the style of
Liubov Popova, n.d. Oil on
canvas, 27.5 × 19.25 inches.

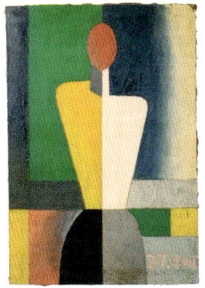

94
Artist unknown. In the style of
Kazimir Malevich, n.d. Oil on
canvas, 20 × 14 inches.

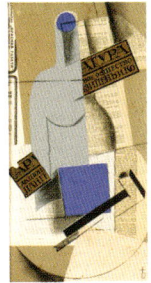

95
Artist unknown, n.d. Collage on
cardboard, 21.75 × 10.25 inches.

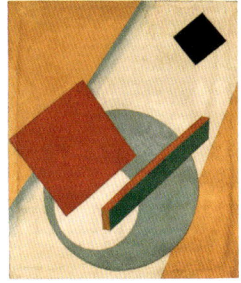

96
Artist unknown. In the style of
El Lissitzky, n.d. Oil on canvas,
27.5 × 23.5 inches.

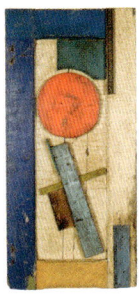

97
Artist unknown. In the style
of Vasilii Ermilov, n.d. Collage
and wood construction,
35.5 × 14.5 inches.

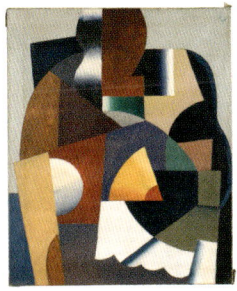

98
Artist unknown, n.d. Oil on
canvas, 28.75 × 23.5 inches.

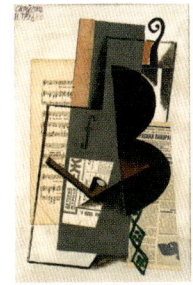

99
Artist unknown, n.d.
Mixed media on cardboard,
24 × 16 inches.

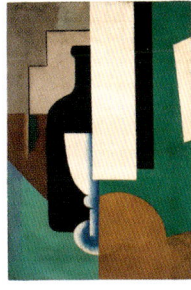

100
Artist unknown. In the style of
Nathan Altman, n.d. Oil on
canvas, 36 × 28.75 inches.

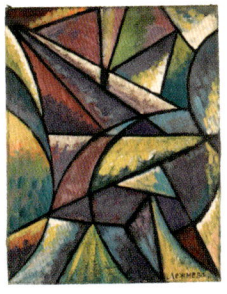

101
Artist unknown. In the style of
Alexander Bogomazov, n.d. Oil
on canvas, 17.75 × 14 inches.

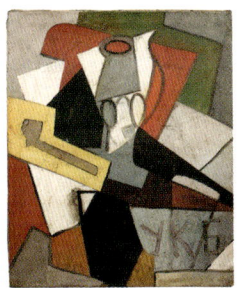

102
Artist unknown, n.d. Oil on
canvas, 23.5 × 19.5 inches.

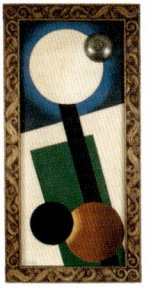

103
Artist unknown. In the style of
Aleksandr Rodchenko, n.d.
Mixed media on plywood,
27.5 × 13.75 inches.

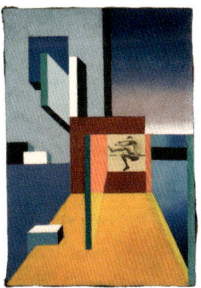

104
Artist unknown. In the style
of Sándor Bortnyik, n.d.
Mixed media on canvas,
19.5 × 14 inches.

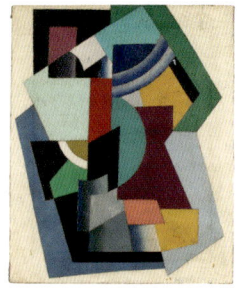

105
Artist unknown, n.d. Oil on canvas, 23.6 × 19.5 inches.

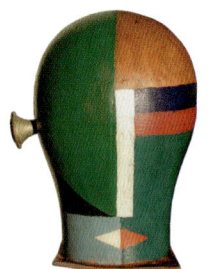

106
Artist unknown, n.d. In the style of Sophie Taeuber-Arp. Mixed media on wooden hatblock, 12 × 7 × 7.75 inches.

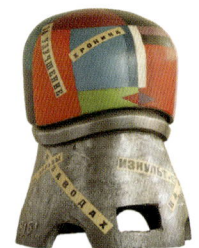

107
Artist unknown, n.d. In the style of Sophie Taeuber-Arp. Mixed media on metal hatblock, 11 × 7.75 × 7 inches.

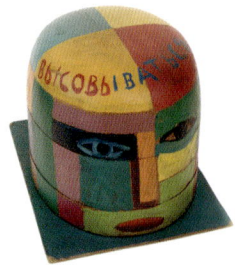

108
Artist unknown, n.d. In the style of Sophie Taeuber-Arp. Mixed media on wooden hatblock, 6.5 × 8.25 × 7 inches.

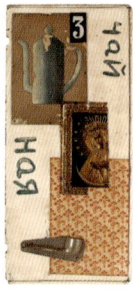

109
Artist unknown, n.d. Mixed media on wood, 28.25 × 13.75 inches.

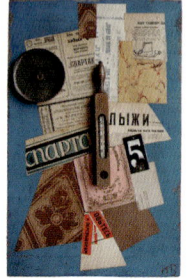

110
Artist unknown, n.d. Mixed media on plywood, 21.5 × 15.75 inches.

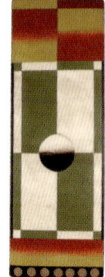

111
Artist unknown. In the style of Pavel Mansurov, n.d. Oil on wooden plank, 35 × 11.75 × .75 inches.

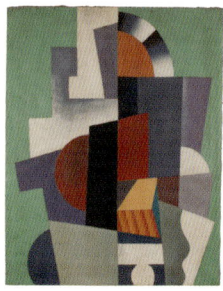

112
Artist unknown, n.d. Oil on canvas, 43 × 27.5 inches.

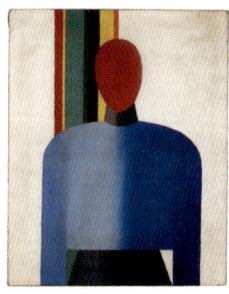

113
Artist unknown. In the style of Kazimir Malevich, n.d. Oil on canvas, 29 × 23.5 inches.

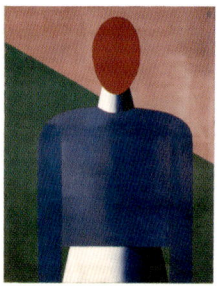

114
Artist unknown. In the style of Kazimir Malevich, n.d. Oil on canvas, 29 × 23.5 inches.

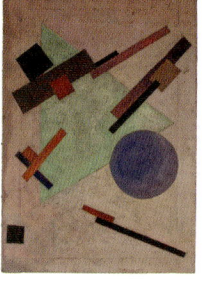

115
Artist unknown. In the style of Kazimir Malevich, n.d. Oil on canvas, 19.5 × 14 inches.

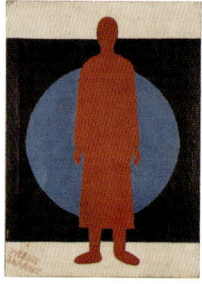

116
Artist unknown. In the style of Kazimir Malevich, n.d. Oil on canvas, 31.5 × 22 inches.

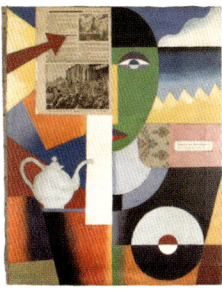

117
Artist unknown, n.d.
Mixed media on canvas,
31.5 × 25.5 inches.

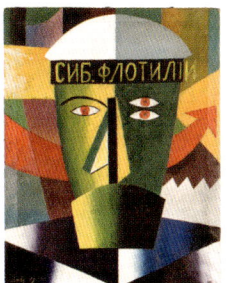

118
Artist unknown, n.d. Oil on
canvas, 18 × 15 inches.

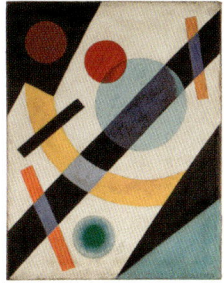

119
Artist unknown. In the style of
Ivan Kliun, n.d. Oil on canvas,
29.25 × 20.25 inches.

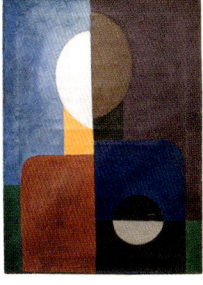

120
Artist unknown, n.d. Oil on
canvas, 27 × 21.5 inches.

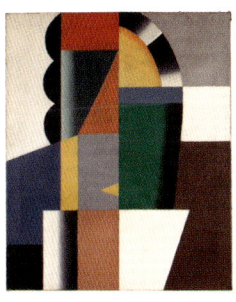

121
Artist unknown, n.d. Oil on
canvas, 29 × 24 inches.

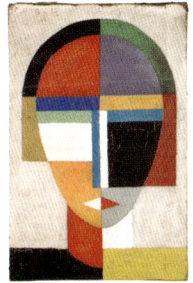

122
Artist unknown, n.d. Oil on
canvas, 18 × 11.75 inches.

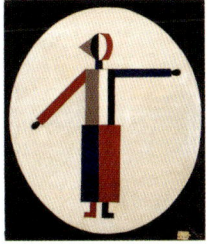

123
Artist unknown. In the style of
Il'ia Chashnik, n.d. Oil on
canvas, 27.5 × 24 inches.

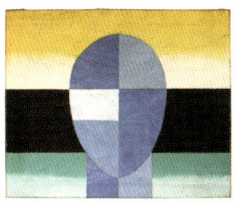

124
Artist unknown, n.d. Oil on
canvas, 23.5 × 27.5 inches.

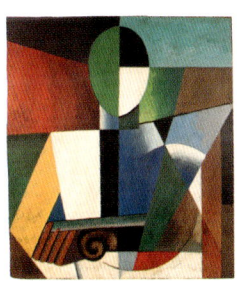

125
Artist unknown, n.d. Oil on
plywood, 37.5 × 33.5 inches.

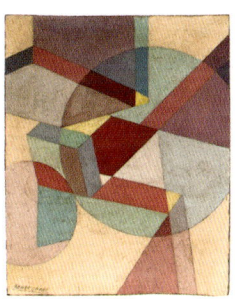

126
Artist unknown, n.d. Oil on
plywood, 23.5 × 19.25 inches.

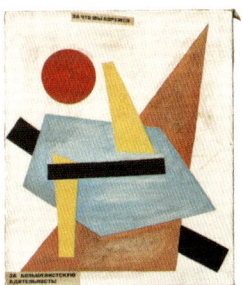

127
Artist unknown. In the style
of Nadezhda Udaltsova, n.d.
Mixed media on canvas,
19.5 × 15.75 inches.

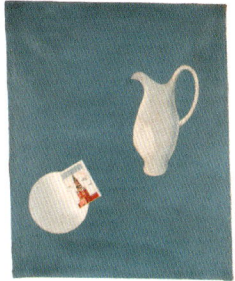

128
Artist unknown. In the style
of David Shterenberg, n.d.
Mixed media on canvas,
27.75 × 23.25 inches.

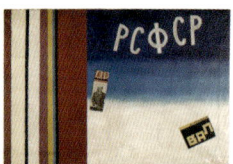

129
Artist unknown, n.d.
Mixed media on canvas,
20.5 × 31.25 inches.

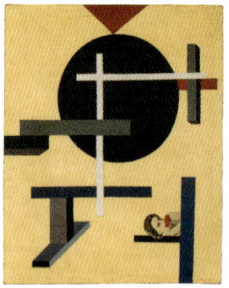

130
Artist unknown, n.d.
Mixed media on canvas,
23.5 × 19.5 inches.

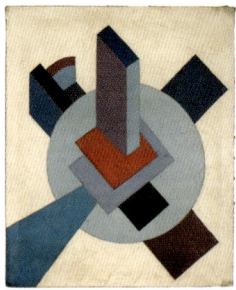

131
Artist unknown. In the style of
Gustav Klutsis, n.d. Oil on
canvas, 19 × 15.75 inches.

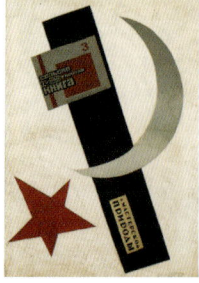

132
Artist unknown, n.d.
Mixed media on canvas,
23.25 × 14.5 inches.

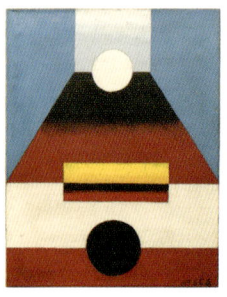

133
Artist unknown, n.d. Oil on
canvas, 19.5 × 15.75 inches.

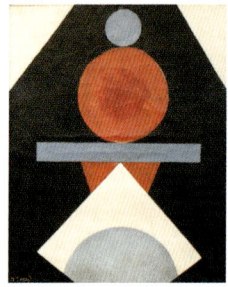

134
Artist unknown, n.d. Oil on
canvas, 25.5 × 20 inches.

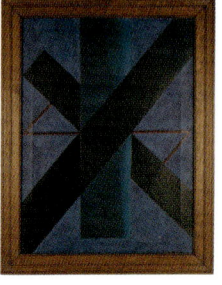

135
Artist unknown. In the style of
Kliment Redko, n.d. Oil on
canvas, 31.5 × 23.5 inches.

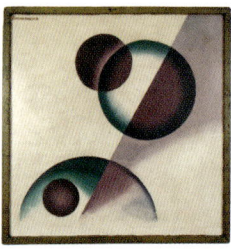

136
Artist unknown, n.d. Oil on
canvas, 25.5 × 25.5 inches.

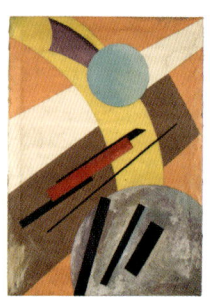

137
Artist unknown, n.d. Oil on
canvas, 27.5 × 19.5 inches.

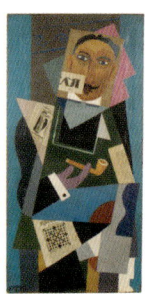

138
Artist unknown, n.d.
Oil and collage on wood,
39 × 17.75 inches.

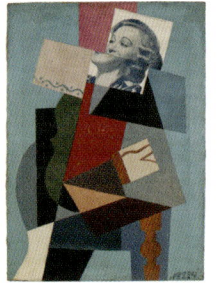

139
Artist unknown, n.d.
Mixed media on canvas,
27.5 × 19.5 inches.

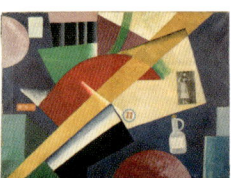

140
Artist unknown, n.d.
Mixed media on canvas,
22 × 29.5 inches.

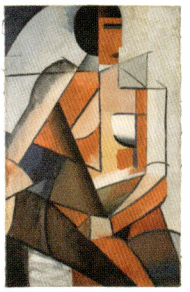

141
Artist unknown. In the style of
Nadezhda Udaltsova, n.d. Oil on
canvas, 39 × 25.5 inches.

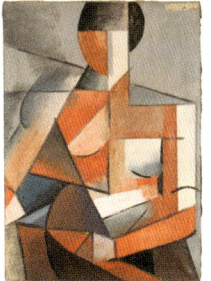

142
Artist unknown. In the style of
Nadezhda Udaltsova, n.d. Oil on
canvas, 17.75 × 12.5 inches.

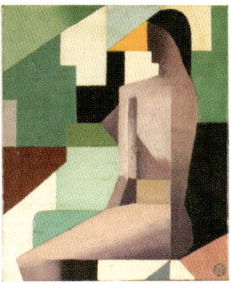

143
Artist unknown. In the style of
Alexei Grishenko, n.d. Oil on
canvas, 19 × 15 inches.

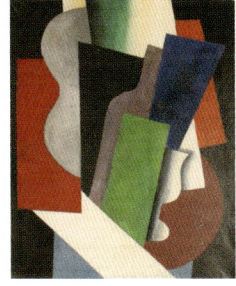

144
Artist unknown. In the style of
Liubov Popova, n.d. Oil on
canvas, 23.5 × 19.5 inches.

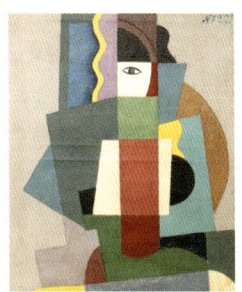

145
Artist unknown, n.d. Oil on
canvas, 23.5 × 19.5 inches.

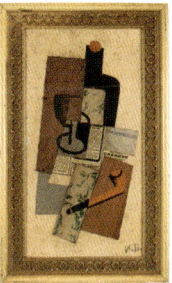

146
Artist unknown, n.d.
Mixed media on cardboard,
15 × 8.5 inches.

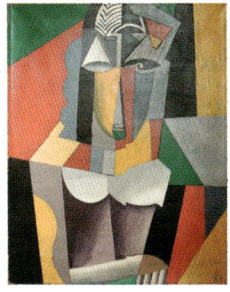

147
Artist unknown, n.d. Oil on
canvas, 32 × 25 inches.

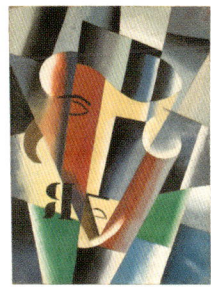

148
Artist unknown. In the style of
Liubov Popova, n.d. Oil on
canvas, 25.5 × 19.5 inches.

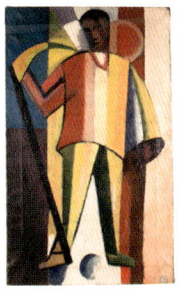

149
Artist unknown. In the style of
Alexei Morgunov, n.d. Oil on
canvas, 25 × 19.5 inches.

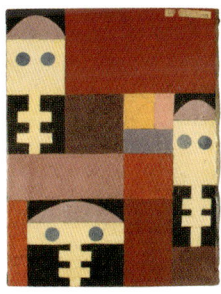

150
Artist unknown, n.d. Oil on
canvas, 15.75 × 12.25 inches.

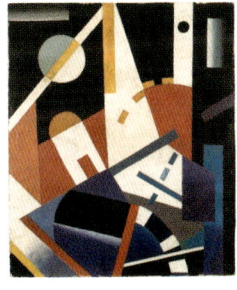

151
Artist unknown. In the style of
Alexandra Exter, n.d. Oil on
plywood, 28 × 23.5 inches.

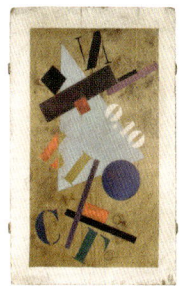

152
Artist unknown. In the style of
Kazimir Malevich, n.d. Oil on
panel, 25 × 15.75 inches.

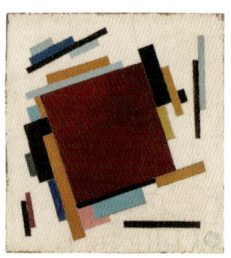

153
Artist unknown, n.d. Oil on
plywood, 11 × 11 inches.

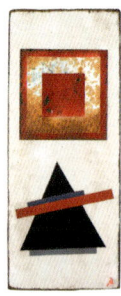

154
Artist unknown. In the style of
Il'ia Chasnik, n.d. Mixed media
on wood, 25 × 10.25 inches.

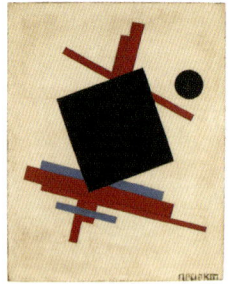

155
Artist unknown. In the style of
Nikolai Suetin, n.d. Oil on
canvas, 29.5 × 23.5 inches.

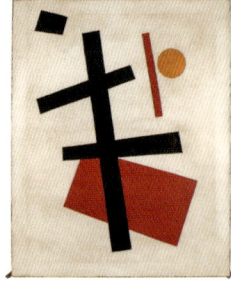

156
Artist unknown. In the style of
Ivan Chervinko, n.d. Oil on
canvas, 32 × 25.5 inches.

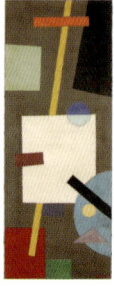

157
Artist unknown. In the style of
Ivan Kliun, n.d. Oil on canvas,
35.5 × 13.75 inches.

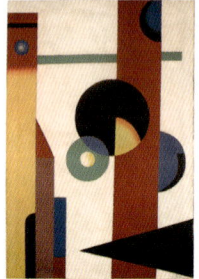

158
Artist unknown. In the style of
Anna Kagan, n.d. Oil on canvas,
43 × 31 inches.

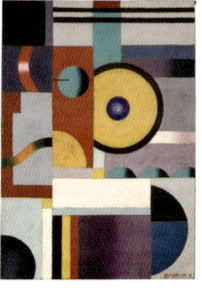

159
Artist unknown. In the style of
Anna Kagan, n.d. Oil on canvas,
26.25 × 18.5 inches.

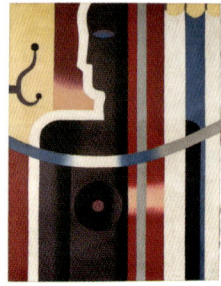

160
Artist unknown, n.d. Oil on
canvas, 39 × 27.5 inches.

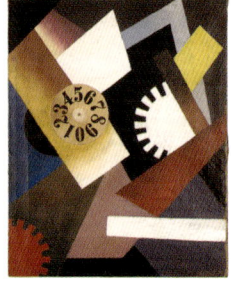

161
Artist unknown. In the style of
Ivan Kliun, n.d. Mixed media on
canvas, 23.5 × 19.75 inches.

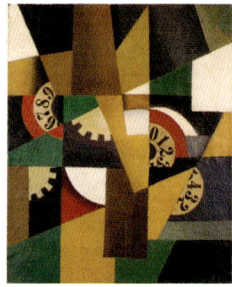

162
Artist unknown. In the style of
Ivan Kliun, n.d. Mixed media on
canvas, 22.5 × 18.5 inches.

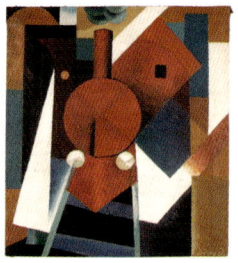

163
Artist unknown. In the style of
Sándor Bortnyik, n.d. Oil on
canvas, 18.5 × 16 inches.

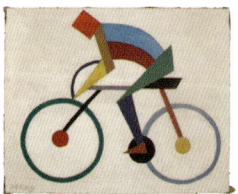

164
Artist unknown, n.d. Oil on
canvas, 15.75 × 19.5 inches.

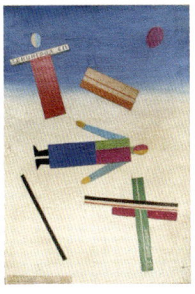

165
Artist unknown, n.d.
Mixed media on plywood,
22.5 × 16 inches.

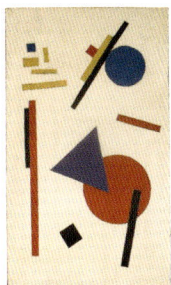

166
Artist unknown, n.d. Oil on
canvas, 18.5 × 11.5 inches.

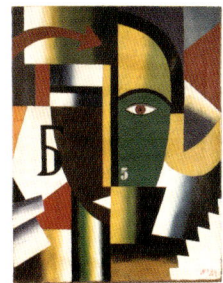

167
Artist unknown, n.d. Oil on
canvas, 25.5 × 19.5 inches.

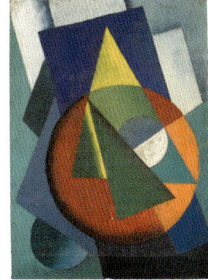

168
Artist unknown, n.d. Oil on
canvas, 19 × 14 inches.

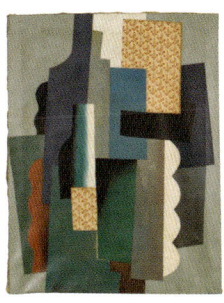

169
Artist unknown. In the style
of Liubov Popova, n.d.
Mixed media on canvas,
35.5 × 27.5 inches.

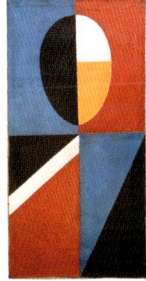

170
Artist unknown. In the style of
Nikolai Suetin, n.d. Oil on
canvas, 48 × 24 inches.
.

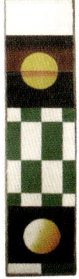

171
Artist unknown. In the style
of Pavel Mansurov, n.d.
Oil on wooden panel,
31 × 9 × 1.5 inches.

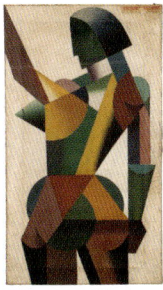

172
Artist unknown. In the style of
Liubov Popova, n.d. Oil on
canvas, 27.5 × 15.75 inches.

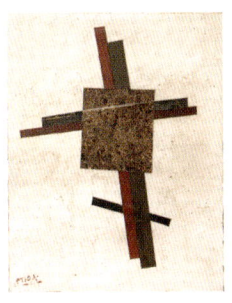

173
Artist unknown. In the
style of Nikolai Suetin, n.d.
Paper and oil on canvas,
19.25 × 15.25 inches.

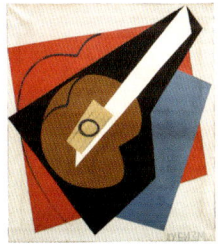

174
Artist unknown, n.d. Oil on
canvas, 31.5 × 28.5 inches.

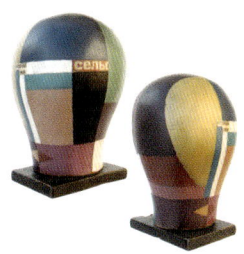

175
Artist unknown, n.d. In the
style of Sophie Taeuber-Arp.
Oil and paper on wood,
10.5 × 6.25 × 6.5 inches.

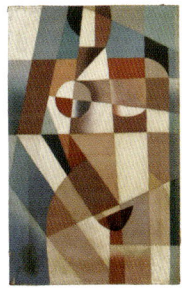

176
Artist unknown, n.d. Oil on
canvas, 21.5 × 13.75 inches.

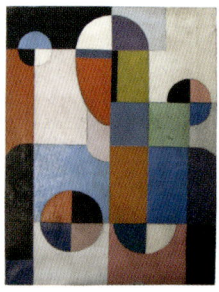

177
Artist unknown, n.d. Oil on
canvas, 25.5 × 19.5 inches.

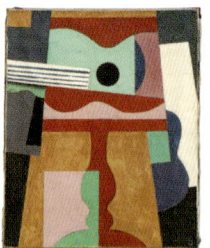

178
Artist unknown, n.d. Oil on
canvas, 22 × 18.5 inches.

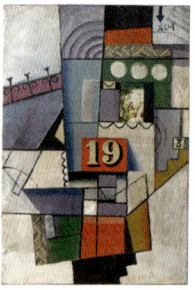

179
Artist unknown, n.d.
Oil and paper on canvas,
21.5 × 14.5 inches.

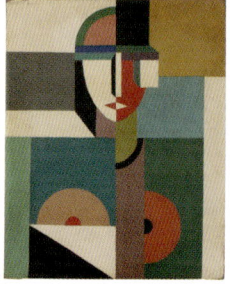

180
Artist unknown, n.d. Oil on
canvas, 23.5 × 19 inches.

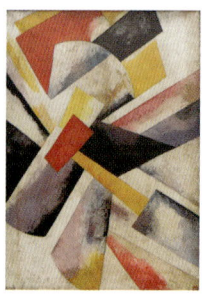

181
Artist unknown, n.d. Oil on
canvas, 37 × 26 inches.

IMAGE CREDITS

Except as indicated below, all images are courtesy of
Ron Pollard.

Fig. 26: Reproduced in *Vladimir Evgrafovich Tatlin*, 1915.
From Christina Lodder, *Russian Constructivism* (New Haven
and London: Yale University Press, 1983), 16.

Fig. 27: Unknown photographer. Central State Archives of Cinema
and Photography, St. Petersburg.

Fig. 28: Malevich, Kazimir (1878–1935). *Suprematist Composition:
Airplane Flying*. 1915 (dated on reverse 1914). Oil on canvas,
22 7/8 × 19 inches (58.1 × 48.3 cm). 1935 acquisition confirmed in
1999 by agreement with the Estate of Kazimir Malevich and made
possible with funds from the Mrs. John Hay Whitney Request
(by exchange). Museum of Modern Art, New York, NY, USA.
Photo credit: The Museum of Modern Art/Licensed by SCALA/
Art Resource, NY.

Fig. 34: Malevich, Kazimir (1878–1935). *Black Square*, around
1923. Oil on canvas, 106 × 106 cm. Sch-9484. Russian State
Museum, Saint Petersburg, Russia. Photo credit: Erich Lessing/
Art Resource, NY.

Fig. 35: Unknown photographer. From Kasimir Malevich,
The Non-Objective World: The Manifesto of Suprematism
(Mineola, NY: Dover, 2003), 25.

Fig. 36: Malevich, Kazimir (1878–1935). *Black Cross*, around 1923.
Canvas, 106 × 106.5 cm. Sch-9485. Russian State Museum, Saint
Petersburg, Russia. Photo credit: Erich Lessing/Art Resource, NY.

Fig. 47: Malevich, Kazimir (1878–1935). *Torso, Transformation
to a New Shape*, 1928–32. Oil on canvas. Russian State Museum,
Saint Petersburg, Russia. Photo credit: Bridgeman Art Library, NY.

Fig. 55: Malevich, Kazimir (1878–1935). *Suprematist Composition*,
1915. Wilhelm-Hack-Museum, Ludwigshafen, Germany. Photo
Credit: Erich Lessing/Art Resource, NY.

Fig. 62: Unknown photographer. From Larissa Alekseevna
Zhadova, ed., *Tatlin* (New York: Rizzoli, 1984), 421.

PUBLISHED BY

Princeton Architectural Press
37 East 7th Street
New York, NY 10003

Visit our website at www.papress.com

© 2014 Adam Lerner
All rights reserved
Printed and bound in China
17 16 15 14 4 3 2 1 First edition

No part of this book may be used or reproduced in any manner
without written permission from the publisher, except in the
context of reviews.

Every reasonable attempt has been made to identify owners of copyright.
Errors or omissions will be corrected in subsequent editions.

EDITORS: Nicola Brower and Megan Carey
BOOK DESIGN: Paul Wagner
DESIGN ASSISTANCE: Benjamin English

SPECIAL THANKS TO: Meredith Baber, Sara Bader, Janet Behning,
Carina Cha, Andrea Chlad, Barbara Darko, Russell Fernandez,
Will Foster, Jan Hartman, Jan Haux, Diane Levinson, Jennifer Lippert,
Katharine Myers, Margaret Rogalski, Elana Schlenker, Dan Simon,
Sara Stemen, Andrew Stepanian, and Joseph Weston of
Princeton Architectural Press —Kevin C. Lippert, publisher

LIBRARY OF CONGRESS CATALOGING-IN-PUBLICATION DATA
Lerner, Adam, 1966–
From Russia with doubt : the quest to authenticate 150 would-be
masterpieces of the Russian avant-garde / Adam Lerner. — First edition.
    pages   cm
ISBN 978-1-61689-162-6 (pbk.)
1. Pollard, Ron—Art collections. 2. Pollard, Roger—Art collections.
3. Painting, Russian—Appreciation. 4. Authentication. I. Title.
ND1301.6.P65L47 2013
759.947—dc23

2013017231

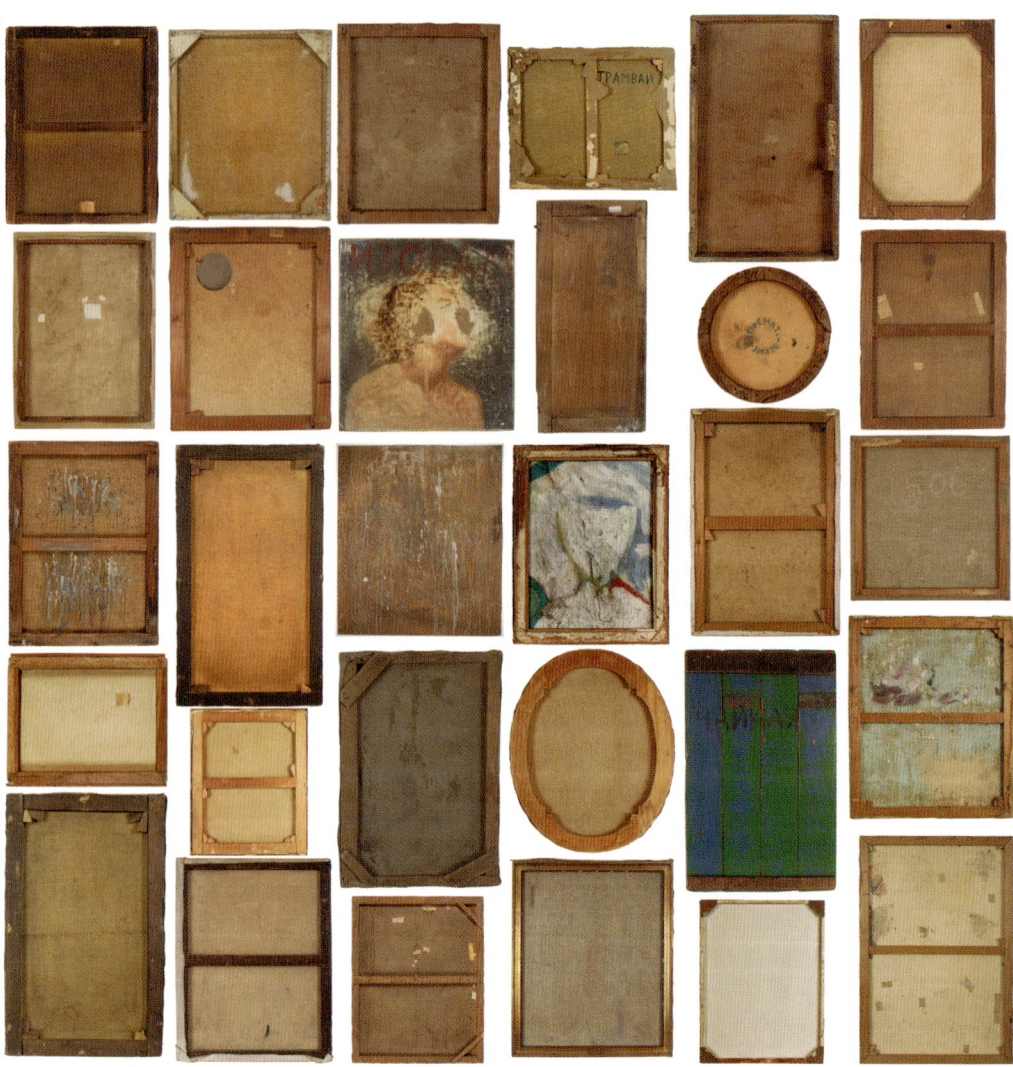